STARS IN THEIR
COURSES

STARS IN THEIR COURSES

THE GETTYSBURG CAMPAIGN
JUNE–JULY 1863

SHELBY FOOTE

THE MODERN LIBRARY

NEW YORK

SHELBY FOOTE

Although he now makes his home in Memphis, Tennessee, Shelby Foote comes from a long line of Mississippians. He was born in 1916 in Greenville, Mississippi, and has had a consuming interest in the history of the Civil War since boyhood. From an early age he devoured books on the subject much as others read detective stories. Foote attended high school in Greenville, and later the University of North Carolina, with novelist and essayist Walker Percy, who later joked that his literary example launched Foote on a writing career. Yet Percy's guardian, William Alexander Percy—the free-spirited planter-poet-lawyer whose autobiographical *Lanterns on the Levee* (1941) paid eloquent tribute to the bygone agrarian traditions of the Mississippi Delta while gloomily assessing the spiritual health of Western civilization—greatly influenced both young men, introducing them to the world of books, music and art. A literary figure and something of a spokesman for the South, the elder Percy was a bachelor who oversaw a great rambling house that became a standard stopover for all manner of visitors, including William Faulkner (who came to play tennis, but whose racket never made contact with the ball) and Carl Sandburg (who broke out his guitar and sang). Meanwhile, Foote and Walker Percy set up shop in another section of the house building model airplanes.

Shelby Foote's own career as a writer began and advanced rapidly in the years following World War II (during which he had served in the European theater as a captain of field artillery). After working briefly as a reporter for the Associated Press and selling the first postgraduate short story he ever wrote to *The Saturday Evening Post*, he published his first novel, *Tournament*, in 1949. The story of a delta landowner who revives a plantation that has been blighted by the Reconstruction years, the book was hailed by *The Christian Science Monitor* as "a tragic tale of frustrated energy, ambition and pride." Foote's next novel, *Follow Me Down* (1950), a mesmerizing account of faith, passion, and murder set in modern-day Mississippi, was praised by *The New Yorker*: "Mr. Foote's writing is marvelously exact and positive. His attitude toward his people is respectful and human, as though he had thought about them a great deal and knew too much about them ever to take them for granted." *Love in a Dry Season* (1951), the story of a small cotton town that is turned into a sexual battleground as two wealthy Mississippi families are manipulated by a fortune hunter from the North, further consolidated Foote's reputation. "Shelby Foote ably fashions a drama as modern as today's newspaper, as old as Mosaic law," said *The New York Times*.

But it was *Shiloh*, a genuine tour de force that appeared in 1952, which proved to be Foote's breakthrough composition. A fictional recreation of the battle of Shiloh—a work that conveys not only the bloody choreography of Union and Confederate troops through the woods near Pittsburg Landing, Tennessee, in April 1862, but the inner movements of the lower-ranking combatants' hearts and minds—it was acclaimed by *The New York Times* as "imaginative, powerful, filled with precise visual details . . . a brilliant book." "*Shiloh* is the best novel of the Civil War I have ever read," wrote Van Allen Bradley in the *Chicago Daily News*. Foote's next novel, *Jordan County* (1954), was a fictional chronicle—"a landscape in narrative"—of seven haunted generations in a Mississippi county, a place where the traumas of slavery, war, and Reconstruction are as tangible as rock formations. An ambitious, troubling work of fiction that builds on the traditions of William Faulkner and Stark Young, *Jordan County* was praised by *The Saturday Review* for its "extraordinary inventiveness of narrative and descriptive detail . . . and a supple prose style which supplies a whiplash effect to the unexpected turns of events with which its stories bristle."

While completing *Jordan County*, Foote received a letter from publisher Bennett Cerf asking him if he'd like to do a short history of the Civil War. "They wanted only about two hundred thousand words," Foote recalled, "and it seemed like a good way to spend a year or two." Before finishing one hundred pages, he realized that he would have "to go spread-eagle, whole hog on the thing." The result, of course, became the epic three-volume narrative, *The Civil War*, that took twenty years (during which time Foote was awarded three Guggenheim fellowships) to complete. The first part, *Fort Sumter to Perryville*, came out in 1958 and was immediately deemed a classic of its kind. "Here, for a certainty, is one of the great historical narratives of our century, a unique and brilliant achievement, one that must be firmly placed in the ranks of the masters," said the *Chicago Daily News*. When the second installment, *Fredericksburg to Meridian*, appeared in 1963, the *Washington Post Book World* called it "one of the historical and literary achievements of our time." By the time the last volume, *Red River to Appomattox*, was published in 1974, *Newsweek* wrote: "To read this chronicle is an awesome and moving experience. History and literature are rarely so thoroughly combined as here; one finishes this volume convinced that no one need undertake this particular enterprise again."

In between researching and writing *The Civil War*, Foote took time out to serve as novelist-lecturer at the University of Virginia and playwright-in-residence at the Arena Stage in Washington, D.C. After completing the twenty-year project, he returned to fiction with *September September* (1977), a tense and haunting novel of the South set on the eve of integration in Little Rock and Memphis. More recently, he served as consultant and presiding spirit on the celebrated nine-part PBS television series *The Civil War* that aired in 1990. At the time he remarked: "Any understanding of this nation has to be based, and I mean really based, on an understanding of the Civil War. I believe that firmly. It defined us. The Revolution did what it did. Our involvement in European wars, beginning with the First World War, did what it did. But the Civil War defined us as what we are and it opened us to being what we became, good and bad things. And it is very necessary, if you're going to understand the American character in the twentieth century, to learn about this enormous catastrophe of the mid-nineteenth century. It was the crossroads of our being, and it was a hell of a crossroads."

STARS IN THEIR COURSES

★ 1 ★

Whatever lack of nerve or ingenuity had been demonstrated in Mississippi throughout the long hot hungry weeks that Vicksburg shuddered under assault and languished under siege, there had been no shortage elsewhere in the Confederate States of either of these qualities on which the beleaguered city's hopes were hung. Indeed, a sort of inverse ratio seemed to obtain between proximity and daring, as if distance not only lent enchantment but also encouraged boldness, so far at least as the western theater was concerned. A case in point was P. G. T. Beauregard, 650 airline miles away on the eastern seaboard. Charleston's two-time savior was nothing if not inventive: especially when he had time on his hands, as he did now. In mid-May with the laurels still green on his brow for the repulse of Samuel Du Pont's ironclad fleet the month before, he unfolded in a letter to the regional commander, Joseph E. Johnston—with whom he had shared the triumph of Manassas, back in the first glad summer of the war, and to whom, under pressure from Richmond, he had just dispatched 8000 of his men—a plan so sweeping in its concept that the delivery of the Gibraltar of the West, whose plight had started him thinking along these lines, was finally no more than an incidental facet of a design for sudden and absolute victory over all the combinations whereby the North intended to subjugate the South.

According to his "general views of the coming summer campaign," propounded in the letter to his friend, Johnston would be reinforced by troops from all the other Confederate commanders, who would stand on the defensive, east and west, while Johnston joined Braxton Bragg south of Nashville for an all-out offensive against the Union center, wrecking William S. Rosecrans and driving the frazzled remnant of his army beyond the Ohio. Johnston would follow, picking up 10,000 recruits in Middle Tennessee and another 20,000 in Kentucky, and if this threat to the Federal heartland had not already prompted a withdrawal by the bluecoats from in front of Vicksburg, he could march west to the Mississippi, above Memphis, "and thus cut off Grant's communications with the north." When the besiegers moved upriver, as they would be obliged to do for want of supplies, Johnston would draw them into battle on a field of his choice, "and the result could not be doubtful for an instant." With Ulysses S. Grant thus disposed of, the victorious southern Army of the Center, some 150,000 strong by then, could split in two, one half crossing the big river to assist Kirby Smith and Sterling Price in the liberation of Louisiana and Missouri, while the other half joined Robert E. Lee in Virginia to complete "the terrible lesson the enemy has just had at Chancellorsville." Meanwhile, by way of lagniappe, a fleet of special torpedo boats would be constructed in England, from designs already on hand at Charleston, to steam westward across the Atlantic and "resecure" the Mississippi, upwards from its mouth. The war would be over: won.

Thus Beauregard. But after waiting five weeks and receiving no sign that his suggestions had been received, much less adopted, he felt, as he told another friend, "like Samson shorn of his locks." Time was slipping away, he complained in a postscript to his retained copy of the letter, despite the fact that "the whole of this brilliant campaign, which is only indicated here, could have been terminated by the end of June." On July 1 he heard at last from Johnston, though only on an administrative matter and without reference to his proposals of mid-May. Assuming that the original must have gone astray, he sent him at once a copy of the letter, together with the postscript stressing the need for haste in the adoption of the plan which he called brilliant. "I fear, though, it is now too late to undertake it," he admitted, and added rather lamely: "I hope everything will yet turn out well, although I do not exactly see how."

Nothing came of the Creole general's dream of reversing the blue flood, first in the center and then on the left and right; but others with easier access to the authorities in Richmond had been making similar, if less flamboyant, proposals all the while. James Longstreet, for example, on his way to rejoin Lee in early May, hard on the heels of Chancellorsville and the aborted Siege of Suffolk, outlined for Secretary of War James A. Seddon a plan not unlike Beauregard's, except that it had the virtue of comparative simplicity. It was Old Peter's conviction "that the only way to equalize the contest was by skillful use of our interior lines," and in this connection he proposed that Johnson give over any attempt to go directly to John C. Pemberton's assistance at Vicksburg, and instead reinforce Bragg at Tullahoma, while Longstreet, with his two divisions now en route from Suffolk under John B. Hood and George E. Pickett, moved by rail to that same point for that same purpose; Rosecrans would be swamped by overwhelming numbers, and the victors then could march for the Ohio. Grant's being the only force that could be used to meet this threat, his army would be withdrawn upriver and Vicksburg thereby would be relieved.

Seddon listened attentively. Though he liked the notion of using Hood and Pickett to break the enemy's grip on the Mississippi south of Memphis, he preferred the more direct and still simpler method of sending them southwestward for a movement against Grant where he then was. However, this presupposed the approval of Lee: which was not forthcoming. Lee replied that he would of course obey any order sent him, but he considered the suggestion less than wise. "The adoption of your proposition is hazardous," he wired Seddon, "and it becomes a question between Virginia and the Mississippi." The date was May 10; Stonewall Jackson died that afternoon. But Lee suppressed his grief in order to expand his objections to the Secretary's proposal in a letter that same Sunday. He not only thought the attempt to rescue Pemberton by sending troops from Virginia unduly risky; he also considered it unnecessary. "I presume [the reinforcements] would not reach him until the last of this month," he wrote. "If anything is done in that quarter, it will be over by that time, as the climate in June will force the enemy to retire."

Seddon doubted that climate alone would be enough to cause the Federals to abandon, even for a season, their bid for source-to-mouth control of the Mississippi. Whatever Lee might think of Grant, the Secretary considered him "such an obstinate fellow that he could only be induced to quit Vicksburg by terribly hard knocks." In fact, that had been his objection to Longstreet's claim that a strike at Rosecrans would abolish the threat downriver; Grant might simply ignore the provocation and refuse to loosen his grip. Jefferson Davis agreed. Moreover, he shared Seddon's reservations about Johnston, who had just been ordered to the Mississippi capital, as a deliverer of hard knocks. Between them, under pressure of the knowledge that something had to be done, and done quickly, now that the bluecoats were on the march in Pemberton's rear, the President and the Secretary decided that the time had come for a high-level conference to determine just what that something was to be. On May 14, the day Johnston abandoned Jackson to Union occupation, they summoned Lee to Richmond for a full discussion of the problem.

He arrived next day, which was one of sorrow and strain for the whole Confederacy; Stonewall Jackson was being buried, out in the Shenandoah Valley, and Joe Johnston was retreating to Canton, a day's march north of the Mississippi capital, while Grant turned west for a leap at Vicksburg from the rear. Davis and Seddon hoped that, face to face with Lee, they might persuade him to continue the risk of facing Joseph Hooker with a depleted army, so that Longstreet could join Johnston for a strike at Grant. However, they found him still convinced that such an attempt, undertaken for the possible salvation of the Mississippi for a season, would mean the loss of Virginia forever; and that for him was quite unthinkable. "Save in defense of my native State, I never again desire to draw my sword," he had said two years ago, on the day he resigned from the U.S. Army.

Apparently he still felt that way about it: with one refinement. His proposal now—for he agreed that something drastic had to be done to reverse the blue flood of conquest in the center and on the far left of the thousand-mile Confederate line of battle—was that he launch a second invasion of the North. The first, back in September, had come to grief in Maryland because of a combination of mishaps, not the least of which had been

George McClellan's luck in finding the lost order issued by Lee when he snapped at the bait left dangling at Harpers Ferry. This time, though, he would profit by that experience. He would march without delay into Pennsylvania, deep in Washington's rear, where a victory might well prove decisive, not only in his year-long contest with the Army of the Potomac, in which he had never lost a major battle, but also in the war. It might or might not cause the withdrawal of Grant from in front of Vicksburg, but at least it would remove the invaders from the soil of Virginia during the vital harvest season, while at best it would accomplish the fall of the northern capital and thus encourage the foreign intervention which Davis long had seen as the key to victory over the superior forces of the Union.

The President and Seddon were impressed. Having heard Lee out, Davis asked him to return the following morning for a presentation of his views to the entire cabinet.

That too was a critical day for the young republic. Before it was over, Grant had thrown Pemberton into retreat from Champion Hill, continuing his lunge for the back door of Vicksburg, and Nathaniel Banks had ended his week-long occupation of Alexandria, Louisiana, in order to move against Port Hudson. Lee spent most of it closeted with Davis and the cabinet at the White House, presenting his solution to the national crisis. He spoke not in his former capacity as military adviser to the President, and certainly not as general-in-chief—no such office existed in the Confederacy; Henry Halleck's only counterpart was Davis, or at least a fraction of him—but rather as commander of the Department of Northern Virginia. Having rejected the notion of reinforcing Vicksburg—"The distance and the uncertainty of the employment of the troops are unfavorable," he told Seddon—Lee based his present advice on what was good or bad for his department and the soldiers in his charge. "I considered the problem in every possible phase," he subsequently explained, "and to my mind, it resolved itself into a choice of one of two things: either to retire to Richmond and stand a siege, which must ultimately have ended in surrender, or to invade Pennsylvania."

Placed in that light, the alternatives were much the same as if the cabinet members were being asked to choose between certain defeat and possible victory. In fact, "possible" became *probable* with Robert E. Lee in charge of an invasion launched as the aftermath of Fredericksburg and Chancellorsville, triumphs scored against the same adversary and against longer odds than he would be likely to encounter when he crossed the Potomac with the reunited Army of Northern Virginia. Seddon and Secretary of State Judah P. Benjamin, Secretary of the Treasury Christopher G. Memminger, Attorney General Thomas H. Watts, and Secretary of the Navy Stephen R. Mallory all agreed with the gray-bearded general "whose fame," as one of them said, "now filled the world." They were not only persuaded by his logic; they were awed by his presence, his aura of invincibility. And this included Davis, who had seldom experienced that reaction to any man.

It did not include Postmaster General John H. Reagan. He was by no means persuaded by Lee, and such awe as he felt for any living man was reserved for Jefferson Davis, whom he considered self-made and practical-minded like himself. Born in poverty forty-five years ago in Tennessee, Reagan had been a schoolteacher and a Mississippi plantation overseer before he was eighteen, when he moved to Texas with all he

owned tied up in a kerchief. Passing the bar, he had gone
into Lone Star politics and in time won election to Con-
gress, where service on the postal committee prepared
him for his present assignment. In this he already had
scored a singular triumph, unequaled by any American
postmaster in the past seventy-five years or indeed in
the next one hundred. Under Reagan's watchful eye, the
Confederate postal department did not suffer an annual
deficit, but yielded a clear profit. He accomplished this
mainly by forcefulness and vigor, and now he employed
these qualities in an attempt to persuade Davis and his
fellow cabinet members that no victory anywhere, even
in Washington itself, could offset the disaster that would
result from the loss of the Mississippi.

The only man present whose home lay beyond that
river, he said plainly that he thought Lee was so
absorbed in his masterful defense of Virginia that he did
not realize the importance of the Transmississippi,
which would be cut off from the rest of the country with
the fall of Vicksburg. It had been claimed that Lee's
advance might result in Grant's withdrawal to meet the
challenge, but Reagan did not believe this for an instant.
Grant was committed, he declared. The only way to
stop him from accomplishing his object was to destroy
him, and the only way to destroy him was to move
against him with all possible reinforcements, including
Longstreet's two divisions from Lee's army. As for the
talk of cooperation expected from those with antiwar
sentiments in the North—this too had been advanced as
an argument for invasion; the peace movement had been
growing beyond the Potomac—Reagan agreed with
Beauregard as to "the probability that the threatened
danger to Washington would arouse again the whole
Yankee nation to renewed efforts for the protection of

their capital." In short, he saw everything wrong with Lee's plan and everything right about the plan it had superseded. Grant was the main threat to the survival of the Confederacy, and it was Grant at whom the main blow must be aimed and struck.

Davis and the others heard both men out, and when the two had had their say a vote was taken. In theory, the cabinet could reject Lee's proposal as readily as that of any other department commander, Bragg or Pemberton or Beauregard, for example, each of whom was zealous to protect the interests of the region for which he was responsible. But that was only in theory. This was Lee, the first soldier of the Confederacy—the first soldier of the world, some would assert—and this was, after all, a military decision. The vote was five to one, in the general's favor. Davis concurring, it was agreed that the invasion would begin at the earliest possible date.

Pleased with the outcome and the confidence expressed, Lee went that evening to pay his respects to a Richmond matron who had done much to comfort the wounded of his army. As he took his leave, it seemed to a young lady of the house—much as it had seemed earlier to five of the six cabinet members—that he was clothed in glory. "It was broad moonlight," she was to write years later, "and I recall the superb figure of our hero standing in the little porch without, saying a last few words, as he swung his military cape around his shoulders. It did not need my fervid imagination to think him the most noble looking mortal I had ever seen. We felt, as he left us and walked on up the quiet leafy street in the moonlight, that we had been honored by more than royalty."

Again Reagan had a different reaction. Unable to sleep because of his conviction that a fatal mistake had been made that day at the White House, he rose before dawn—it was Sunday now, May 17; Pemberton would be routed at high noon on the Big Black, and Johnston was advising the immediate evacuation of Vicksburg— to send a message urging Davis to call the cabinet back into session for a reconsideration of yesterday's decision. Davis did so, having much the same concern for Mississippi as Lee had for Virginia—his brother and sisters were there, along with many lifelong friends who had sent their sons to help defend the Old Dominion and now looked to him for deliverance from the gathering blue host—but the result of today's vote, taken after another long discussion, was the same as yesterday's: five to one, against Reagan. Lee returned to the Rappahannock the following day, which was the first of many in the far-off Siege of Vicksburg.

The problems awaiting him at Fredericksburg were multitudinous and complex. Chancellorsville, barely two weeks in the past and already being referred to as "Lee's masterpiece," had subtracted nearly 13,000 of the best men from his army. Of these, in time, about half would be returning; but the other half would not. And of these last, as all agreed, the most sorely missed was Jackson. "Any victory would be dear at such a price," Lee declared. He found it hard to speak of him, so deep was his emotion at the loss. "I know not how to replace him," he said—and, indeed, he did not try.

Instead he reorganized the army, abandoning the previous grouping of the infantry into two corps, of four divisions each, for a new arrangement of three corps, each with three divisions. The new ninth division thus required was created by detaching two brigades from A. P. Hill's so-called Light Division, the largest in the army, and combining them with two brought up from

Richmond and North Carolina; Henry Heth, Hill's senior brigadier, was given command, along with a promotion to major general. Similarly, one division was taken from each of the two existing corps—Richard Anderson's from the First and what was left of Hill's from the Second—in order to fill out the new Third. The problem of appointing corps commanders was solved with equal facility. Longstreet of course would remain at the head of the First Corps, whose composition was unchanged except for the loss of Anderson; Lafayette McLaws, Pickett, and Hood were in command of their three divisions, as before. The Second Corps went to Richard S. Ewell, Jackson's former chief subordinate, who opportunely returned to the army at this time, having recovered from the loss of a leg nine months ago at Groveton. A. P. Hill got the new Third Corps, which was scarcely a surprise; Lee had praised him weeks ago to Davis as the best of his division commanders, and moreover a good half of the troops involved had been under him all along. Promotion to lieutenant general went to both Ewell and Hill. Jubal Early kept the division he had led since Ewell's departure, and W. Dorsey Pender succeeded Hill, under whom he had served from the outset. He was promoted to major general, as was Robert Rodes, who was confirmed as commander of the division that had spearheaded the flank attack on Hooker. Edward Johnson, returning to duty after a year-long absence spent healing the bad leg wound he had suffered at McDowell, the curtain raiser for Jackson's Valley Campaign, completed the roster of corps and division commanders by taking over the Second Corps division which had been temporarily under Raleigh Colston. The artillery was reshuffled, too, and the general reserve abolished, so that each corps now had five battalions; William Pendleton, the former Episcopal rector, retained his assignment as chief of the army's artillery, though the title was merely nominal now that the reserve battalions had been distributed, and he remained a brigadier. J.E.B. Stuart, on the other hand, gained three new brigades of Virginia cavalry, brought in from various parts of the state in order to add their weight to the three he already had for the offensive.

As a result of all these acquisitions, supplemented by volunteers and conscripts forwarded from all parts of the nation as replacements for the fallen, the army was almost up to the strength it had enjoyed before the sub- tractions of Fredericksburg and Chancellorsville. Approximately 75,000 effectives—in round figures, 5000 artillery, 10,000 cavalry, and 60,000 infantry— stood in its ranks. The infantry order of battle was as follows:

I. LONGSTREET	II. EWELL	III. A. P. HILL
McLaws	Early	Anderson
Pickett	Johnson	Heth
Hood	Rodes	Pender

The arrangement seemed pat and apt enough, but there were those who had objections no less sharp for being silent. Longstreet, for instance, perhaps chagrined that Lee had not consulted him beforehand, resented Hill's promotion over the head of McLaws, whom he considered better qualified for the job. Aside from that, Old Peter was of the opinion that the post should have gone to Harvey Hill, on duty now in his home state of North Carolina. "His record was as good as that of Stonewall Jackson," the Georgian later wrote, "but, not being a Virginian, he was not so well advertised." There was, he thought, "too much Virginia" on the roster—and there were, in fact, apparent grounds for the complaint. Of the fifteen most responsible assignments in the army, ten were held by natives of the Old Dominion, including Lee himself, Ewell and Hill, Stuart, Early and Johnson, Pickett, Rodes and Heth, and Pendleton. Georgia had two, Longstreet and McLaws; Texas had Hood, South Carolina Anderson, and North Carolina, which furnished more than a quarter of Lee's troops, had only the newly promoted Pender; while Mississippi and Alabama, which furnished three brigades apiece, had no representative on the list at all.

Lee too saw possible drawbacks and shortcomings to the arrangement, though not with regard to the states his leading generals came from. His concern was rather with the extent of the reorganization, which placed two of his three corps and five of his nine divisions under men who previously had served either briefly or not at all in their present capacities. Moreover, though his brigadiers were the acknowledged backbone of his army, six of the thirty-seven brigades were under new commanders, and another half dozen were under colonels whom he considered unready for promotion. This troubled him, though not as much as something else. Always in his mind was the missing Jackson, whose death had been the occasion for the shake-up now in progress and of whom he said, "I never troubled myself to give him detailed instructions. The most general suggestions were all that he needed."

Lee's proposed solution was characteristically simple. "We must all do more than formerly," he told one general. And this applied as much to himself as it did to anyone; especially so far as "detailed instructions" were concerned. The sustaining factor was the army itself, the foot soldiers, troopers, and cannoneers who had never failed him in the year since the last day of May, 1862, when Davis gave him the command amid the half-fought confusion of Seven Pines. He was convinced, he declared within ten days of the anniversary of his appointment, "that our army would be invincible if it could be properly organized and officered." Of the troops themselves, the rank and file who carried the South's cause on their bayonets, he had no doubts at all. "There never were such men in an army before," he said. "They will go anywhere and do anything if properly led."

Another known quantity, or at any rate an assumed one, was James Longstreet. "My old warhorse," Lee had called him after Sharpsburg, a battle which Old Peter had advised against fighting—"General," he had said to Lee on entering Maryland, "I wish we could stand still and let the damned Yankees come to us"—but which at least was fought in the style he preferred, with the Confederates taking up a strong defensive position against which the superior blue forces were shattered, like waves against a rock. Fredericksburg, where his corps had suffered fewer than 2000 casualties while inflicting about 9000, had confirmed his predilection in that respect, and he considered Chancellorsville the kind of flashy spectacle the South could ill afford. Facing what Abraham Lincoln called "the arithmetic," he perceived that four more such battles, in which the Confederates were outnumbered two to one and inflicted casualties at a rate of three for four, would reduce Lee's army to a handful, while Hooker would be left with the number Lee had had at the outset.

Disappointed by the rejection of his proposal that he take Hood and Pickett west for an assault on Rosecrans, the burly Georgian listened with disapproval as Lee announced his intention to launch an offensive in the East. He protested, much as Reagan had done, but with no more success; Lee's mind was made up. So Longstreet contented himself with developing his theory—or, as he thought, advancing the stipulation—that the proposed invasion be conducted in accordance with his preference for receiving rather than delivering attack when the two armies came to grips, wherever that might be. As he put it later, quite as if he and Lee had been joint commanders of the army, "I then accepted his proposition to make a campaign into Pennsylvania, provided it should be offensive in strategy but defensive in tactics, forcing the Federal army to give us battle when we were in strong position and ready to receive them."

Lee heard him out with the courtesy which he was accustomed to extend to all subordinates, but which in this case was mistaken for a commitment. He intended no such thing, of course, and when he was told years later that Longstreet had said he so understood him, he refused to believe that his former lieutenant had made the statement. But Old Peter had said it, and he had indeed received that impression at the time; whereby trouble was stored up for all involved.

In any case, once Lee had completed the ground-work for his plans, he wasted no time in putting them into execution. Four days after his May 30 announce-ment of the army's reorganization, and just one month after Chancellorsville, he started McLaws on a march up the south bank of the Rappahannock to Culpeper, near which Hood and Pickett had been halted on their return from Suffolk. Rodes followed on June 4, and Early and Johnson the next day, leaving Hill's three divisions at Fredericksburg to face alone the Union host across the river. Hooker's balloons were up and apparently spotted the movement, for the bluecoats promptly effected a crossing below the town. It was rumored that Lee had expressed a willingness to "swap queens," Richmond for Washington, in case Hooker plunged south while his back was turned. However, the validity of the rumor was not tested; Hill reported the bridgehead was nothing he could not handle, and Lee took him at his word. Riding westward in the wake of Longstreet and Ewell, he joined them at Culpeper on June 7.

Stuart had been there more than two weeks already, getting his cavalry in shape for new exertions, and two days before Lee's arrival he had staged at nearby Brandy Station a grand review of five of his brigades, including by way of finale a mock charge on the guns of the horse artillery, which lent a touch of realism to the pageant by firing blank rounds as the long lines of grayjackets bore down on them with drawn sabers and wild yells. Stirred or frightened by this gaudy climax, several ladies fainted, or pretended to faint, in the grandstand which Jeb had had set up for them along one side of the field. To his further delight, the army commander agreed to let him restage the show for his benefit on the day after his arrival, though he insisted that the finale be omitted as a waste of powder and horseflesh. Despite this curtailment, the performance was a source of pride to the plumed chief of cavalry, who, as Lee wrote home, "was in all his glory." It was something more, as well; for another result of this second review was that he still had most of his 10,000 troopers concentrated near Brandy on June 9 for what turned out to be the greatest cavalry battle of the war.

Thirty-nine-year-old Alfred Pleasonton, recently

promoted to major general as successor to George Stoneman, had eight brigades of cavalry, roughly 12,000 men, grouped in three divisions under John Buford, David Gregg, and Judson Kilpatrick. All were West Pointers, like himself, and all were of the new hell-for-leather style of horsemen who had learned to care more for results than they did for spit and polish. Buford, the oldest, was thirty-seven; Gregg was thirty; Kilpatrick was twenty-seven. Supported by two brigades of infantry, Pleasonton moved upriver from Falmouth on June 8, with six of his brigades, which gave him a mounted force equal in strength to Stuart's, and crossed at dawn next morning at Beverly and Kelly's fords, above and below Rappahannock Station. Instructed to determine what Lee was up to, there in the V of the rivers where John Pope had nearly come to grief the year before, he got over under cover of the heavy morning fog and surprised the rebel pickets, who were driven back toward Brandy, five miles away, with the blue riders hard on their heels.

And so it was that Stuart, who had pitched his headquarters tent on Fleetwood Hill overlooking the field where the two reviews were held, got his first sight of the Yankees at about the same time he received the first message warning him that they were over the river at Beverly Ford. Two of his present five brigades, under Rooney Lee and William E. Jones, were already in that direction, contesting the advance. Fitz Lee's brigade was seven miles north, beyond the Hazel River, and the other two, under Wade Hampton and Beverly Robertson, were in the vicinity of Kelly's Ford, where John Pelham had fallen twelve weeks ago today. Stuart sent couriers to alert the brigades to the north and south, then rode forward to join the fight Lee and Jones were making, about midway between Beverly Ford and Fleet-wood Hill. However, he had no sooner gotten the situation fairly well in hand on that quarter of the field than he learned that another enemy column of equal strength had eluded the pickets at Kelly's Ford and was riding now into Brandy Station, two miles in his rear.

The result, as he regrouped his forces arriving from north and south to meet the double threat, was hard fighting in the classic style, headlong charges met by headlong countercharges, with sabers, pistols, and carbines employed hand to hand to empty a lot of saddles. He lost Fleetwood Hill, retook it, lost it again, and again retook it. Near sundown, spotting rebel infantry on the march from Brandy—his own infantry had been engaged only lightly—Pleasonton fell back the way he had come, effecting an orderly withdrawal. He had lost 936 men, including 86 taken prisoner, as compared to the Confederate total of 523, but he was well satisfied with his troopers and their day's work on the rebel side of the Rappahannock.

Stuart expressed an equal if not greater satisfaction. After all, he retained possession of the field, along with three captured guns, and had inflicted a good deal more damage than he had suffered: except perhaps in terms of pride. For there could be no denying that he had been surprised, on his own ground, or that the Yankees had fought as hard—and, for that matter, as well—as his own famed gray horsemen, at least one of whom was saying, even now, that the bluecoats had been successful because he and his fellows had been "worried out," all the preceding week, by the grand reviews Jeb staged out of fondness for "military foppery and display."

One thing was clear to Stuart at any rate. Such

exploits as he hoped to perform in the future, enhancing his already considerable reputation, were going to be more difficult to bring off than those he had accomplished in the days when the blue troopers were comparatively inept. Doubtless his solution was the same as the army commander's. "We must all do more than formerly," Lee had said, and for Jeb this meant more, even, than the two "rides" around McClellan.

Approaching the field of battle that afternoon, Lee experienced the double shock of learning that his normally vigilant chief of cavalry had suffered a surprise and of seeing his son Rooney being carried to the rear with an ugly leg wound. However, he did not let either development change his plans for the march northward, which were as follows. While Longstreet remained at Culpeper, in position to reinforce Hill in case Hooker tried to swamp him, Ewell would move into and down the Shenandoah Valley, preceded by Stuart's sixth brigade of cavalry, en route from Southwest Virginia under Albert Jenkins. When Ewell reached the Potomac, he was to cross into Maryland and strike out for Pennsylvania without delay. Longstreet then would advance northward, east of the Blue Ridge, thus preventing Union penetration of the passes, while Hill marched west from Fredericksburg and followed Ewell northward down the Valley and over the Potomac, to be followed in turn by Longstreet, who would leave Stuart to guard the Blue Ridge passes until the combined advance of 60,000 butternut infantry into Pennsylvania caused the Washington authorities to call the Army of the Potomac northward across the river from which it took its name.

Lee's plan was a bold one, but it had worked well against Lincoln and McClellan in September and it seemed likely to work as well against Lincoln and

Hooker nine months later. The most questionable factor was Ewell, whose corps would not only set the pace for the rest of the army, but would also be the first to encounter whatever trouble lay in store for the Confederates in the North. In effect, this meant that he was being required to march and fight with the same fervor and skill as his former chief and predecessor, and whether he could ever become another Jackson was extremely doubtful, especially since he was not even the same Ewell, either to the ear or eye, who had fought under and alongside the dead Wizard of the Valley. In partial compensation for the loss of his leg—though this seemed in fact to bother him very little, either on horseback or afoot—he had made two acquisitions. One was religion, which tempered his language, and the other was a wife, which tempered his whole outlook. Formerly profane, he now was mild in manner. Formerly of modest means, he now was wealthy, having won the hand of a rich widow who in her youth had rejected his suit in order to marry a man with the undistinguished name of Brown. Now that she and her extensive property were in his charge, Old Bald Head could scarcely believe his luck, and sometimes he forgot himself so far as to introduce her as "My wife, Mrs Brown."

Whether this new, gentled Ewell would measure up to such high expectations was the subject of much discussion around the campfires of all three corps, particularly his own; but it soon appeared that all the worry had been for nothing. Out in the Valley, the scene of former military magic, his firm grasp of strategy and tactics, coupled with a decisiveness of judgment, a good eye, and an eagerness to gather all the fruits of sudden victory, made it seem to former doubters that another

Stonewall had indeed been found to lead the Second Corps and inspire the army.

He moved northward on the day after Stuart's fight at Brandy Station, entered the Valley by way of Chester Gap, and on June 13, having divided his corps at Front Royal the day before, marched on Winchester with Early and Johnson while Rodes and the cavalry struck at Berryville, ten miles east. Robert Milroy had 5100 bluecoats at the former place, and Ewell was out to get them, along with an 1800-man detachment at the latter, ten miles east. As it turned out, the Berryville force made its getaway due to blunders by Jenkins, who was unfamiliar with the kind of work expected of horsemen in Lee's army, but the success of the operation against Winchester more than made up for the disappointment. Warned to fall back, Milroy chose to stand his ground, much as Banks had done in a similar predicament the year before. That hesitation had led to Banks's undoing, and so now did it lead to Milroy's. Charged by Early on the 14th from the west, he retreated northeastward in the darkness, only to be intercepted at dawn by Johnson some four miles up the Harpers Ferry road at Stevenson's Depot, where he was routed. The Union general managed to escape with a couple of hundred of his troopers, but his unmounted men had no such luck in outrunning their pursuers, who gathered them up in droves. Johnson himself—called "Old Clubby" by his soldiers because he preferred to direct their combat maneuvers with a heavy walking stick instead of a sword—asserted happily that he had taken thirty prisoners "with his opera glass" before he ended his private chase by falling off his horse and into Opequon Creek.

Milroy was presently removed from command by

Lincoln, but that was a rather superfluous gesture, since practically all of his command had already been removed from him by Ewell. The total bag, in addition to the infliction of 443 casualties on the immediate field of battle, was 700 sick and 3358 able-bodied prisoners, 23 fine guns, and some 300 well-stocked wagons: all at a cost of 269 Confederate casualties, less than fifty of whom were killed. Ewell's triumph over Milroy was even greater than Jackson's had been over Banks on that same field: a fact that was not lost on the men of the Second Corps, whose final doubts as to the worth of their new commander were forgotten. Moreover, like Stonewall, Old Bald Head did not sit down to enjoy in leisure the spoils and glory he had won. Pushing Jenkins forward to the Potomac before sundown, he had Rodes follow on June 16 for a crossing at Williamsport, Maryland, where a halt was called to allow the other two divisions to catch up for a combined advance into Pennsylvania.

Lee had already put the other two corps in motion. On June 15, while Ewell was gathering prisoners in the woods and fields near Winchester, Longstreet started north from Culpeper, and Hill—who reported that Hooker had abandoned his west-bank bridgehead and withdrawn his army from its camps around Falmouth the day before, apparently for a concentration at or near Manassas, where he would stand athwart Lee's path in case the unpredictable Virginian launched a direct drive on Washington from Culpeper—left Fredericksburg, under instructions to follow Ewell's line of march to the Potomac. Two days later, Lee himself moved north, establishing headquarters at Berryville on the 19th, while Stuart fought a series of thunderous cavalry engagements at Aldie, Middleburg, and Upperville, in all of which he was successful at keeping his hard-riding blue opponents from discovering what was afoot beyond the mountains that screened the Valley from the Piedmont.

Pleased with Jeb's recovery of his verve, the army commander listened with sympathy to the cavalry chief's suggestion that he leave two brigades of horsemen to plug the gaps of the Blue Ridge and move with the other three into Hooker's rear, the better to annoy and delay him when he started north across the Potomac. Lee approved, in principle, but warned that once it became clear that Fighting Joe was crossing the river, Stuart "must immediately cross himself and take his place on our right flank," where he would be needed to screen the northward advance and keep the invading army informed of the movements of the defenders. Aware of his former cadet's fondness for adventure at any price, Lee sent him written instructions on June 22, repeating the warning that he must not allow himself to be delayed in joining the rest of the column when the time came. Next day, when Stuart reported the bluecoats lying quiet in their camps north of Manassas and suggested that a crossing of the Potomac to the east of them by his three mobile brigades would help to mislead Hooker as to Lee's intentions, Lee followed his first message with a second, re-emphasizing the need for close observance of the Federals, but adding: "You will, however, be able to judge whether you can pass around their army without hindrance, doing them all the damage you can, and cross the river east of the mountains. In either case, after crossing the river, you must move on and feel the right of Ewell's troops, collecting information, provisions, etc." The dispatch ended on a note of caution. "Be watchful and circumspect in all your movements," Lee told Stuart.

Meanwhile the infantry was marching rapidly. By June

24, Ewell's main body had cleared Hagerstown and his lead division was at Chambersburg, twenty miles beyond the Pennsylvania line, with orders to press on to the Susquehanna. Presumably the North was in turmoil, having been warned that the penetration would be deep. "It is said," the Richmond *Whig* had reported the week before, "that an artificial leg ordered some months ago awaits General Ewell's arrival in the city of Philadelphia."

Hill and Longstreet crossed the Potomac that same day, at Shepherdstown and Williamsport, and Lee himself made camp that night on the south bank, opposite the latter place, intending to cross over in the morning. Before he did so, however, he received from the President a reply to a letter written two weeks before, in which Lee had made certain admissions in regard to the present national outlook and had suggested some maneuvers he thought might be available to the Confederacy, not only on the military but also on the diplomatic front. "Our resources in men are constantly diminishing," he had written, "and the disproportion in this respect between us and our enemies, if they continue united in their efforts to subjugate us, is steadily augmenting." This being so, he thought the proper course would be to promote division in the northern ranks by encouraging those who favored arbitration as a substitute for bloodshed. "Should the belief that peace will bring back the Union become general," Lee continued, "the war would no longer be supported, and that, after all, is what we are interested in bringing about. When peace is proposed to us, it will be time enough to discuss its terms, and it is not the part of prudence to spurn the proposition in advance, merely because those who wish to make it believe, or affect to believe, that it will result in bringing us back to the Union."

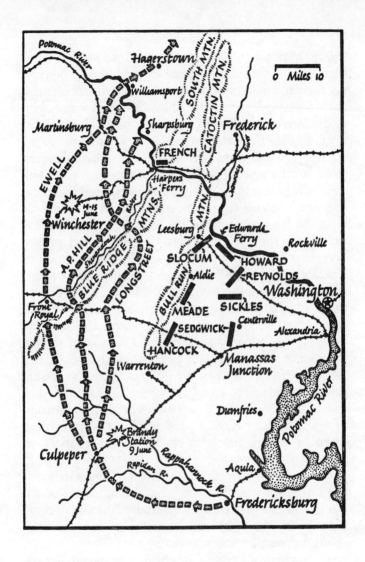

If this was sly, it was also rather ingenuous, particularly in its assumption of such a contrast between the peoples of the North and South that the latter would be willing to resume fighting if negotiations produced no better terms than a restoration of the Union, whereas the former would be willing to concede the Confederacy's independence rather than have the war begin again. Perceiving the risk involved—after all, it might turn out the other way around—Davis contented himself with remarking that encouragement of the followers of the northern peace party was a commendable notion, especially now that a second invasion was being launched at them. Lee replied next morning, as he prepared to cross the Potomac, that he was "much gratified" by the President's approval of his views. He suggested, moreover, that Bragg at Tullahoma and Simon Buckner at Knoxville take the offensive against the Union center and thus "accomplish something in Ohio." Beauregard, too, could share in the delivery of the all-out blow about to be struck for southern independence, Lee said, by bringing to Culpeper such troops as he could scrape together on the seaboard for a feint at Washington. This "army in effigy," as Lee called it, would have at least a psychological effect, particularly with the Hero of Manassas at its head, since it probably would cause Lincoln to make Hooker leave a portion of his army behind when he started north to challenge the invaders of Pennsylvania.

Of course, it was rather late for such improvisations, but Lee suggested them anyhow. "I still hope that all things will end well for us in Vicksburg," he said in closing. "At any rate, every effort should be made to bring about that result." And with that, having advanced such recommendations as he thought proper in connection with the supreme endeavor he was about to make with the Army of Northern Virginia, he mounted Traveller and rode in a heavy rain across the shallow Potomac.

This was the week of the summer solstice, and the land was green with promise as Lee rode northward, this day and the next. "It's like a hole full of blubber to a Greenlander!" Ewell had exclaimed as he passed this way the week before. Hill and Longstreet agreed, finding that his heavy requisitions of food and livestock had scarcely diminished the pickings all around. Marches were so rapid over the good roads that some outfits enjoyed "breakfast in Virginia, whiskey in Maryland, and supper in Pennsylvania." Struck by the contrast to the ravaged, fought-over region in which they had spent most of the past two years, the Confederates gazed wide-eyed at the lush fields and sleek cattle and the prosperity of the citizens who tilled and tended them. A Texas private wrote home in amazement that the barns hereabouts were "positively more tastily built than two thirds of the houses in Waco." The sour looks of the natives had no repressive effect on the soldiers, who "would ask them for their names so we could write them on a piece of paper, so we told them, and put it in water as we knew it would turn to vinegar." Spirits were high all down the long gray column. "Och, mine contree!" the lean marchers called out to the stolid men along the roadside, or: "Here's your played-out rebellion!" The Pennsylvanians in turn were impressed by the butternut invaders, so different from their own well-turned-out militiamen, who had fallen back northward at the approach of Ewell's outriders the week before. "Many were ragged, shoeless, and filthy," a civilian wrote, but all were "well armed and under perfect discipline. They seemed to move as one vast machine."

Others found that the obvious admiration the rebels felt for this land of plenty did not necessarily mean that they preferred it to their homeland. The farms were too close together for their liking, and they complained of the lack of trees and shade, which made the atmosphere seem cramped and unfit for leisure. Even the magnificent-looking horses, the great Percherons and Clydesdales, turned out to be a disappointment in the end. Consuming about twice the feed, they could stand only about half the hardship required of what one artilleryman called "our compact, hard-muscled little horses. . . . It was pitiful later," he added, "to see these great brutes suffer when compelled to dash off at full gallop with a gun, after pasturing on dry broom sedge and eating a quarter of feed of weevil-eaten corn." Nor was the qualified reaction limited to those from whom it might have been expected. A housewife, questioning a Negro body servant who was attending his North Carolina master on the march, tested his loyalty by asking him if he was treated well, and she got a careful answer. "I live as I wish," he told her, "and if I did not, I think I couldn't better myself by stopping here. This is a beautiful country, but it doesn't come up to home in my eyes."

Apparently Lee felt much the same way about it, for at Chambersburg on June 27—he had arrived the day before and pitched his headquarters tent just east of town in a roadside grove called Shetter's Woods, where the townspeople came in normal times for picnics and such celebrations as the one planned for the Fourth of July, a week from now—he told "a true Union woman" who asked him for his autograph: "My only desire is that they will let me go home and eat my bread in peace." He said this despite the fact that his ride northward had in some ways resembled a triumphal procession, beginning with a gift of fresh raspberries just after he crossed the Potomac. Though Marylanders noted that he had aged considerably in the ten months since his previous visit, the gray commander on the iron-gray horse still impressed them as quite the handsomest man they had ever seen. "Oh, I wish he was ours!" a girl who was waving a Union flag exclaimed with sudden fervor as he passed through Hagerstown, and in Pennsylvania when a civilian whispered in awe as he rode by, "What a large neck he has," a nearby Confederate was quick with an explanation: "It takes a damn big neck to hold his head."

The "perfect discipline" remarked on by civilians as the butternut columns wound past their houses and left them unmolested was the result of a decision Lee had made before leaving Virginia. "I cannot hope that Heaven will prosper our cause when we are violating its laws," he said. "I shall therefore carry on the war in Pennsylvania without offending the sanctions of a high civilization and of Christianity." Accordingly, he had instructed his commissary officers to meet all the necessities of the army by formal requisition on local authorities or by direct purchase with Confederate money. Exhorting his troops "to abstain with most scrupulous care from unnecessary or wanton injury to private property," he issued at Chambersburg today a general order commending them for their good behavior so far on the march. "It must be remembered that we make war only upon armed men," he told them, "and that we cannot take vengeance for the wrongs our people have suffered without lowering ourselves in the eyes of all whose abhorrence has been excited by the atrocities of our enemies, and offending against Him to whom vengeance belongeth, without whose favor and support our efforts must all prove in vain."

In part these words were written, and enforced, with an eye to the encouragement of the northern peace movement. Whether anything would come of that remained to be seen, but the effect on the men to whom the order was addressed was all that could have been desired. No army had ever marched better or with so little straggling. Longstreet and Hill had their two corps in bivouac at Chambersburg and Fayetteville, six miles east, and their men were in excellent spirits, well rested and far better shod and clad and fed than they had been when they were up this way the year before.

Ewell by now was well along with his independent mission. Early was within half a dozen miles of York, and the other two divisions were at Carlisle, a short day's march from the Susquehanna and Harrisburg, which Ewell had been authorized to capture if it "comes within your means." This now seemed likely, and Lee was prepared to follow with the other two corps as soon as Stuart arrived to shield his flank and bring him news of what the Federals were up to on the far side of the Potomac.

But there was the rub; Lee had heard nothing from Stuart in three days. This probably meant that Jeb and his picked brigades were off on the "ride" Lee had authorized on the 23d, but he seemed either to have ignored the admonition to "take his place on our right flank," which was highly improbable, or else to have run into unforeseen difficulties: which might mean almost anything, including annihilation, except that it was hard to imagine the irrepressible Stuart being caught in any box he could not get out of. Still, the strain of waiting was beginning to tell on Lee, who spent much of his time poring over a large-scale map of western Maryland and southern Pennsylvania which Stonewall Jackson had had prepared that winter, with just such a campaign as the present one in mind.

Another legacy from Jackson was a sixty-one-year-old

West Pointer named Isaac Trimble, one of his favorite brigadiers, who reported for duty to Lee in Shetter's Woods today, having recovered at last from a leg wound received ten months ago. "Before this war is over," he had told Stonewall, "I intend to be a major general or a corpse." His promotion having come through in April, he had been slated for command of the division that had gone to Edward Johnson, but his injuries had been so slow to heal—in part, no doubt, because of his age—that it had been necessary to go ahead without him. There could be no question of his superseding Old Clubby, who had done so well at Winchester, yet Lee had no intention of losing the services of so hard a fighter as this veteran of all the Second Corps victories from First through Second Manassas, even though there was no specific command to give him that was commensurate with his rank. Ewell was moving against Harrisburg, Lee told Trimble; "go and join him and help him take the place."

Before he left, however, Lee drew him into conversation about the terrain just beyond the mountains to the east. Trimble, who had been chief engineer of a nearby railroad before the war, replied that there was scarcely a square mile in that direction that did not contain excellent ground for battle or maneuver. Lee seemed pleased at that, and he told why. "Our army is in good spirits, not overfatigued, and can be concentrated in twenty-four hours or less." Not having heard from Stuart to the contrary—as he surely would have done if such had been the case—he assumed that the Federals were still on the far side of the Potomac, and he outlined for Trimble his plans for their destruction. "When they hear where we are, they will make forced marches to interpose their forces between us and Baltimore and Philadelphia. They will come up, probably through Frederick, broken down with hunger and hard marching, strung out on a long line and much demoralized. When they come into Pennsylvania, I shall throw an overwhelming force on their advance, crush it, follow up the success, drive one corps back on another, and by successive repulses and surprises, before they can concentrate, create a panic and virtually destroy the army."

Stirred by this vision of the Army of the Potomac being toppled like a row of dominoes, Trimble said that he did not doubt the outcome of such a confrontation, especially since the morale of the Army of Northern Virginia had never been higher than it was now. "That is, I hear, the general impression," Lee replied, and by way of a parting gesture he laid his hand on the dead Jackson's map, touching the region just east of the mountains that caught on their western flanks the rays of the setting sun. "Hereabouts we shall probably meet the enemy and fight a great battle," he said, "and if God gives us the victory, the war will be over and we shall achieve the recognition of our independence."

One of the place names under his hand as he spoke was the college town of Gettysburg, just over twenty miles away, from which no less than ten roads ran to as many disparate points of the compass, as if it were probing for trouble in all directions.

★ ★ ★

At sundown of that same June 27, as Trimble said good-bye to Lee and left for Carlisle to join Ewell, a courier left Washington aboard a special train for Hooker's headquarters, established just that afternoon at Frederick. Though he thus was risking capture by rebel cavalry, which was known to be on the loose, the documents he carried would admit of no delay. In the past ten months, the army had fought four major battles under as many different commanders—Bull Run under Pope, Antietam under McClellan, Fredericksburg under Ambrose Burnside, and Chancellorsville under Hooker—all against a single adversary, Robert Lee, who could claim unquestionable victory in three out of the four: especially the first and the last, of which about the best that could be said, from the Northern point of view, was that the Federal army had survived them. Now it was about to fight its fifth great battle, and the import of the messages about to be delivered was that it would fight it under still a fifth commander.

Not that Hooker had not done well in the seven weeks since Chancellorsville. He had indeed: especially in the past few days, when by dint of hard and skillful marching he managed to interpose his 100,000 soldiers between Lee and Washington without that general's knowledge that the blue army had even crossed the river from which it took its name. The trouble was that, despite his efforts to shift the blame for the recent Wilderness fiasco—principally onto George Stoneman and John Sedgwick and O. O. Howard's rattled Dutchmen—he could not blur a line of the picture fixed in the public mind of himself as the exclusive author of that woeful chapter. In early June, for example, the Chicago *Tribune* defined its attitude in an editorial reprinted in papers as far away as Richmond: "Under the leadership of 'fighting Joe Hooker' the glorious Army of the Potomac is becoming more slow in its movements, more unwieldy, less confident of itself, more of a football to the enemy, and less an honor to the country than any army we have yet raised."

There was much in this that was unfair—particularly in regard to slowness, a charge Hooker had refuted once and would refute again—but it was generally known, in and out of army circles, that his ranking corps commander, Darius Couch, had applied for and been granted transfer to another department in order to avoid further service under a man he judged incompetent. Moreover, this mistrust was shared to a considerable extent by the authorities in Washington. Secretary of War Edwin M. Stanton and General-in-Chief Henry W. Halleck had never liked Joe Hooker, and Lincoln had sent him at the outset a letter which made only too clear the doubts that had attended his appointment. These doubts had been allayed for a time by the boldness and celerity of his movements preceding the May Day confrontation in the Wilderness, when he came unglued under pressure and revived them. Now they were back, and in force: as was shown by the day-to-day correspondence between himself and Lincoln, made voluminous by his determination to avoid all possible contact with Halleck, whom he regarded with reciprocal distaste.

On June 4, when Thaddeus Lowe's balloonists reported some Confederates gone from their camps across the Rappahannock, Hooker interpreted this as the opening movement of an offensive elsewhere, probably upriver, and reasoned that the most effective way to stop it was to launch one of his own, here and now. Next morning, after directing the establishment of a west-bank bridgehead for this purpose, he wired Lincoln that he thought his best move would be "to pitch into [Lee's] rear," and he asked: "Will it be within the sphere of my instructions to do so?" Lincoln replied promptly, to the effect that it would not. He had, he said, "but one idea which I think worth suggesting to you, and that is, in case you find Lee coming to the north of the Rappahannock, I would by no means cross to the south of it. . . . In one word, I would not take any risk of being entangled upon the river, like an ox jumped half over a fence and liable to be torn by dogs, front and rear, without a fair chance to gore one way or kick the other." Halleck followed this up with some advice of his own. "Lee will probably move light and rapidly," he warned. "Your movable force should be prepared to do the same." Hooker did as he was told, alerting his troops for a sidling movement up the north bank, but he maintained the bridgehead, not only as a possible means of learning what the enemy was up to, but also on the off-chance that the authorities might decide to give him his head after all.

On June 10, hearing from Pleasonton that rebel infantry had been spotted in force at Brandy Station the day before, he showed that he too, though he considered the Washington defenses quite strong enough to withstand attack, was willing to risk a swap of queens in the presently deadly chess game. If Lee had taken a good part of his army west to Culpeper, Hooker wired Lincoln, "will it not promote the true interest of the cause for me to march to Richmond at once? . . . If left to operate from my own judgment, with my present information, I do not hesitate to say that I should adopt this course as being the most speedy and certain mode of giving the rebellion a mortal blow."

Once more Lincoln was prompt in reply. Unlike Davis, who believed that the best defense of his capital was a threat to the enemy's, he was plainly horrified at this notion of removing the army from its present tactical position between Lee and Washington. Besides, he said, "If you had Richmond invested today, you would not be able to take it in twenty days; meanwhile your communications, and with them your army, would be ruined. I think Lee's army, and not Richmond, is your true objective point. If he comes toward the Upper Potomac, follow on his flank and on his inside track, shortening your lines whilst he lengthens his. Fight him, too, when opportunity offers. If he stays where he is, fret him and fret him."

Next morning Hooker began the movement north, conforming to the pattern set by Lee, but maintaining what Lincoln called the "inside track." This meant that he was required to keep between the Confederates and the capital in his rear, a limitation he found irksome. Moreover, though he knew the rebels had been reinforced for the campaign now fairly under way, his own army was far below the strength it had enjoyed when it marched on Chancellorsville. Nearly 17,000 men had fallen there, and an equal number of short-term enlistments had expired in the past six weeks. As a result of these subtractions, by no means offset by the trickle of recruits, barely 100,000 effectives left the familiar camps around Falmouth in the course of the next four days.

To facilitate the march, which would be a hard one, he divided his army into two unequal wings, one led by John Reynolds, consisting of his own corps and those under Daniel Sickles and Howard, and the other by Hooker himself, consisting of those under George G. Meade, John Sedgwick, Henry W. Slocum, and Winfield Scott Hancock, who had succeeded Darius Couch. "If the enemy should be making for Maryland, I will make the best dispositions in my power to come up with him," he assured Lincoln on June 14: only to receive from him a message sent at the same time. Foreseeing the disaster in the present threat to Milroy, the Commander in Chief wanted something more from Fighting Joe than words of reassurance. "If the head of Lee's army is at Martinsburg and the tail of it on the Plank road between Fredericksburg and Chancellorsville," he wired, "the animal must be very slim somewhere. Could you not break him?" Strung out on the roads as he was by now, having abandoned the bridgehead he had held for more than a week, there was nothing Hooker could do for the present but keep marching, and that was what he did.

Hancock's corps, the last to go, pulled out of Falmouth on June 15, the day that A. P. Hill left Fredericksburg and Ewell's lead division began its crossing of the Potomac. A simultaneous dispatch from Halleck, warning against "wanton and wasteful destruction of public property," snapped the string of Hooker's patience, and he got off an urgent wire to Lincoln: "You have long been aware, Mr President, that I have not enjoyed the confidence of the major general commanding the army, and I can assure you so long as this continues we may look in vain for success." This sounded as if he was saying he lacked confidence in himself, "the major general commanding the army," but it was Old Brains he meant, and Lincoln knew it. "To remove all misunderstanding," he replied, "I now place you in the strict military relation to General Halleck of a commander of one of the armies to the general-in-chief of all the armies. I have not intended differently, but as it seems to be differently understood, I shall direct him to give you orders and you to obey them."

The sting of this was somewhat relieved by a covering letter in which the Chief Executive explained that all he asked was "that you will be in such mood that we can get into our action the best cordial judgment of yourself and General Halleck, with my own poor mite added, if indeed he and you shall think it entitled to any consideration at all." However, it had begun to seem to Hooker that Lincoln's advice in regard to Lee—"fret him and fret him"—was also being applied in regard to himself, not only by the general-in-chief but also by the President, whose "poor mite" often made up in sharpness for what it lacked in weight. It seemed to Hooker that he was being goaded, and unquestionably he was. One after another his proposals had been dismissed as rash, or else they had been urged upon him only after subsequent instructions had placed his army in an attitude from which they could no longer be accomplished. Urgent appeals for reinforcements were rejected out of hand, as were others that his authority be extended to include the soldiers in the capital defenses. More and more, as the long hot days of hard and dusty marching went by, it came to seem to Fighting Joe that he commanded his army only in semblance, though it was clear enough at the same time that his was the head on which the blame would fall in event of the disaster he saw looming.

Leapfrogging his headquarters northward, first to Dumfries and then to Fairfax, with no information as to what was occurring beyond his immediate horizon, he complained at last to Halleck, on June 24, that "outside of the Army of the Potomac I don't know whether I am standing on my head or feet." The next two days were spent crossing the Potomac at Edwards Ferry and effecting a concentration around Frederick.

His plan was to strike westward into the Cumberland Valley, severing Lee's communications with Virginia, and for this he wanted the co-operation of the 10,000 men at Harpers Ferry, which was beyond the limits of his control, but which he thought should be evacuated before Lee turned and gobbled up the garrison as he had done in September. On the evening of June 26, believing that the authorities might have learned from that example—at least they had learned to post the troops on Maryland Heights, occupation of which had permitted the Confederates to take the place in short order the time before, along with some 12,000 men and 73 cannon—Hooker wired Halleck: "Is there any reason why Maryland Heights should not be abandoned after the public stores and property are removed?" Halleck replied next morning: "Maryland Heights have always been regarded as an important point to be held by us, and much expense and labor incurred in fortifying them. I cannot approve their abandonment, except in case of absolute necessity."

Convinced that the garrison was "of no earthly account" on its perch above the Ferry, Hooker decided to appeal through channels to Stanton and Lincoln. "All the public property could have been secured tonight," he wired back, "and the troops marched to where they could have been of some service. Now they are but a bait for the rebels, should they return. I beg that this may be presented to the Secretary of War and His Excellency the President." While waiting for an answer, he either decided the appeal should be strengthened or else he lost his head entirely. Or perhaps, having taken all he could take from above, he really wanted to get from under. At any rate, before the general-in-chief replied, Fighting Joe got off a second wire to him, hard on the heels of the first. "My original instructions require me to cover Harpers Ferry and Washington," it read. "I have now imposed upon me, in addition, an enemy in my front of more than my number. I beg to be understood, respectfully, but firmly, that I am unable to comply with this condition with the means at my disposal, and earnestly request that I may at once be relieved from the position I occupy."

This was sent at 1 p.m. The long afternoon wore slowly away; the sun had set and night had fallen before he received an answer addressed to "Major General Hooker, Army of the Potomac." Whether the word *commanding* had been omitted by accident or design he could not tell. Nor was the body of the message at all conclusive on that point. "Your application to be relieved from your present command is received," Halleck told him. "As you were appointed to this command by the President, I have no power to relieve you. Your dispatch has been duly referred for Executive action."

The wire was headed 8 p.m. and that was where duplicity came in. Halleck knew that the special train had left Washington half an hour before that time, for the courier aboard it was James A. Hardie, his own assistant adjutant general, and Old Brains himself had written the documents he carried, one an order relieving Hooker of command and the other a letter of instructions for his successor. Reaching Frederick well after midnight, Hardie did not wait for morning. Nor did he call first on Joe Hooker. Rather, he went directly to the tent of the man who would succeed him: George Meade.

This would come as something of a shock to the army, especially to Reynolds and Sedgwick, who ranked him, but no one was more surprised than Meade himself. His immediate reaction, on waking out of a sound sleep at 3 o'clock in the morning to find the staff colonel standing beside his cot, was alarm. He thought he was about to be arrested. Sure enough, after a brief exchange of greetings, during which Meade wondered just what military sin he had committed, Hardie's first words were: "General, I'm afraid I've come to make trouble for you." And with that, changing the nature if not the force of the shock, he handed him Halleck's letter of instructions, which began: "You will receive with this the order of the President placing you in command of the Army of the Potomac."

Shortly before, in a letter to his wife, Meade had commented on "the ridiculous appearance we present of changing our generals after each battle," and only two days ago, amid rumors that Hooker was slated for removal, he had written her that he stood little chance of receiving the appointment, not only because he was outranked by two of his six fellow corps commanders, but also "because I have no friends, political or others, who press or advance my claims or pretensions." Yet now he had it, against all the odds, and with it a cluster of problems inherited on what was obviously the eve of battle. Partly, though—if he could believe what Halleck told him—these problems were reduced at the very outset. "You will not be hampered by any minute instructions from these headquarters," the letter read. "Your army is free to act as you may deem proper under the circumstances as they arise." His main duty would be to cover Washington and Baltimore. "Should General Lee move upon either of these places, it is expected that you will either anticipate him or arrive with him so as to give him battle."

By way of stressing the fact that the new commander would have a free hand, Halleck added: "Harpers Ferry and its garrison are under your direct orders." Knowing the difficulties Hooker had encountered on this question, Meade could scarcely believe his eyes. "Am I permitted, under existing circumstances," he inquired

by telegraph, later that same day, "to withdraw a portion
of the garrison of Harpers Ferry, providing I leave sufficient force to hold Maryland Heights against a *coup de
main*?" Promptly the reply came back: "The garrison at
Harpers Ferry is under your orders. You can diminish or
increase it as you think the circumstances justify."

Meanwhile the new commander had called on
Hooker, who reacted to the order with as much apparent relief as Lincoln and Halleck had felt in issuing it. In
fact, nothing in Fighting Joe's five-month tenure, in the
course of which the army had experienced much of
profit as well as pain, became him more than the manner in which he brought it to a close. Conferring with
Meade on his plans and dispositions, he was coopera-
tive and pleasant, except for one brief flare-up when
Meade, looking over the situation map, remarked that
the various corps seemed "rather scattered." Then
Hooker quieted down, issued a farewell address urging
support for his successor—"a brave and accomplished
officer, who has nobly earned the confidence and esteem
of this army on many a well-fought field"—and got into
a spring wagon, alongside Hardie, for the ride to the
railroad station. Meade shook his hand, stood for a
moment watching the wagon roll away, then turned and
entered the tent Hooker had just vacated.

Presently he was interrupted by Reynolds, who had
put on his dress uniform to come over and congratulate
his fellow Pennsylvanian. This had a good effect on
those who had wondered what his reaction would be:
the more so because those closest to him knew that he
had gone to Washington early that month, when it was
rumored that Fighting Joe was about to get the ax, to
tell Lincoln that he did not want the command—for
which, with Couch gone, he was next in line—unless he

was allowed more freedom of action than any of the army's five unfortunate chieftains had been granted up to then. Now, if not before, Reynolds had his answer, and he took it with aplomb.

Sedgwick too arrived to offer congratulations and assurance of support, having managed to assuage the burning in his bosom which the announcement had provoked. News that it was Meade who would head the army, and not himself, had reached "Uncle John," as the men of his corps liked to call him, while he was out for his morning ride. For him, as for most old soldiers, the tradition of seniority was a strong one. Putting the spurs to his horse, he led his staff on a hard gallop for some distance to relieve his agitation, then rode over to shake the hand of the man who had passed him by.

That hand was a busy one just now, getting the feel of the controls even as the vehicle was headed for a collision. Meade's own elevation called for other promotions and advancements beyond those recently conferred in the wake of Chancellorsville, which in turn had followed hard upon another extensive shake-up after bloody Fredericksburg. As a result, not one of the seven army corps was commanded now by the general who had led it into battle at Antietam, and the same was true of all but two of the nineteen infantry divisions—Andrew Humphreys' and Alpheus S. Williams'—only four of which were commanded by major generals: Abner Doubleday, David Birney, John Newton, and Carl Schurz. Of the fifteen brigadiers in charge of divisions, seven had been appointed to their posts since early May: John C. Caldwell, Alexander Hays, James Barnes, Romeyn B. Ayres, Samuel W. Crawford, Horatio G. Wright, and Francis Barlow. Equally new to their positions were Hancock and George Sykes, successors to Couch and

Meade as corps commanders. In fact, only Reynolds and Slocum had the same division commanders they had had at Chancellorsville: Doubleday, James S. Wadsworth, and John C. Robinson with the former, Williams and John W. Geary with the latter.

Other drawbacks there were, too. In contrast to Lee, all of whose corps and division commanders were West Pointers except for one V.M.I. man, Meade had only fourteen academy graduates among the twenty-six generals who filled those vital positions in the Army of the Potomac. This meant that nearly half were nonprofessionals, and of these a number were political appointees: Dan Sickles, for example, for whom Meade had small use, either military or private. He had, however, for whatever it was worth, a better geographical distribution among his generals than Lee had achieved. Eight were Pennsylvanians and seven were New Yorkers, while three were from Connecticut, two from Maine, two from Germany—Schurz and Adolf von Steinwehr, both in Howard's corps—and one each from Vermont, Massachusetts, Maryland, and Virginia. The revised order of battle was as follows:

I. REYNOLDS	II. HANCOCK	III. SICKLES	V. SYKES
Wadsworth	Caldwell	Birney	Barnes
Doubleday	Gibbon	Humphreys	Ayres
Robinson	Hayes		Crawford

VI. SEDGWICK	XI. HOWARD	XII. SLOCUM
Wright	Barlow	Williams
Howe	Steinwehr	Geary
Newton	Schurz	

Doubtful as were the qualities of a sizable proportion of these men, one third of whom had been assigned to their current posts within the past eight weeks, none was more of a military question mark than the man who had just been given the most responsible job of all. This doubt was not so much because of any lack of experience; Meade had performed well, if not brilliantly, in combat as the commander of a brigade, a division, and a corps. If at Chancellorsville, through no fault of his own, he had been denied an appreciable share in the battle, at Fredericksburg his had been the only division to achieve even a brief penetration of the rebel line, and surely this had been considered by Lincoln—along with Reynolds' unacceptable stipulation and Sedgwick's alleged poor showing in early May, of which Hooker had complained—in making his choice as to who was to become the army's sixth commander. The question, rather, was whether Meade could inspire that army when pay-off time came round, as it was now about to do. He seemed utterly incapable of provoking the sort of personal enthusiasm McClellan and Hooker could arouse by their mere presence; Burnside and Pope, even the hapless Irvin McDowell, seemed downright gaudy alongside Meade, who gave an impression of professorial dryness and lack of juice.

What he lacked in fact was glamour, not only in his actions and dispatches, but also in his appearance, which a journalist said was more that of "a learned pundit than a soldier." Two birthdays short of fifty, he looked considerably older, with a "small and compact" balding head, a grizzled beard, and outsized pouches under eyes that were "serious, almost sad," and "rather sunken" on each side of what the reporter charitably described as "the late Duke of Wellington class of nose." The over-all effect, although "decidedly patrician and distinguished," was not of the kind that brought forth cheers or a wholesale tossing of caps, particularly when it was known to be combined with a hair-trigger temper and a petulance which tested in turn the patience of his staff. "What's Meade ever done?" was a common response among the men—those outside his corps, at least—when they heard that he was their new commander. The general himself had few delusions on this score. "I know they call me a damned old snapping turtle," he remarked.

Whatever other shortcomings he might have, in addition to lacking glamour, it presently was shown that indecision was not one of them: at least not now, in these first hours. "So soon as I can post myself up, I will communicate more in detail," he had closed an early-morning telegram accepting the appointment to command. By midafternoon, having studied Hooker's plans and dispositions, along with intelligence reports on Lee—reports which, incidentally, turned out to be extremely accurate; "The enemy force does not exceed 80,000 men and 275 guns," he was told by Maryland observers who kept tally on what passed through Hagerstown, and this was within 5000 men and 3 guns of agreement with Lee's own figures, which included his scattered cavalry—Meade had decided on a course of action and had already begun to issue orders that would put it into execution. "I propose to move this army tomorrow in the direction of York," he wired Halleck at 4.45 p.m. This meant that he had rejected Hooker's plan for a westward strike at Lee's supply line. Moreover, the decision was made irrevocable by dispatches, not only recalling the units that had gone in that direction, but also ordering William French to march eastward to Frederick with 7000 men while the remainder of the garrison served as train guards for the Harpers Ferry stores, which were to be removed at once to the capital defenses.

Meade thus was adopting what had seemed to him at the outset the only proper course for him to take in conformity with his orders from above: "I must move toward the Susquehanna, keeping Washington and Baltimore well covered, and if the enemy is checked in his attempt to cross the Susquehanna, or if he turns toward Baltimore, to give him battle." Reynolds was retained as commander of the three corps in the lead on the swing north, and a warning order went out soon after sundown for the whole army to "be ready to march at daylight tomorrow. . . . Strong exertions are required."

That meant early reveille and breakfast in the dark, but the men had grown accustomed to this in the two weeks they had spent on the road since leaving the Rappahannock. All the same, and even though they had taken what Lincoln called the "inside track," the pace had been killing—Slocum's corps, as an extreme example, had covered thirty-three hot dusty miles in a single day while moving up to Fairfax—with the result that straggling had been worse than at any time since the berry-picking jaunt to First Bull Run, just three weeks short of two full years ago. For the most part, those who fell out managed to catch up at night and start out with their units in the morning, but enough had dropped out permanently, skulking in barns along the way, to bring the army's total down to 94,974 effectives of all arms. Then—on June 28, by coincidence a Sunday—had come a day of rest, occasioned by the change of commanders, and now they were off again. Although they did not know just where they were going, at any rate they were glad it was not back to the Old Dominion. "We have marched through some beautiful country," a colonel wrote home. "It is refreshing to get out of the barren desert of Virginia and into this land of thrift and plenty."

One thing was practically certain, however, and this was that the road they now were taking led to battle. But that was all right, too, apparently, despite the tradition of defeat which had been lengthened under Burnside and Hooker and was a part of Meade's inheritance. "We felt some doubt about whether it was ever going to be our fortune to win a victory in Virginia," another soldier afterwards recalled, "but no one admitted the possibility of a defeat north of the Potomac."

★ ★ ★

For Lee, this same Sunday had been a day of puzzlement, mounting tension, and frustration. He not only did not know of the early-morning switch in blue commanders; he did not even know that for the past two days the whole Federal army had been on the same side of the Potomac as his own. Such ignorance might have been expected to be the opposite of disturbing—a maxim even described it as "bliss"—except that, as he knew only too well, having had occasion to prove it to several opponents, a lack of information was all too often the prelude to disaster. A recent prime example of this was Hooker, of whom Jackson had said on the ride to Guiney Station: "He should not have sent away his cavalry. That was his great blunder. It was that which enabled me to turn him, without his being aware of it, and to take him by the rear." Now Lee himself was in somewhat the same danger, and for somewhat the same reason.

For the better part of a week he had heard nothing at all from Stuart, on whom he had always depended for information, or from any of his six brigades. One was at Carlisle with Ewell, approaching the Susquehanna; two were guarding the Blue Ridge passes, far to the south; while the other three, presumably, were off on another of those circumferential "rides" that had brought fame to their plumed leader. This last was not in itself the reason for Lee's anxiety. After all, he himself had authorized the adoption of such a course. What bothered him was the silence, which was as complete as if a sound-proof curtain had been dropped between him and his one best source of information. Scarcely an officer who approached him there in Shetter's Woods today escaped the question: "Can you tell me where General Stuart is?" or: "Where on earth is my cavalry?" or even: "Have you any news of the enemy's movements? What is the enemy going to do?"

No one had ever heard him ask such things before, for the simple reason that he had never needed to ask them; Stuart had generally supplied the answers in advance. And now, for lack of answers, he was obliged— as most of his opponents, to their distress in the course of the past year, had been obliged—to fall back on uninformed conjecture. This summoned up a host of alarming possibilities, including the danger that the bluecoats might be contemplating an attack on thinly defended Richmond or on his even more thinly defended supply line in the Cumberland Valley: both of which maneuvers had in fact been proposed by Hooker and disallowed by Lincoln. One would be about as unwelcome to Lee as the other in the present dispersed condition of his army, one third of which was a good forty miles from Chambersburg, where the remaining two thirds were in profitless bivouac and so completely stripped of cavalry that the foraging was being done by soldiers mounted on horses from the artillery and the wagon train.

However, for all his inward anxiety, which he masked

as best he could behind a show of being calm and even
cheerful, Lee not only let his dispositions stand; he sent
word for Ewell to continue the advance on Harrisburg,
and prepared to move the rest of his army in that direction the following day, first Longstreet and then Hill,
both of whom were put on the alert. "If the enemy does
not find us," he explained, "we must try to find him, in the
absence of the cavalry, as best we can." So he said, continuing the attempt to mask his growing concern. But still
he asked all comers: "Can you tell me where General Stuart is?" and "Where on earth is my cavalry?"

Perhaps it was just as well, so far at least as his temper was concerned, that no one within range of his voice
could give him the answer, which was not of a nature to
relieve his qualms. In fact, it might well have upset him
more than did the tantalizing silence. For even as he
inquired of various callers as to the whereabouts of his
cavalry on this Sunday afternoon, Stuart and the more
than 5000 troopers of his three best brigades were on
the northeast fringe of Washington, some seventy miles
away. That was as the crow flew, moreover, and for anyone but a crow it would have been considerably farther,
not only because Jeb had no more notion of Lee's
whereabouts than Lee had of his, but also because a
good many of those intervening miles were occupied by
the Federal army, which Lee mistakenly assumed to be
still south of the Potomac but which in fact was being
alerted even now for a resumption of its northward
march at dawn.

This meant that Stuart would face tomorrow the same
frustration he had faced today, and indeed for the past
three days as well, in attempting to carry out his instructions to make contact with the right flank of the Confederate army of invasion; Hooker had stood in his path,

and so would Meade. It had been that way from the outset, just after midnight June 24, when he first left Salem
and moved east, beyond the Bull Run Mountains, to find
a heavy column of blue infantry marching squarely
athwart the route he had chosen for what was intended
to be not only the greatest of all his "rides," but also
indemnity for the ugly things some of the southern papers
had been saying about him ever since the surprise they
claimed he had suffered a couple of weeks ago at Brandy
Station.

His plan, based on information that the bluecoats
were inactive in their camps east of the mountains and
were scattered over so wide an area that he would be
able to push his way between two of their corps in order
to get beyond them for a crossing of the Potomac in
their rear, had been workable the day before, when the
information was true; but it was true no longer. By coincidence, Hooker began his northward march to the
Potomac shortly before Stuart emerged from Glass-
cock's Gap on the morning of June 25, and that was how
it happened that Jeb found his progress blocked by a
whole corps of Federals in motion across his front.
Promptly he unlimbered the six guns he had brought
along and began to shell the passing column, which
extended north and south for a greater distance than the
eye could follow. He thus was mindful of Lee's instructions to do the enemy "all the damage you can," but the
admonition included in the same letter, that he was not
to attempt his favorite maneuver unless he found he
could do so "without hindrance," was ignored. Turning
off to the south, he camped for the night near Buckland,
intending to swing wide around the enemy rear next
morning. However, dawn showed the Federals gone,
and he rode east through Bristoe and Brentsville, not

sighting a single bluecoat all day long, to bivouac just
south of Occoquan Creek, which he crossed at Wolf
Run Shoals next morning, June 27.

In better than fifty hours he had covered less than
forty miles of road, and he was about as far from the
nearest Potomac ford as he had been when he started.
Moreover, horses and men were beginning to show how
hard they had been worked these past two weeks, fend-
ing off the aggressive blue troopers at such places as
Middleburg and Aldie before undertaking their present
exertions deep in the enemy rear. Frequent halts were
necessary for rest and feeding, no matter how Stuart
chafed when he remembered that his orders had been to
cross the Potomac as soon as practicable after the 24th,
three days ago.

Pressing northward, first through Fairfax Station,
where he captured most of a 100-man detachment of
New York cavalry, and then to Fairfax Court House,
where he called a halt to let his hungry troopers "go
through" several sutler shacks and graze their horses,
he struck the Leesburg-Alexandria turnpike and turned
left along it for Dranesville, which he reached soon after
sundown. Smoldering campfires were evidence that
Federal infantry had recently passed this way and were
still in the vicinity, guarding the better Potomac fords
upstream; so he swung due north for a crossing at
Rowser's Ford, which was deep and wide and booming.
"No more difficult achievement was accomplished by
the cavalry during the war," a staff officer later declared.
The guns went completely out of sight, and the ammunition was distributed among the men, who kept it
above water by carrying it over in their arms. By 3
o'clock in the morning, June 28—as Meade awoke to
find Hardie standing beside his cot—the entire com-

mand, one member said, "stood wet and dripping on the Maryland shore."

Stuart let his troopers sleep till dawn, then resumed the march, mindful of his orders to "take position on General Ewell's right, place yourself in communication with him, guard his flank, keep him informed of the enemy's movements, and collect all the supplies you can for the use of the army." The trouble was he did not know Ewell's position, any more than he knew Lee's, except that Ewell would "probably move toward the Susquehanna." Jeb's decision to move in that direction, too, was easily arrived at. The whole Union army was to the west; the heavily manned Washington defenses were to the east; all that was left—unless he gave the project up and retraced his steps southward, which apparently never crossed his mind—was north, and that was the way he went.

By midday he was in Rockville, a town on the National Road, which ran from Washington through Frederick, present headquarters of the Army of the Potomac, and thence on out to Ohio. Rockville was thus on the main Federal supply route, and scouts reported a train of 150 mule-drawn wagons on the way there from the capital, whose outskirts were less than a dozen miles away. Soon they came in sight and the raiders bore down on them, whooping in hungry anticipation of a feast. "The wagons were brand new, the mules fat and sleek, and the harness in use for the first time," one trooper later wrote. "Such a train we had never seen before and did not see again." Though almost half were captured at that first swoop, the other teamsters got their wagons turned around and took off down the road at a hard trot. For a time it looked as if they might be able to outrun the weary rebel horses, but presently a wagon overturned and caused a pile-up, blocking the road for all but about two dozen of the others, whose drivers continued their race for safety, still pursued, until the gray riders came within full view of Washington itself and abandoned the chase. Even without the ones that got away, the spoils were rich, including 400 teamsters, 900 mules, and 125 wagons loaded with hams, bacon, sugar, hardtack, bottled whiskey, and enough oats to feed the 5000 half-starved mounts of the raiders for several days.

Much time was spent at Rockville, paroling the prisoners, feeding the horses, and accepting the admiring glances of some young ladies from a local seminary, who came out waving improvised Confederate flags and requesting souvenir buttons. While all this was going on, Stuart toyed with the notion of making a quick dash into the northern capital, but then rejected it regretfully—for lack of time, he subsequently explained—and resumed his northward march at sundown, hampered somewhat by the "one hundred and twenty-five best United States model wagons and splendid teams with gay caparisons" which he was determined to turn over to Lee, as a sort of super trophy of the ride, when and if he managed to find him.

A twenty-mile night march brought the raiders into Cooksville, where they captured another detachment of blue cavalry on the morning of June 29 before pushing on to Hood's Mill, a station on the B&O about midway between Baltimore and Frederick. While further disrupting the Federal lines of supply and communication by tearing up the tracks there and burning a bridge at Sykeston, three miles east, Stuart inquired of friendly Marylanders as to Ewell's whereabouts. None of them could tell him anything, but newspapers just in from the north reported Confederate infantry at York and Carlisle, moving against Wrightsville and Harrisburg; so Jeb pressed on to Westminster, fifteen miles north, on the turnpike connecting Gettysburg and Baltimore. Arriving in the late afternoon, he gobbled up another mounted blue detachment and made camp for the night. Scouts brought word that Union cavalry was in strength at Littletown, twelve miles ahead and just beyond the Pennsylvania line.

Next morning—it was now the last day of June, the sixth he had spent out of touch with the rest of the army— he took the precaution of placing Fitz Lee on the left of the column, assigned Hampton to guard the captured wagons, and rode in the lead with John R. Chambliss, successor to the wounded Rooney Lee. His immediate objective, another fifteen miles to the north, was Hanover, where he would be able to choose between two good roads, one leading northwest to Carlisle and the other northeast to York, for a hook-up with one or the other of Ewell's reported columns of invasion.

What he encountered first at Hanover, however, was a fight. It was an unequal affair, the enemy force amounting to no more than a single brigade, but what the blue horsemen lacked in numbers they made up for in vigor. A sudden charge struck and shattered the head of the gray column, and Stuart himself was obliged to take a fifteen-foot ditch jump to avoid being captured along with his blooded mare Virginia. "I shall never forget the glimpse I then saw of this beautiful animal away up in midair over the chasm," a staff officer later wrote, "and Stuart's fine figure sitting erect and firm in the saddle." Bringing up reserves, Jeb drove off the attackers, who in turn were reinforced by another brigade. No serious fighting ensued, however, for while the Federals seemed content to block the road to Gettysburg, a dozen miles to the west, Stuart wanted only to take the road to York, twenty miles to the northeast. After some desultory long-range firing, the two forces drew apart, the Confederates still hampered by the train of captured wagons and some 400 prisoners, taken here and elsewhere in the past two days since leaving Rockville, where the previous 400 had been paroled.

This called for another night march, and the riders who made it remembered it ever after as a nightmare. "It is impossible for me to give you a correct idea of the fatigue and exhaustion of the men and beasts," a lieutenant afterwards said. "Even in line of battle, in momentary expectation of being made to charge, [the men] would throw themselves upon their horses' necks, and even to the ground, and fall to sleep. Couriers in attempting to give orders to officers would be compelled to give them a shake and a word, before they could make them understand." Reaching Dover soon after dawn of the hot first day of July, Stuart learned to his chagrin that there were no Confederates at York, six miles east. They had been there, two days ago, but now they were gone and no one would say where. So he turned the head of the column hard left toward Carlisle, 25 miles northwest, supposing that Ewell had ordered a concentration there.

He was wrong: as he discovered when he approached the town that afternoon and found it occupied by Pennsylvania militia, who peremptorily rejected his demand for a surrender. Jeb and his road-worn troopers were in no shape for a fight, even with raw home guardsmen, one of his officers frankly admitted. "Weak and helpless as we were," he wrote home later, "our anxiety and uneasiness were painful indeed. Thoughts of saving the wagons now were gone, and we thought only of how we, ourselves, might escape." Contenting himself with a token long-range shelling of the U.S. cavalry barracks, the plumed commander was at a loss for a next move until well after nightfall, when two scouts who had left the column near York, with instructions to search westward for signs of the army, reported back to Stuart outside Carlisle. They had found Lee and the main body that day at Gettysburg, where a battle was in progress, and Lee had sent them to find and summon the long-absent Jeb, who thus was placed in the unusual position of having the army commander report to him the location of the infantry he had been ordered to get in touch with and protect.

At 1 o'clock in the morning, July 2—one week, to the hour, since he first set out on the ride that was designed, in part, to retrieve his slipping reputation— Stuart had his troopers on the march for Gettysburg, which was thirty miles away by the nearest road. This was their fifth night march in the past eight days, and it was perhaps the hardest of them all. Southward the weary horses plodded, over Yellow Breeches Creek, through Mount Holly Pass, and across the rolling farmland of Adams County, of which Gettysburg was the county seat. The riders were so exhausted, it was noted, that one who tumbled from his mount slept sprawled across the fence that broke his fall. At dawn they still had miles to go, and even the indefatigable Jeb, though he still clung tenaciously to the train of captured wagons as the one substantial trophy of his ride, could see that a rest halt had to be called if he was to arrive with more than a remnant of his three brigades. It was late afternoon before he reached the field of the greatest battle of the war, having missed all of the first day and

most of the second. Lee received him with an iciness
which a staff officer found "painful beyond description."

Reddening at the sight of his chief of cavalry, the gray
commander raised one arm in a menacing gesture of
exasperation. "General Stuart, where have you been?"
he said. "I have not heard a word from you in days, and
you the eyes and ears of my army." Jeb wilted under this
unfamiliar treatment and became so flustered that he
played his trump card at the outset. "I have brought you
125 wagons and their teams, General," he announced:
only to have Lee reply, "Yes, General, but they are an
impediment to me now."

Then suddenly Lee softened. Perhaps it was Stuart's
obvious dismay or his somewhat bedraggled appearance
after eight days in the saddle; or perhaps it was a recol-
lection of all the service this young man had done him in
the past. At any rate, a witness recalled years later, Lee's
manner became one "of great tenderness" as he added:
"Let me ask your help now. We will not discuss this
longer. Help me fight these people."

The reason Stuart had encountered none of Ewell's
men at York or Carlisle the day before—a Wednesday—
was that Lee, acting on information that reached him
Sunday night, had recalled them Monday morning. As it
was, the tail of Early's column, marching westward on
the road through East Berlin and Heidlersburg, had
been less than ten miles from the head of Stuart's own at
the time he took the risky ditch jump near Hanover on
Tuesday. In fact, the foot soldiers had heard the guns of
that brief engagement, but had not investigated because
Lee, despite his repeated warning to Stuart to be on the
lookout for Ewell, had neglected to warn Ewell to be on

the lookout for Stuart: with the result that the cavalry's roundabout hegira was prolonged for two more days, including some thirty-odd hours beyond the opening of the battle, which in turn resulted from Lee's groping his way across the Pennsylvania landscape, deprived of his eyes and ears, as he said, and with little information as to the enemy's whereabouts or intentions.

Because that ten-mile gap had been ignored—not only ignored, but unsuspected—whatever Lee encountered, good or bad, was bound to come as a surprise, and surprise was seldom a welcome thing in war. And so it was. Coincidence refused to mesh for the general who, six weeks ago in Richmond, had cast his vote for the long chance. Fortuity itself, as the deadly game unfolded move by move, appeared to conform to a pattern of hard luck; so much so, indeed, that in time men would say of Lee, as Jael had said of Sisera after she drove the tent peg into his temple, that the stars in their courses had fought against him.

Such information as he had, and it was meager, had come to him not from Robertson or Jones, whom Stuart had left to guard the Blue Ridge passes, nor from Jenkins, who was off with Ewell, but from a spy—"scout" was the euphemistic word—sent out some weeks before by Longstreet, with instructions to pick up what useful tips he could in the lobbies and barrooms of Washington. His name was Harrison, and no one knew much about him except that he was a Mississippian, bearded and of average height, with sloping shoulders, pale hazel eyes, and an abiding dislike of all Yankees. Lee, for one, apparently considered him unsavory and declined at first to see him when he was brought to Shetter's Woods that Sunday night. "I have no confidence in any scout," he said. Informed by a staff officer, however, that Harrison

claimed the Federal army had crossed the Potomac—
which Lee could scarcely credit, in the absence of any
such report from Stuart—he changed his mind and sent
for him, shortly before midnight.

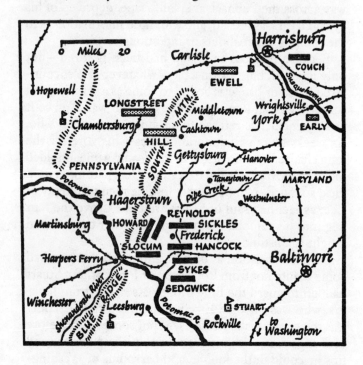

Travel-stained and weary, the spy told Lee that he
had been in Frederick that morning, having heard in
Washington that Hooker had transferred his headquarters to that place. Arriving he had found it true. At least
two corps were there, he said, and others were in the
vicinity, with two more pushed out toward South
Mountain. After observing all this he had procured a
horse and ridden hard for Chambersburg to report to

Longstreet, who had sent him on to Lee. Incidentally, he remarked in closing, Hooker had been replaced that day by Meade.

Lee reacted fast—as well he might—to this news that the blue army had been for the past two days on the same side of the Potomac as his own, one of whose corps, in addition to being divided itself, was thirty-odd miles away from the other two, which were threatened in turn by a possible movement against their rear. It was not so much that he feared for his supply line; he was prepared to abandon contact with Virginia anyhow. The trouble was, if the Federals crossed South Mountain and entered the lower Cumberland Valley—as Harrison had claimed they were about to do, and as Hooker in fact had intended—they would force Lee to conform, in order to meet the threat to his rear, and thus deprive him of the initiative he had to retain if he was to conduct the sort of campaign he had in mind. In the absence of his cavalry, moreover, the dispersed segments of his army were in danger of being surprised and swamped by overwhelming numbers: Meade, in short, might do to him what he had planned to do to Hooker—defeat him in detail. What was called for, in the face of this, was a rapid concentration of all his forces, preferably east of the mountains so as to compel the enemy to abandon the threat to his rear.

Orders designed to effect this went out promptly. Ewell was instructed to give up his advance on Harrisburg and return at once to Chambersburg with all three of his divisions. Hill and Longstreet, who had just been alerted for a northward march to the Susquehanna, were told to prepare instead for a move on Cashtown, eighteen miles to the east and just beyond South Mountain; the former would start today—it was morning by now,

June 29—the latter tomorrow, which would keep the single road from being clogged. On second thought, and for the same purpose of avoiding a jam, Lee sent a follow-up message to Ewell, suggesting that he remain on the far side of the mountains and march directly to Cashtown or Gettysburg, another eight miles to the east. Simultaneously, couriers hurried south to urge Robertson and Jones to leave the Blue Ridge and join the army in Pennsylvania as soon as possible. A seventh brigade of cavalry, under John B. Imboden, assigned to Lee for use on the invasion but so far only used to guard the western approaches to the lower Cumberland Valley, was also summoned, but since it would be at least two days before these horsemen could get to Chambersburg, Lee told Longstreet to leave one division behind to protect the trains until Imboden arrived. Meanwhile the rest of the army would converge on Cashtown, from which point it could threaten both Washington and Baltimore, thus retaining the initiative by forcing the enemy to turn back east or remain there, in order to keep between the gray invaders and those two vital cities.

All this had been arranged within eight hours of Harrison's report to Lee. But neither the spy nor anyone else could tell him anything of Stuart, who had vanished as if into quicksand. However, an officer who arrived from the south that morning reported that he had met two cavalrymen who told him they had left Stuart on June 27, all the way down in Prince William County, on the far side of Occoquan Creek. Lee was startled to hear this, having learned from Harrison that Hooker had begun to cross the Potomac two full days before that time. Though he kept up a show of confidence for the benefit of subordinates—"Ah, General, the enemy is a long time finding us," he told a division commander; "If he does not succeed soon, we must go in search of him"—Lee was obviously disturbed, and he kept asking for news of Stuart from all callers, none of whom could tell him anything.

One more item concerned him, though few of his lieutenants agreed that it should do so. They were saying that Meade was about as able a general as Hooker, but considerably less bold, and they were exchanging congratulations on Lincoln's appointment of another mediocre opponent for them. Lee, who had known the Pennsylvanian as a fellow engineer in the old army, did not agree. "General Meade will commit no blunder on my front," he said, "and if I make one he will make haste to take advantage of it."

While Longstreet marked time at Chambersburg, waiting for Hill to clear the road on which his three divisions were proceeding east to Cashtown, Ewell began his southward march from Carlisle. Greatly disappointed by the cancellation of his plan to occupy the Pennsylvania capital, which he saw as a fitting climax to the campaign that had opened so auspiciously at Winchester and continued for the next two weeks as a triumphal procession through one of the most prosperous regions of the North, Old Bald Head was puzzled by the apparent indecisiveness of his chief. Jackson's orders, enigmatic though they often were, had always been precise and positive; whereas Lee had not only reversed himself by ordering a return to Chambersburg, he had also modified this further by changing the objective to Cashtown or Gettysburg and leaving it up to the corps commander to choose between the two. Unaccustomed to such leeway, which Jackson had never allowed him on any account, Ewell deferred making a final choice until next day, when he would reach Middletown, aptly named because it was equidistant from both of these alternative objectives. Sending word for Early to head west from York and taking up the southward march himself with Rodes while Johnson came along behind with the spoils-laden wagon train, he was also nettled by Lee's additional instructions that if at any point he encountered what he judged to be a large force of the enemy, he was to avoid a general engagement, if practicable, until the other two corps were at hand. This seemed to Ewell a plethora of ifs, and he fumed under the added burden of responsibility, not only for the safety of his corps, but also for the safety of the army, in a situation which, for him at least, was far from clear. Much as he missed his amputated leg, he missed even more the iron guidance of the man under whom he had been serving when he lost it.

Those same precautionary instructions had gone of course to Hill, who was known to have little caution in his make-up. His policy, throughout his year of service under Lee—beginning with the attack that opened the Seven Days offensive, which he had started rolling for the simple reason that he could no longer abide the strain of standing idle—had been to pitch into whatever loomed in his path, with little or no regard for its strength or composition. This had stood the Confederacy in good stead from time to time, especially at Cedar Mountain, where he had saved Stonewall from defeat, and at Sharpsburg, where he had done the same for Lee, whose reference to him in the official report of that battle, "And then A. P. Hill came up," had become a byword in the army. Little Powell was the embodiment of the offensive spirit, here in Pennsylvania as well as back home in Virginia, and so were the troops of his command, who took a fierce pride in the fact.

Completing the march to Cashtown that first day, Heth's division went into camp while the other two were still on the road, and hearing that Early's men had overlooked a supply of shoes while passing through Gettysburg the week before, Heth sent his lead brigade forward next morning, June 30, to investigate the rumor. Its commander, Johnston Pettigrew, mindful of Lee's warning not to bring on a battle until the whole army was at hand, prudently withdrew when he encountered Federal troopers along a creekbank west of town, not knowing what number of blue soldiers of all arms might be lurking in rear of the cavalry outposts. He returned to Cashtown late that afternoon, having put his men into bivouac about midway between there and Gettysburg, and reported on the day's events.

Heth did not think highly of such wariness. What was more, he wanted those shoes. So he took Pettigrew to Hill and had him repeat the account of what he had seen. Hill agreed with Heth. "The only force at Gettysburg is cavalry," he declared, "probably a detachment of observation." Meade's infantry forces were still down in Maryland, he added, "and have not struck their tents."

Heth was quick to take him up on that. "If there is no objection," he said, "I will take my division tomorrow and go to Gettysburg and get those shoes."

"None in the world," Hill told him.

★ ★ ★

One strenuous objector was there, however, in the person of John Buford, a tough, Kentucky-born regular with a fondness for hard fighting and the skill to back it up. And though Hill was strictly correct in saying that the only bluecoats now in Gettysburg were cavalry,

Buford's two brigades were formidable in their own right, being equipped with the new seven-shot Spencer carbine, which enabled a handy trooper to get off twenty rounds a minute, as compared to his muzzle-loading adversary, who would be doing well to get off four in the same span. Moreover, in addition to having five times the firepower of any equal number of opponents, these two brigades were outriders for the infantry wing under Reynolds, whose own corps was camped tonight within six miles of the town, while those under Howard and Sickles were close behind him. Meade had set up army headquarters just south of the state line at Taneytown, about the same distance from Reynolds as Reynolds was from Gettysburg, and all but one of his seven corps—Sedgwick's, off to the east at Manchester—were within easy marching distance of the latter place. He was, in fact, about as well concentrated as Lee was on this last night of June. The Confederates had the advantage of converging on a central point—Ewell at Heidlersburg and Longstreet in rear of Cashtown were each about ten miles from Gettysburg, and Hill was closer than either—whereas the Federals would be marching toward a point that was beyond their perimeter, but Meade had the advantage of numbers and a less congested road net: plus another advantage which up to now, except for the brief September interlude that ended bloodily at Sharpsburg, had been with Lee. The northern commander and his soldiers would be fighting on their own ground, in defense of their own homes.

His march north, today and yesterday, after the day spent getting the feel of the reins, had been made with the intention, announced to Halleck at the outset, "of falling upon some portion of Lee's army in detail" with the full strength of his own. His "main point," he said, was "to find and fight the enemy," since in his opinion "the attitude of the enemy's army in Pennsylvania presents us the best opportunity we have had since the war began." But this morning, receiving information "that the enemy are advancing, probably in strong force, on Gettysburg," he had begun to doubt that that was really what he wanted after all. "Much oppressed with a sense of responsibility and the magnitude of the great interests intrusted to me," as he wrote his wife, he had begun to think that his best course would be to take up a strong defensive position, covering Washington and Baltimore, and there await attack. It was his intention, he declared in a circular issued that afternoon, "to hold this army pretty nearly in the position it now occupies until the plans of the enemy shall have been more fully developed," adding that it was "not his desire to wear the troops out by excessive fatigue and marches, and thus unfit them for the work they will be called upon to perform." He found what he considered an excellent position along the south bank of Pipe Creek, just to the rear of his present headquarters at Taneytown, and he had his engineers start laying it out on the morning of July 1, planning to rally his army there in case Lee came at him in dead earnest.

"The commanding general is satisfied that the object of the movement of the army in this direction has been accomplished," he announced in another circular, "viz. the relief of Harrisburg, and the prevention of the enemy's intended invasion of Philadelphia, &c. beyond the Susquehanna. It is no longer his intention to assume the offensive until the enemy's movements or position should render such an operation certain of success." If this was reminiscent of Hooker in the Wilderness, Meade went Fighting Joe one better by making it plain that every corps commander was authorized to initiate a retirement to the Pipe Creek line, not only by his own corps but also by the others, in the event that the rebels made a lunge at him: "The time for falling back can only be developed by circumstances. Whenever such circumstances arise as would seem to indicate the necessity for falling back and assuming this general line indicated, notice of such movement will be at once communicated to these headquarters and to all adjoining corps commanders."

That was a long way from the intention expressed two days ago, "to find and fight the enemy." But the fact was, Meade had already lost control of events before he made this offer to abide by the decision of the first of his chief subordinates who took a notion that the time had come to backtrack. Even as the circular was being prepared and the engineers were laying out the proposed defensive line behind Pipe Creek, John Reynolds was committing the army to battle a dozen miles north of the headquarters Meade was getting ready to abandon. And Reynolds in turn had taken his cue from Buford, who had spread his troopers along the banks of another creek, just west of Gettysburg; Willoughby Run, it was called. "By daylight of July 1," he later reported, "I had gained positive information of the enemy's position and movements, and my arrangements were made for entertaining him until General Reynolds could reach the scene."

Buford was all business and hard action, now as always. A former Indian fighter, he drove himself as mercilessly as he did his men, with the result that he would be dead within six months, at the age of thirty-seven, of what the doctors classified as "exposure and exhaustion." Convinced now that the fate of the nation was in his hands, here on the outskirts of the little college town, the Kentuckian was prepared to act accordingly. A journalist had recently described him as being "of a good-natured disposition, but not to be trifled with," a "singular-looking party . . . with a tawny mustache and a little, triangular gray eye, whose expression is determined, not to say sinister." The night before, when one of his brigade commanders expressed the opinion that the rebels would not be coming in any considerable strength and that he would be able to hold them off without much trouble, Buford had not agreed at all. "No, you won't," he said. "They will attack you in the morning and they will come booming—skirmishers three-deep. You will have to fight like the devil until supports arrive."

★ 2 ★

That was how they came, three-deep and booming; Heth was on his way to "get those shoes." In the lead today, by normal rotation of the honor, was the Alabama brigade of Maryland-born James Archer. A Princeton graduate who had discovered an aptitude for war in Mexico and had gone on to become a U.S. Army captain and now a Confederate brigadier at the age of forty-six, Archer had fought in every major battle under Lee, from the Seven Days through Chancellorsville, where he led the charge on Hazel Grove that broke the back of the Federal defense. Hill had fallen sick in the night and was confined to his tent in Cashtown this morning, too weak to mount a horse, but with Archer out front he would have all the aggressiveness even he could desire—as was presently demonstrated.

Though Pettigrew had warned him the previous evening that he was likely to run into trouble short of Gettysburg, Archer moved his Alabamians rapidly eastward, down the Chambersburg Pike, until they topped a rise and came under fire, first from the banks of a stream in the swale below and then from the slopes of another north-south ridge beyond, on whose crest a six-gun battery was in action at a range of three quarters of a mile. That was about 8 o'clock. Archer ordered up a battery of his own, and while it took up the challenge of the guns across the way, he shook out a triple line of skirmishers, textbook style, and prepared to continue the advance. But Heth, who had come to the head of the column by now, decided to make doubly sure there would be no further delay. He called up a Mississippi brigade commanded by Joseph R. Davis, put it on the left of Archer, north of the pike, and sent them forward together, down into the shallow valley that was floored with the shimmering gold of ripened wheat fields. The two brigades started downhill through the standing grain, the skirmishers whooping and firing as they went. Just as the Deep South had led the way to secession—Alabama had been fourth and Mississippi second among the original seven states to leave the Union—so was it leading the way into the greatest battle of the war that had been provoked by that withdrawal.

Buford's troopers, back across Willoughby Run by now and in position on McPherson's Ridge, fired their carbines rapidly as the butternut riflemen came at them down the east side of Herr Ridge. But it was obvious to their general, who had a good view of the scene from the cupola of a Lutheran seminary on the crest of the next rearward ridge, about midway between Gettysburg and the one they were defending a mile from town, that his two brigades of dismounted men, one out of four of whom had to stay behind to hold the horses of the other three, were not going to be able to hang on long in the face of all that power. Moreover, reports had reached him from outposts he had established to the north, toward Heidlersburg, that substantial rebel forces were advancing from there as well. Unless Federal infantry came up soon, and in strength, he would have to pull out to avoid being swamped from both directions. At about 8.30, however, as he started down the ladder, perhaps to give the order to retire, he heard a calm voice asking from below: "What's the matter, John?"

It was Reynolds, whom many considered not only the highest ranking but also the best general in the army. Buford shook his head. "The devil's to pay," he said, and he came on down the ladder. But when Reynolds asked if this meant that he could not hang on till the I Corps got there, most likely within an hour, the cavalryman said he reckoned he could; at any rate he would try. That was enough for Reynolds. He sent at once for Howard and Sickles, urging haste on the march to join him, then turned to an aide and gave him a verbal message for Meade at Taneytown. "Tell him the enemy are advancing in strong force, and that I fear they will get to the heights beyond the town before I can. I will fight them inch by inch, and if driven into the town I will barricade the streets and hold them back as long as possible."

He himself rode back to bring up Wadsworth's division, which was leading the march up the Emmitsburg

Road, and guided it cross-country, over Seminary Ridge and up the Chambersburg Pike toward McPherson's Ridge, where by now, after two full hours of fighting, Buford's troopers were approaching both the crest of the ridge, uphill in their rear, and the limit of their endurance. Reynolds directed one of Wadsworth's two brigades to the right and the other to the left, to bolster the cavalry and oppose the rebel infantry coming at them. The race was close; he knew that unless he hurried he would lose it. Already the time was past 10 o'clock, and he could see Confederates among the trees of an apple orchard just to the left of where the pike went out of sight beyond the ridge. He turned in the saddle and called back over his shoulder to the infantry trudging behind him: "Forward, forward, men! Drive those fellows out of that! Forward! For God's sake, forward!"

Those were his last words. He suddenly toppled from his horse and lay quite still, face-down on the soil of his native Pennsylvania. No one knew what had hit him— including Reynolds himself, most likely—until an aide saw the neat half-inch hole behind his right ear, where the rifle bullet had struck. When they turned him over he gasped once, then smiled; but that was all. He was dead at the age of forty-two, brought down by a rebel marksman in the orchard just ahead. "His death affected us much," a young lieutenant later wrote, "for he was one of the *soldier* generals of the army."

Beyond the ridge, Heth had decided by now that the time had come for him to press the issue with more than skirmishers. He passed the word and Davis and Archer went in with their main bodies, left and right of the turnpike, intending to overrun the rapid-firing blue troopers spread out on the slope before them. Archer's men were thrown into some disorder by a fence they had to climb just west of Willoughby Run, but at last they got over and splashed across the stream. As they started up McPherson's Ridge, however, the woods along the crest were suddenly filled with flame-stabbed smoke and the crash of heavy volleys. This was musketry, not sporadic carbine fire, and then they saw why. Not only were these new opponents infantry, but their black hats told the startled and stalled attackers that this was the Iron Brigade, made up of hard-bitten Westerners with a formidable reputation for hard fighting and a fierce pride in their official designation as the first brigade of the first division of the first corps of the first army of the Republic. Staggered by the ambush and outnumbered as they were, the butternut survivors perceived that the time had come to get out of there, and that was what they did. Splashing back across the stream, however, they piled up again at the high fence and were struck heavily on the outer flank by a Michigan regiment that had worked its way around through the woods to the south.

Most got over, but about 75 Confederates were captured while awaiting their turn at the fence: including Archer, who was grabbed and mauled by a hefty private named Patrick Maloney. Exuberant over the size of his catch—as well he might be; no general in Lee's army had ever been captured before—Maloney turned Archer over to his captain, who refused to accept the sword that was offered in formal surrender. "Keep your sword, General, and go to the rear," he told him. "One sword is all I need on this line." A staff lieutenant who had taken no part in the fighting did not see it that way, however, and insisted on having the trophy even after the prisoner explained that it had been declined by the man who was entitled to it. Archer was furious, not only at this but also because of the roughing-up the big Irishman had given him, which accounted in part for his reaction when he was presented to Doubleday, who had succeeded Reynolds as corps commander. "Archer! I'm glad to see you," the New Yorker cried, striding forward with his hand out. They had been friends in the old army, but apparently that meant nothing to Archer now. "Well, I'm not glad to see you by a damn sight," he said coldly, and he kept his hand at his side.

North of the turnpike, the other half of Heth's attack had better success, at least at the start. Though Reynolds even in death had won his race on the Union left, where the Iron Brigade arrived in time to prepare for what was coming, the brigade on the right not only had a longer way to go, and consequently less time for getting set, it also found no covering woods along that stretch of McPherson's Ridge. Davis's men—five regiments scraped together from the Richmond defenses and the Carolina littoral, none of whom had worked together previously and only two of which had ever fought in Virginia—could see what lay before them, and they advanced with all the eagerness of green troops glad of a chance to demonstrate their mettle. One of the five was a North Carolina outfit whose colonel went down early in the charge, shot as he took up the fallen colors, and when another Tarheel officer bent over him to ask if he was badly hurt, he replied: "Yes, but pay no attention to me. Take the colors and keep ahead of the Mississippians."

By then the whole line was going in on the double. On the crest ahead, the Federals wavered and then, as Wadsworth sought to forestall a rout by ordering a withdrawal, fell back hastily toward Seminary Ridge. Davis was elated. The President's nephew, he was aware

of muttered complaints of nepotism, and he was happy
to be proving his worth and his right to the wreathed
stars on his collar. Yelling in anticipation of coming to
grips with the fleeing bluecoats, the attackers swept over
the crest of McPherson's Ridge and into the quarter-
mile-wide valley beyond. There they funneled into the
deep cut of an unfinished railroad bed, which seemed to
offer an ideal covered approach to the Federal rear, but
which in fact turned out to be a trap. Once in, they
found the sides of the cut so high and steep that they
could not fire out, and Doubleday, spotting the opportunity, quickly took advantage of it by sending two regiments over from south of the pike, where Archer had
just been routed. "Throw down your muskets! Throw
down your muskets!" the men in the cut heard voices
calling from overhead, and they looked up into the muzzles of rifles slanted down at them from the rim above.
Caught thus in a situation not unlike that of fish in a
rainbarrel, some 250 graybacks surrendered outright,
dropping their weapons where they stood, while casualties were heavy among those who chose to attempt
escape by running the gauntlet westward.

The reversal was complete. Davis and his survivors
fell back across McPherson's Ridge, profoundly shaken
by the sudden frown of fortune and considerably
reduced from the strength they had enjoyed when they
first came whooping over the crest, headed in the opposite direction. Here on the Confederate left, after so
brave a beginning, the attackers had wound up with an
even worse disaster than had been suffered on the right.
Though Davis himself, unlike Archer, had avoided capture, a good half of his men had either been taken prisoner or shot, and the rest were too demoralized to be of
any present use at all.

Doubleday was as elated as Davis had been, a short while back. Moreover, his hard-won feeling of security was strengthened by the arrival of the other two divisions of the corps, his own and Robinson's, and close on their heels came Howard, riding in advance of his own corps, which was coming fast and would be there within an hour. Eleven years younger than forty-four-year-old Doubleday, Howard assumed command of the field by virtue of his seniority. While the skirmishers of both armies kept up a racket down in the valley, banging away at each other from opposite banks of Willoughby Run, he reinforced Wadsworth on McPherson's Ridge and continued the long-range artillery duel with rebel batteries on Herr Ridge. It was noon by now; the XI Corps was arriving, under Schurz, and the lines were much the same as they had been four hours ago, when Buford's dismounted troopers were all that held them. Unquestionably, there were a great many butternut soldiers on the field—you could see them plainly across the valley, "formed in continuous double lines of battle," a staff man noted, adding that "as a spectacle it was striking"— but Howard believed he was ready for whatever came his way. Sickles ought to be arriving soon, and he had sent for Slocum as well; that would give him five more divisions, a total of eleven, perhaps by nightfall.

Just then, however, a shell burst in rear of the Union center, followed quickly by another and another, all with such startling accuracy that one regimental commander sent an angry complaint that the supporting guns were firing short. But those were not friendly shells, dropped in error; they were Confederate. A mile north of the Chambersburg Pike, the two eastern ridges merged at a dominant height called Oak Hill, and there an enemy battery was in action, signaling danger to the Federal

right, which extended only about half that distance. Coming south across the fields around Oak Hill, directly toward the vulnerable flank, was another gray flood of rebel infantry. One-armed Howard, knowing he had to move fast to meet the threat, bent the north end of Doubleday's line back east, astride Seminary Ridge, and hurried the first two divisions of his own corps across the rolling farmland north of Gettysburg, with instructions for Schurz to form a new line there, at right angles to the first. They barely had time to arrive before the storm burst.

This new gray pressure was brought to bear by Rodes. Like Heth, he was going into battle for the first time as a major general, and just as his fellow Virginian had faced the test without his corps commander at hand to advise him, so too was Rodes on his own, not because Ewell lay sick in his tent, as had been the case with Hill, but because he preferred to ride near the tail of the column in his buggy. Old Bald Head was in a strange mood any how, confused by discretionary orders and aggrieved the sudden abandonment of his advance on Harrisb just as he had the place within his grasp. At Middle that morning, confronted with the necessity for ch between his alternate objectives, he had had h made up for him at last by a note from Hill, in him that the Third Corps was on its way to G so he had directed Rodes to take the left fork there. Besides, that seemed a convenient poi tion with Early, who was marching from t Johnson, off to the east with the train, c there by turning east when he reache nightfall the corps would be reunited in a week, but until then Ewell pre three division commanders to functi

Rodes no doubt appreciated the confidence this implied. At any rate, hearing heavy firing up ahead at noon, he quickened the pace and reached Oak Hill about 1.30 to find a golden opportunity spread before him. On parallel ridges extending south from where he stood, Confederates and Federals were disposed in an attitude not unlike that of two animals who had just met and scrapped and then drawn back, still growling, for a better assessment of each other before coming to grips again. What attracted Rodes at first glance was the fact that the enemy flank, half a mile down the eastern ridge, was wide open to an oblique attack from the road along which his division was advancing. He would have to move fast, however, for already the near end of the Union line was beginning to curl back in response to his appearance, and reinforcements were pouring in large numbers from the streets of Gettysburg, taking up positions from which to defend it. This last was quite all right with Rodes. It was not the town he wanted, dead ahead; it was the blue force on the ridge to his right front.

Accordingly, after posting one of his five brigades out to the left, with instructions to hold off the still-arriving defenders of the town in case they went over to the offensive—which they well might do; their number by now was larger than his own—he held another brigade reserve and put the remaining three in line abreast, facing south, for a charge against the flank of the blue-coats on the ridge. All this was quickly done, with no time spared for a preliminary reconnaissance or even the advancement of a skirmish line. By 2 o'clock the alignment had been completed, and Rodes gave his three brigades the order to go forward.

They did go forward, but into chaos. Left on its own

by the other two brigades—one stalled at the outset; the other drifted wide—the center brigade stepped in midstride into slaughter when a line of Federals, hidden till then, rose from behind a low stone wall, diagonal to the front, and killed or wounded about half of the advancing men with a series of point-blank volleys pumped directly into their flank. Such was the price they paid for the time Rodes saved by forgoing a reconnaissance. The survivors hit the ground alongside the fallen, some making futile attempts to return the decimating fire, while others began waving scraps of cloth in token of surrender. Observing this, their shaken commander, Alfred Iverson, sent word to Rodes that one whole regiment had raised the white flag and gone over to the enemy on first contact. Though Rodes did not credit the hysterical report, he saw only too clearly that he had the makings of a first-class disaster on his hands. Like Heth to the south, he had paid in disproportionate blood for the ready aggressiveness which in the past had been the hallmark of the army's greatest victories, but which now seemed mere rashness and the hallmark of defeat. It had been so for the captured Archer and for Davis, and now it was the same for Iverson, who was so demoralized by what he had seen, or thought he had seen, that he had to turn over to his adjutant the task of trying to extricate his shattered regiments.

It was at this critical juncture that Lee drew near. Riding through the mountains east of Chambersburg that morning, he had heard the rumble of guns in the distance and wondered what it meant. Hill, who had risen from his sickbed at the sound, pale and feeble though he was, and called for his horse in order to go forward and investigate, could tell Lee nothing more than he already knew—namely, that Heth had marched

on Gettysburg, with Pender in support—nor could
Anderson, whose division was just beyond Cashtown
and within half a dozen miles of the ominous booming.
Despite repeated warnings that a general engagement
was to be avoided until the army was reunited, the noise
up ahead was too loud, or anyhow too sustained, for a
mere skirmish. Moreover, Lee was aware of Napoleon's
remark that at certain edgy times a dogfight could bring
on a battle, and it seemed to him that with his infantry
groping its way across unfamiliar hostile terrain, in an
attempt to perform the proper function of cavalry, this
might well be one of those times. He was worried and
he said so.

"I cannot think what has become of Stuart," he told
Anderson. "I ought to have heard from him long before
now. He may have met with disaster, but I hope not."
As he spoke he gazed up the road, where the guns continued to rumble beyond the horizon. "In the absence of
reports from him, I am in ignorance of what we have in
front of us here. It may be the whole Federal army, or
it may be only a detachment. If it is the whole Federal
force, we must fight a battle here." For once, he did not
seem pleased at the prospect of combat, and he spoke
of a withdrawal before he knew what lay before him: "If
we do not gain a victory, those defiles and gorges which
we passed this morning will shelter us from disaster."
And having used the word disaster twice within less than
a minute, he hurried ahead, as Hill had done before him,
to see for himself what grounds there might be for such
forebodings.

About 2.30, after passing through Pender's division,
which was formed for attack on both sides of the pike
but was so far uncommitted, he ascended Herr Ridge to
find the smoky panorama of a battle spread before

him—a battle he had neither sought nor wanted. Heth had three brigades in line on the slope giving down upon Willoughby Run, and Lee now learned that he had attacked some three hours earlier, due east and on a mile-wide front, only to encounter Federal infantry whose presence he had not even suspected until he saw what was left of his two attack brigades streaming back from a bloody repulse. Since then, belatedly mindful of the warning not to bring on a battle, he had contented himself with restoring his shattered front while engaging the enemy guns in a long-range contest. Lee could see for himself the situation that had developed.

Across the way, disposed along the two parallel ridges that intervened between the one on which he stood and Gettysburg, plainly visible two miles to the southeast, the Federals confronted Heth in unknown strength, their right flank withdrawn sharply in the direction of the town, from whose streets more bluecoats were pouring in heavy numbers, in order to meet a new Confederate threat from the north. This was Rodes, just arrived from Heidlersburg, Lee was told, and though his attack was opportune, catching the bluecoats end-on and almost unawares, he was making little headway because he had launched it in a disjointed fashion.

At that point Heth came riding up, having heard that Lee was on the field. Anxious to make up for a slipshod beginning, he appealed to the commanding general to let him go back in. "Rodes is heavily engaged," he said. "Had I not better attack?"

Lee was reluctant. "N-no," he said slowly, continuing to sweep the field with his glasses. It was not that he lacked confidence in Heth, who was not only a fellow Virginian and a distant cousin, but was also the only officer in the army, aside of course from his own sons, whom he addressed by his first name. It was because Lee still had no real notion of the enemy strength, except that it was obviously considerable, and he was by no means willing to risk the apparent likelihood of expanding a double into a triple repulse. "No," he said again, more decisively than before; "I am not prepared to bring on a general engagement today. Longstreet is not up."

But suddenly his mind was changed by what he saw before him. Rodes's right brigade, after drifting wide, came down hard on the critical angle where the Union line bent east, and his reserve brigade, committed after the wreck of Iverson, dislodged the Federals from their position behind the diagonal stone wall, while his left brigade recovered momentum and plunged into a quarter-mile gap between the two blue corps, north and west of Gettysburg. Assailed and outflanked, the eastward extension of Doubleday's line began to crumble as the men who had held it retreated stubbornly down Seminary Ridge. Simultaneously, Howard's two divisions under Schurz—his own, now led by Alexander Schimmelfennig, and Barlow's; the third, Von Steinwehr's, had been left in reserve on the other side of the town—were assaulted by a new gray force that came roaring down the Harrisburg Road—it was Early, arriving from York—to strike their right at the moment when Rodes was probing the gap beyond their left. As a result, this line too began to crumble, but much faster than the other.

On Herr Ridge, Lee saw much of this through his binoculars. Blind chance having reproduced in miniature the conditions of Second Manassas, with Chancellorsville thrown in for good measure, he dropped his unaccustomed cloak of caution and told Hill, who rode up just then, to send both Heth and Pender forward to sweep the field.

They did just that, but only after fierce and bloody fighting, particularly on McPherson's Ridge, south of the pike, where the Iron Brigade was posted. Unleashed at last, Heth's men went splashing across Willoughby Run and up the opposite slope, to and finally over the fuming crest. Heth himself did not make it all the way, having been unhorsed by a fragment of shell which struck him on the side of the head, knocked him unconscious, and probably would have killed him, too, except that the force of the blow was absorbed in part by a folded newspaper tucked under the sweatband of a too-large hat acquired the day before in Cashtown.

Hundreds of others in both armies were not so fortunate. Told by Doubleday to maintain his position at all costs, Solomon Meredith, commander of the Iron Brigade, came close to following these instructions to the letter, although he himself, like Heth, was knocked out

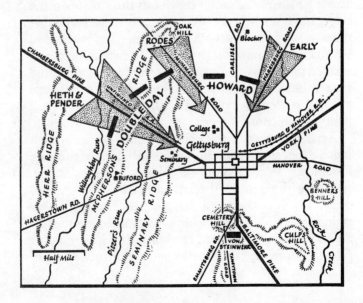

before the action was half over. The 24th Michigan, for example, had come onto the ridge with 496 officers and men; it left with 97. This loss of just over eighty percent was exceeded only by the regiment that inflicted it, Pettigrew's 26th North Carolina, whose two center companies set new records for battlefield losses that would never be broken, here or elsewhere; one took 83 soldiers into the fight and emerged with only 2 unhit, while the other went in with 91, and all were killed or wounded.

Pender, sent forward by Hill as the struggle approached a climax, overlapped the south flank of the defenders and added the pressure that forced them off the ridge. The men of the Iron Brigade fell back at last—600 of them, at any rate, for twice that many were casualties out of the original 1800—ending the brief half hour of concentrated fury. "I have taken part in many hotly contested fights," Pettigrew's adjutant later declared, "but this I think was the deadliest of them all." Coming up in the wake of the attack he heard "dreadful howls" in the woods on the ridge, and when he went over to investigate he found that the source of the racket was the wounded of both sides. Several were foaming at the mouth, as though mad, and seemed not even to be aware that they were screaming. He attributed their reaction to the shock of having been exposed to "quick, frightful conflict following several hours of suspense."

Across the way, Ewell's two divisions were having a much easier time than Hill's. While Rodes was pressing Doubleday steadily southward down Seminary Ridge, widening the gap on the left of the line Schurz had drawn north of the town, Early struck hard at the far right of the Union front, which was exposed to just such a blow as the one that had crumpled that same flank at Chancellorsville, two months ago tomorrow. Most of the men opposing him had been through that experience, and now that they foresaw a repetition of it, they reacted in the same fashion. They broke and ran. First by ones and twos, then by squads and platoons, and finally by companies and regiments, they forgot that they had welcomed the chance to refute in action the ugly things the rest of the army had been saying about them; instead, they took off rearward in headlong flight. Barlow, a twenty-nine-year-old New York lawyer who had finished first in his class at Harvard and volunteered at the start of the war as a private in a militia company, tried desperately to rally the division he had commanded for less than six weeks, but was shot from his horse and left for dead on the field his men were quitting. It was otherwise with Schimmelfennig. A former Prussian officer, ten years older than Barlow and presumably that much wiser, he went along with the rush of his troops, all the way into Gettysburg, until he too was unhorsed by a stray bullet while clattering down a side street, and took refuge in a woodshed, where he remained in hiding for the next three days.

Yelling with pleasure at the sight of the blue flood running backwards across the fields as if the landscape had been tipped, the rebel pursuers cut down and gathered in fugitives by the hundreds, all at comparatively small cost to themselves, since but little of their fire was being returned. "General, where are your dead men?" an elated young officer called to John B. Gordon, whose six Georgia regiments had led the charge that threw the bluecoats into retreat before contact was established. Still intent on the pursuit, Gordon did not pause for an answer. "I haven't got any, sir!" he shouted as he rode past on his black stallion. "The Almighty has covered my men with his shield and buckler."

Lee observed from atop Herr Ridge the sudden climax of this latest addition to his year-long string of victories. Riding forward in the wake of Pender's exultant attack, which was delivered with the cohesive, smashing power of a clenched fist, he crossed McPherson's Ridge, thickly strewn with the dead and wounded of both armies, and mounted the opposite slope just as the Federals abandoned a fitful attempt to make a stand around the seminary. Ahead of him, down the remaining half mile of the Chambersburg Pike, they were retreating pell-mell into the streets of Gettysburg, already jammed with other blue troops pouring down from the north, under pressure from Ewell, as into a funnel whose spout extended south. Those who managed to struggle free of the crush, and thus emerge from the spout, were running hard down two roads that led steeply up a dominant height where guns were emplaced and the foremost of the fugitives were being brought to a halt, apparently for still another stand; Cemetery Hill it was called because of the graveyard on its lofty plateau, half a mile from the town square. Another half mile to the east, about two miles from where Lee stood, there was a second eminence, Culp's Hill, slightly higher than the first, to which it was connected by a saddle of rocky ground, similarly precipitous and forbidding.

These two hills, their summits a hundred feet above the town, which in turn was about half that far below the crest of Seminary Ridge, afforded the enemy a strong position—indeed, a natural fortress—on which to rally his whipped and panicky troops, especially if time was allowed for the steadily increasing number of defenders to improve with their spades the already formidable advantages of terrain. Lee could see for himself, now that he had what amounted to a ringside view of the action, that his victory had been achieved more as the result of tactical good fortune than because of any great preponderance of numbers, which in fact he did not have. Prisoners had been taken from two Union corps, six divisions in all, and they reported that the rest of the blue army was on the march to join them from bivouacs close at hand. Some 25,000 attackers, just under half of Lee's infantry, had faced 20,000 defenders, just over one fourth of Meade's, and the resultant casualties had done little to change the over-all ratio of the two armies, on and off the field. Nearly 8000 Confederates had fallen or been captured, as compared to 9000 Federals, about half of whom had been taken prisoner. It was clear that if the tactical advantage was not pressed, it might soon be lost altogether, first by giving the rattled bluecoats a chance to recompose themselves, there on the dominant heights just south of town, and second by allowing time for the arrival of heavy reinforcements already on the way. Moreover, both of these reasons for continuing the offensive were merely adjunctive to Lee's natural inclination, here as elsewhere, now as always, to keep a beaten opponent under pressure, and thus off balance, just as long as his own troops had wind and strength enough to put one foot in front of the other.

Ill though he was, ghostly pale and "very delicate," as one observer remarked, A. P. Hill was altogether in agreement that the new Federal position had to be carried if the victory was to be completed. But when Lee turned to him, there on Seminary Ridge, and proposed that the Third Corps make the attack, Little Powell declined. Anderson's division was still miles away; Heth's was shattered, the commander himself unconscious, and Pender's blown and disorganized by its furious charge and wild pursuit. The survivors were close to exhaustion and so was their ammunition, which would have to be replenished from the train back up the pike. Regretfully Hill replied that his men were in no condition for further exertion just now, and Lee, knowing from past experience that Hill invariably required of them all that flesh could endure, was obliged to accept his judgment.

That left Ewell. Rodes had been roughly handled at the outset, it was true, but Early was comparatively fresh, had suffered only light casualties in driving the skittish Dutchmen from the field, and was already on the march through the streets of the town, rounding up herds of prisoners within half a mile of the proposed objective; besides which, it seemed fitting that the Second Corps continue its Jacksonian tradition of hard-legged mobility and terrific striking power, demonstrated recently at Winchester, a month after Stonewall was laid to rest nearby in the Shenandoah Valley, and redemonstrated here today in Pennsylvania. Having made the decision, Lee gave a staff officer oral instructions to take to Ewell. As usual, not being in a position to judge for himself the condition of the troops or the difficulties the objective might present when approached from the north, he made the order discretionary; Ewell was "to carry the hill occupied by the enemy, if he found it practicable"—so Lee paraphrased the instructions afterwards in his formal report—"but to avoid a general engagement until the arrival of the other divisions of the army."

That was about 4.30; barely an hour had passed since Hill threw Pender into the follow-up attack on Seminary Ridge, sweeping it clear of defenders within less than half an hour, and a good four hours of daylight remained for Ewell's follow-up attack on Cemetery Hill, which would complete the victory by annihilating or received. Down below, the streets of the town were still crowded with Confederates, busy flushing Union fugitives out of cellars and back alleys, and there was no sign whatsoever that Ewell was preparing to launch the attack he had twice been told to make if he believed it would be successful. Meantime, the sun was dropping swiftly down the sky and the survivors of the two blue corps were hard at work improving their defenses.

One welcome interruption there was, in the form of a pair of Stuart's troopers who brought word to Seminary Ridge of the skirmish near Hanover the day before, the fruitless grope toward York, and the subsequent decision to push on to Carlisle. Relieved to learn that Jeb had managed to avoid personal disaster, whatever trouble he might have made for others, Lee told the horsemen to ride the thirty miles north at once, with orders for the cavalry to rejoin the army as soon as possible. That could not be sooner than tomorrow, of course, but at least he could anticipate removal of the blindfold he had worn throughout the week of Stuart's absence.

Near 7 o'clock, with sunset half an hour away and full darkness a good hour beyond that—which left just time enough, perhaps, for launching the attack on Cemetery Hill—Lee mounted Traveller and rode toward Gettysburg, intending not only to pay Ewell the visit he had promised, but also to discover for himself the reason for long delay.

* * *

...neytown, a dozen miles from the hill where the ...f the two wrecked blue corps were plying their ...in frantic anticipation of the overdue assault, ...ad heard nothing of the eight-hour battle aside

driving the survivors from the scene before Meade could accomplish his convergence there.

Presently, as Lee continued to search the field for signs that the intended attack was under way, Longstreet arrived, riding well in advance of his troops, who had marked time short of Cashtown all morning, under instructions to yield the single eastward road to Johnson, who was hurrying to join the other divisions of the Second Corps. While Lee explained what had happened so far today, and pointed out the hill aswarm with bluecoats across the valley, Old Peter took out his binoculars and made a careful examination of the front.

A broad low ridge, parallel to and roughly three quarters of a mile east of the one on which he stood, extended two miles southward from Cemetery Hill to a pair of conical heights, the nearer of which, called Little Round Top, was some fifty feet taller than the occupied hill to the north, while the farther, called simply Round Top, was more than a hundred feet taller still. On the map, and in the minds of students down the years, this complex of high ground south of Gettysburg conformed in general to the shape of a fishhook, with Round Top as the eye, Cemetery Ridge as the shank, Cemetery Hill as the bend, and Culp's Hill as the barb. Neither of the dominant heights to the south appeared to have been occupied yet by the enemy, though it was fairly clear that either would afford the Federals another rallying point in the event of another retreat. However, if this bothered Lee, he did not show it as he stood waiting for Ewell to open the attack from the north. Certainly it did not bother Longstreet, who had the look of a man whose prayers had been answered. Completing his survey of the field, he lowered his glasses, turned to his chief, and declared with evident satisfaction that conditions were ideal for pursuing the offensive-defensive campaign on which he presumed they had agreed before they left Virginia.

"If we could have chosen a point to meet our plans of operation," he said, "I do not think we could have found a better one than that upon which they are now concentrating. All we have to do is throw our army around by their left, and we shall interpose between the Federal army and Washington. We can get a strong position and wait, and if they fail to attack us we shall have everything in condition to move back tomorrow night in the direction of Washington, selecting beforehand a good position into which we can place our troops to receive battle next day. Finding our object is Washington and that army, the Federals will be sure to attack us. When they attack, we shall beat them, as we proposed to do before we left Fredericksburg, and the probabilities are that the fruits of our success will be great."

The southern commander's reaction to this proposed surrender of the initiative to Meade was immediate and decisive. "No," he said, and gestured with his fist in the direction of Cemetery Hill as he spoke. "The enemy is there, and I am going to attack him there."

"If he is there," Old Peter countered, unimpressed, "it will be because he is anxious that we should attack him: a good reason, in my judgment, for not doing so."

Lee still did not agree. He had made an auspicious beginning on his plan for toppling the Federal units piecemeal as they came up, like a row of dominoes, and he was determined to go ahead with it. "No," he said again. "They are there in position, and I am going to whip them or they are going to whip me."

For the present, Longstreet let it go at that, observing that his chief "was in no frame of mind to listen to fur-

ther argument," but he resolved to return to the subject as soon as Lee had simmered down. "In defensive warfare he was perfect," he wrote years later. "When the hunt was up, his combativeness was overruling."

Just then a courier arrived with a message from Ewell, sent before the one from Lee had reached him. Rodes and Early believed they could take Cemetery Hill, he reported, if Hill would attack it simultaneously from the west. Lee replied that he was unable to furnish this support, except by long-range artillery fire, and after repeating his instructions for Ewell to take the height alone, if possible, added that he would ride over presently to see him.

Once more Longstreet spoke up. Minute by minute, he had watched the number of bluecoats increasing on the hill, while those already there were making the dirt fly as they worked at improving the natural strength of the position. He was still opposed to the attack, he said, but if it was going to be made at all, it had better made at once. Lee did not reply to this immedia[te] Instead, after sending the courier back to Ewe[ll] asked where the First Corps divisions were b[y] McLaws was a couple of miles this side of Ca[shtown] Old Peter replied, with Hood somewhere be[hind] awaiting road space on the pike. When Le[e] that he could not risk a general assault unti[l] units arrived, Longstreet again fell silent agreement or disagreement, he did not rode off, apparently to hasten the marc[h] whose head was half a dozen miles aw[ay]

It was now past 5.30 and the gun[s] growling on both sides. The staf[f] report that he had delivered th[e] Ewell, but there was no other e[

from the note in which Reynolds announced that he would "fight [the rebels] inch by inch . . . and hold them back as long as possible." Not even the booming of the guns came through; for though the east wind carried their rumble as far as Pittsburgh, 150 miles to the west, it was not audible ten miles to the south, apparently having been absorbed by the Round Tops and the sultry air, which served as a soundproof curtain in that direction. In the early afternoon, however, a *New York Times* correspondent came riding back from Gettysburg on a lathered horse and requested the use of the army telegraph in order to file a story on the fighting. Taken at once to headquarters, he could only report that the conflict had been fierce, that the issue had been in doubt when he left, and that one among the many who had fallen was John Reynolds.

All of this was a shock for Meade. Not only had he lost the officer on whom he had depended most for guidance during these first days of command, but one fourth of his army had been committed, perhaps beyond the possibility of disengagement, a hard day's march north of his chosen position along Pipe Creek, which the engineers were still mapping and preparing for occupation. Moreover, a 2 o'clock dispatch from Howard, confirming the newsman's statement and adding that he had sent for Sickles and Slocum—which would mean the commitment, once they arrived, of just over half the army—was followed by one from Buford, addressed to Pleasonton, announcing that two enemy corps—two thirds of the rebel army, it would seem—had made a junction on the heights northwest of town and seemed determined to press the issue to a conclusion, however bloody. Outnumbered and outflanked on the left and right, the defenders had been severely crippled, Buford

added, by the untimely death of Reynolds and the
resultant loss of co-ordination all along the line. "In my
opinion," the cavalryman closed his dispatch, "there
seems to be no directing person. . . . P.S. We need help
now."

The note was headed 3.20 p.m., by which time help
had been on the way for better than an hour: substantial help, moreover, though it consisted of only one general and his staff. Hancock's corps had reached
Taneytown shortly before noon, and Meade had held it
there while waiting to hear from Reynolds. When he
heard instead of that general's death, he told Hancock to
turn his corps over to Gibbon and ride to Gettysburg
as a replacement for their fellow Pennsylvanian, with
full authority to assume command of all units there and
recommend whether to reinforce or withdraw them. He
himself would remain in Taneytown, Meade said, to
control the movements of the other corps and continue
work on the Pipe Creek line, which would be needed
worse than ever in the event of a northward collapse.
Hancock was thirty-nine, a year older than Sickles and
six years older than Howard; all three had been promoted to major general on the same day, back in
November, but the other two had been made brigadiers
before him and therefore outranked him still. When he
suggested that this might make for trouble up ahead,
Meade showed him a letter from Stanton, stating that he
would be sustained in such arrangements by the President and the Secretary of War. So Hancock set out.

He rode part of the way in an ambulance, thus avail-
ing himself of the chance to study a map of the Gettysburg area, which he had never previously visited though
he was born and raised at Norristown, less than a hundred miles away. Coming within earshot of the guns,

which swelled to a sudden uproar about 3.30, he shifted
to horseback and rode hard toward the sound of firing.
At 4 o'clock, the hour that Lee climbed Seminary Ridge
to find a Confederate triumph unfolding at his feet,
Hancock appeared on Cemetery Hill, a mile southeast
across the intervening valley, to view the same scene in
reverse. "Wreck, disaster, disorder, almost the panic that
precedes disorganization, defeat and retreat were everywhere," a subordinate who arrived with him declared.

One-armed Howard was there by the two-story
arched brick gateway to the cemetery, brandishing his
sword in an attempt to stay the rout, but he was doing
little better now than he had done two months ago at
Chancellorsville, under similar circumstances. Von
Steinwehr, an old-line Prussian and a believer in fortifications, had put his troops to digging on arrival, and the
work had gone well, even though one of his two
brigades had been called forward when the line began to
waver north of town. The trouble was, there were so few
men left to hold the hilltop, intrenched or not. Out of
the 20,000 on hand for the battle, nearly half had fallen
or been captured, while practically another fourth were
fugitives who had had their fill of fighting: as was indicated by the fact that the provost guardsmen of a corps
that came up two hours later herded ahead of them
some 1200 skulkers encountered on the Baltimore Pike,
which was only one of the three roads leading south.
Fewer than 7000 soldiers—the equivalent of a single
Confederate division—comprised the available remnant
of the two wrecked Union corps, including the brigade
that had remained in reserve on the hilltop all along.

With all too clear a view of the jubilant mass of rebels
in the town and on the ridge across the way, Howard
foresaw an extension of the disaster, the second to be

charged against his name in the past two months. Anxious as ever to retrieve his reputation, which had been grievously damaged in the Wilderness and practically demolished north of Gettysburg today, he was chagrined to hear from Hancock that Meade had sent him forward to take charge:

"Why, Hancock, you cannot give orders here," he exclaimed. "I am in command and I rank you." When the other repeated that such were Meade's instructions all the same, he still would not agree. "I do not doubt your word, General Hancock," he said stiffly, "but you can give no orders while I am here."

Possessed of a self-confidence that required no insistence on prerogatives, Hancock avoided having the exchange degenerate into a public squabble by pretending to defer to Howard's judgment in deciding whether to stand fast or fall back. "I think this is the strongest position by nature on which to fight a battle that I ever saw," he said, looking east and south along the fishhook line of heights from Culp's Hill to the Round Tops, "and if it meets with your approbation I will select this as the battlefield." When Howard replied that he agreed that the position was a strong one, Hancock concluded: "Very well, sir. I select this as the battlefield."

Howard later protested that he had selected and occupied Cemetery Hill as a rallying point long before Hancock got there. This was true; but neither could there be any doubt, when the time came for looking back, that it was the latter who organized the all-round defense of the position, regardless of who had selected it in the first place.

Meade had chosen well in naming a successor to the fallen Reynolds. Fourteen months ago, in the course of his drive up the York-James peninsula, McClellan had characterized Hancock as "superb," and the word stuck; "Hancock the Superb," he was called thereafter, partly because of his handsome looks and regal bearing—"I think that if he were in citizen's clothes, and should give commands in the army to those who did not know him," one officer observed, "he would be likely to be obeyed at once"—but also because of his military record, which was known and admired by those below as well as by those above him. The army's craving for heroes, or at any rate a hero, had not been diminished by the fact that so many who supposedly qualified as such had melted away like wax dolls in the heat of combat; Hancock seemed an altogether likelier candidate. A Maine artilleryman, for example, recalling the Pennsylvanian's sudden appearance on Cemetery Hill, later asserted that his "very atmosphere was strong and invigorating," and added: "I remember (how refreshing to note!) even his linen clean and white, his collar wide and free, and his broad wrist bands showing large and rolling back from his firm, finely molded hands." Carl Schurz, who might have been expected to side with Howard, his immediate superior, found Hancock's arrival "most fortunate" at this juncture. "It gave the troops a new inspiration," he declared. "They all knew him by fame, and his stalwart figure, his proud mien, and his superb soldierly bearing seemed to verify all the things that fame had told about him. His mere presence was a reinforcement, and everybody on the field felt stronger for his being there.

His first order was for the troops to push forward to the stone walls that ran along the northern face of the hill, in order to present a show of strength and thus discourage an advance by the rebels down below. "I am of the opinion that the enemy will mass in town and make an effort to take this position," he told the captain of a battery posted astride the Baltimore Pike at the rim of the plateau, "but I want you to remain here until you are relieved by me or by my written order, and take orders from no one." It was clear to all who saw him that he meant business, and though Howard had chosen to defend only a portion of the hill, Hancock soon extended the line to cover it from flank to flank, after which he turned his attention to Culp's Hill.

Half a mile to the east and slightly higher than the ground his present line was drawn on, that critical feature of the terrain had not been occupied, despite the obvious fact that Cemetery Hill itself could not be held if this companion height was lost. He told Doubleday to send a regiment over there at once. "My corps has been fighting, General, since 10 o'clock," the New Yorker protested, "and they have been all cut to pieces." Hancock replied: "I know that, sir. But this is a great emergency, and everyone must do all he can." With that he turned away, as if there could be no question of not obeying, and when he came back presently he found that Doubleday, whose regiments had been reduced to the size of companies in the earlier fighting, had sent Wadsworth's whole division to occupy the hill and the connecting saddle of high ground. It was, in fact, the shadow of a division, no larger than a small brigade, but the position was a strong one, heavily timbered and strewn with rocks that varied in size, as one defender wrote, "from a chicken coop to a pioneer's cabin." Moreover, the lead division of Slocum's corps soon arrived and was posted there, too. Feeling considerably more secure, Hancock got off a message to Meade in which he stated that he believed he could hold his ground till nightfall and that he considered his present position an excellent one for fighting a battle, "although somewhat exposed to be turned by the left."

Across the way, on Seminary Ridge, Longstreet was expressing that same opinion even now. The difference was that Old Peter was a subordinate, whereas Hancock was in actual command and therefore in a position to do something about it. Weak though the line was on those two hills to the north, the Pennsylvanian saw that it could not be held, even in strength, if those two commanding heights to the south—the Round Tops—were occupied by the enemy, whose batteries then would enfilade all the rest of the fishhook. And having noted this, he acted in accordance with his insight. Slocum's second division (but still not Slocum himself; he refused to come forward in person and take command by virtue of his rank, judging that Meade's plans for the occupation of the Pipe Creek line were being perverted by this affair near Gettysburg, which seemed to be going very badly. He would risk his men, but not his career; heads were likely to roll, and he was taking care that his would not be among them) was approaching the field soon after 5 o'clock, when its commander reported to Hancock near the cemetery gate.

"Geary, where are your troops?" he was asked, and replied: "Two brigades are on the road advancing." Hancock gestured south, down Cemetery Ridge. "Do you see this knoll on the left?" He was pointing at Little Round Top. "That knoll is a commanding position. We must take possession of it, and then a line can be formed here and a battle fought. . . . In the absence of Slocum, I order you to place your troops on that knoll."

This was promptly done, and with the continuing forbearance of the Confederates, who obligingly refrained from launching the attack Hancock had predicted, Federal confidence gradually was restored. Here and there, along the heights and ridges, men began to say they hoped the rebels would come on, because when they did they were going to get a taste of Fredericksburg in reverse.

Arriving with his lead division about 6 o'clock, Sickles was posted on the northern end of Cemetery Ridge, just in rear of Howard's and Doubleday's position on Cemetery Hill, which thus was defended in considerable depth. His other division would arrive in the night, as would Hancock's three under Gibbon, if Meade released them, to extend the line southward along the ridge leading down to the Round Tops. Once this had been done, the fishhook would be defended from eye to barb, and if Meade would also send Sykes and Sedgwick, reserves could be massed behind the high ground in the center, where they would have the advantage of interior lines in moving rapidly to the support of whatever portion of the convex front might happen to be under pressure at any time. All this depended on Meade, however, and when Slocum at last came forward at 7 o'clock (apparently he had decided to risk his reputation after all, or else he had decided that it was more risky to remain outside events in which his soldiers were involved) Hancock transferred the command to him and rode back to Taneytown to argue in person for a Gettysburg concentration of the whole army, nine of whose nineteen divisions were there already, with a tenth one on the way.

He arrived at about 9.30 to find his chief already persuaded by the message he had sent him four hours earlier. "I shall order up the troops," Meade had said, after brief deliberation, and orders had gone accordingly to Gibbon, Sykes, and Sedgwick, informing them that the Pipe Creek plan had been abandoned in favor of a rapid concentration on the heights just south of Gettysburg, where the other half of the army was awaiting their support. However, instead of going forward at once himself—there would be no time for a daylight reconnaissance anyhow—Meade decided to get some badly needed sleep. At 1 a.m. he came out of his tent, mounted his horse, and rode the twelve miles north with his staff and escort, a full moon floodlighting the landscape of his native Pennsylvania.

At 3 o'clock, barely an hour before dawn, he dismounted at the cemetery gate, through which there was a rather eerie view of soldiers sprawled in sleep among the tombstones. Across the way, on the western ridge and down in the moon-drenched town below, he saw another sobering sight: the campfires of the enemy, apparently as countless as the stars. Slocum, Howard, and Sickles were there to greet him, and though he had seen but little of the position Hancock had so stoutly recommended, all assured him that it was a good one. "I am glad to hear you say so, gentlemen," Meade replied, "for it is too late to leave it."

By the time he had made a brief moonlight inspection of Culp's and Cemetery hills, dawn was breaking and Hancock's three divisions were filing into position on Cemetery Ridge, having completed their all-night march from Taneytown. Sykes had reached Hanover and turned west in the darkness; he would arrive within a couple of hours. Only Sedgwick's corps was not at hand, the largest of the seven. Uncle John had promised to make it from Manchester by 4 o'clock that afternoon, and though it seemed almost too much to hope that so large a body of men could cover better than thirty miles of road in less than twenty hours, Meade not only took him at his word; he announced that he would attack on the right, as soon as Sedgwick got there.

★ 3 ★

Lee's headquarters tents were pitched in a field beside the Chambersburg Pike, on the western slope of Seminary Ridge. When he rose from sleep, an hour before dawn—about the same time Meade drew rein beside the gate on Cemetery Hill—his intention, like his opponent's, was to attack on the right. He had arrived at this decision the previous evening, in the course of a twilight conference north of Gettysburg with Ewell, whom he found gripped by a strange paralysis of will, apparently brought on, or at any rate intensified, by Lee's stipulation that an assault on the bluecoats attempting a rally on the hilltop south of town, though much desired, not only could not be supported by troops outside his corps, as Ewell had requested, but also was to be attempted only if he found it "practicable," which Ewell interpreted as meaning that he must be certain of success. It occurred to him that in war few things were certain, least of all success; with the result that he refrained from taking any risk whatever. First he waited for Johnson, whose division did not come onto the field until past sundown, and finally called the whole thing off, finding by then that the heights beyond the town bristled with guns and determined-looking infantry, deployed in overlapping lines, well dug in along much of the front, and heavily reinforced.

Though it was not Lee's way to challenge an assessment made by a general on ground which he himself had not examined, when he arrived for the conference he indicated his regret by expressing the hope that Ewell's decision would not apply to next day's operations. "Can't you, with your corps, attack on this front tomorrow?" he asked. Ewell said nothing; nor did Rodes, whose accustomed fieriness had been subdued by his narrow escape from disaster in his first action as a major general, and Johnson was not present.

That left Early, who did not hesitate to answer for his chief that an offensive here on the left, after the Federals had spent the night preparing for such a move, would be unwise. However, he added, indicating the Round Tops looming dimly in the distance and the dusk, an attack on the right, with the mass of bluecoats concentrated northward to meet the expected threat from Ewell, offered the Confederates a splendid opportunity to seize the high ground to the south and assail the Union flank and rear from there. Ewell and Rodes nodded agreement, but when Lee replied: "Then perhaps I had better draw you around towards our right, as the line will be very long and thin if you remain here, and the enemy may come down and break through," Early again was quick to disagree. In his view, that would spoil the whole arrangement by allowing the foe to turn and give his full attention to the blow aimed at his rear. As for the integrity of the present line, Lee need have no qualms; whatever its shortcomings as a base from which to launch an offensive, the position was an excellent one for defense. Besides, Early went on to say, much captured material and many of the wounded could not be moved on such brief notice, not to mention the effect on morale if the troops were required to give up ground they had won so brilliantly today.

Lee heard him out, then pondered, head bent forward. The main thing he disliked about the proposal was that it would require a change in his preferred style of fighting, typified by Manassas, where he had used the nimble Second Corps to set his opponent up for the delivery of a knockout punch by the First Corps, whose specialty was power. Early was suggesting what amounted to a change of stance, which was neither an easy nor a wise thing for a boxer to attempt, even in training, let alone after a match was under way, as it was now. Head still bowed in thought, Lee mused aloud: "Well, if I attack from the right, Longstreet will have to make the attack." He raised his head. "Longstreet is a very good fighter when he gets in position and gets everything ready, but he is so slow."

The extent of his perplexity was shown by this criticism of one subordinate in the presence of another, a thing he would never have done if he had not been upset at finding the commander of the Second Corps, famed for its slashing tactics under Jackson, content to fall back on the defensive with a victory half won. However, when Early, still speaking for his chief, who seemed to have lost his vocal powers along with those employed to arrive at a decision, assured him that the three divisions would be prompt to join the action as soon as the attack was launched across the way, Lee tentatively accepted the plan and rode back through the darkness to Seminary Ridge.

Once he was beyond the range of Early's persuasive tongue, however, his doubts returned. He reasoned that the blow, wherever it was to be delivered—and he had not yet decided on that point—should be struck with all the strength he could muster. If Ewell would not attempt it on the left, he would bring him around to the right, thus shortening the line while adding power to the punch. Accordingly, he sent him instructions to shift his three divisions west and south at once if he was still of the opinion that he could launch no drive from where they were. This not only restored Ewell's powers of speech; it brought him in person to army headquarters. Dismounting with some difficulty because of his wooden leg, he reported that Johnson had examined the Federal position on Culp's Hill and believed he could take it by assault. This changed the outlook completely; for if Culp's Hill could be taken, so could the main enemy position on Cemetery Hill, which it outflanked. Happy to return to his accustomed style, which was to use his left to set his opponent up for the knockout punch he planned to throw with his right, Lee canceled Ewell's instructions for a shift and directed instead that he remain where he was, with orders to seize the high ground to his front as soon as possible. By now it was close to midnight; Ewell rode back to his own head-quarters north of Gettysburg.

Lee pondered the matter further. Since Longstreet, who would deliver the major blow, was not yet up, whereas Ewell was already in position, he decided to time the latter's movements by the former's, and sent a courier after Ewell with instructions for him not to advance against Culp's Hill until he heard Longstreet open with his guns across the way. This done, Lee turned in at last to get some sleep, telling his staff as he did so: "Gentlemen, we will attack the enemy as early in the morning as practicable."

Rising at 3 a.m. he ate breakfast in the dark and went forward at first light to the crest of the ridge, preceded by a staff engineer whom he sent southward, in the direction of the Round Tops, to reconnoiter the ground where the main effort would be made. To his relief, as he focused his glasses on the enemy position, though he saw by the pearly light of dawn that the Federals still held Cemetery Hill in strength, the lower end of the ridge to the south appeared to be as bare of troops as it had been at sunset. Longstreet soon arrived to report that McLaws and Hood were coming forward on the pike, having camped within easy reach of the field the night before—all but one of Hood's brigades, which was on the way from New Guilford, more than twenty miles to the west. Pickett too was on the march, having been relieved by Imboden the day before at Chambersburg, but could scarcely arrive before evening. Glad at any rate to learn that Hood and McLaws were nearby, Lee then was startled to hear Old Peter return to yesterday's proposal that the Confederates maneuver around the Union left and thus invite attack instead of attempting one themselves against so formidable a position as the enemy now held.

While Longstreet spoke, the force of his words was increased by the emergence on Cemetery Ridge of brigade after brigade of blue-clad soldiers, extending the line southward in the direction of the Round Tops. However, Lee rejected his burly lieutenant's argument out of hand, much as he had done the previous after-noon, although by sunup it was apparent that his plan for a bloodless occupation of the enemy ridge would have to be revised. Longstreet lapsed into a troubled silence, and at that point A. P. Hill came up, still pale and weak from illness. Except to report that his whole corps was at hand, Anderson having arrived in the night, he had little to say. Heth was with him, his head wrapped in a bandage, too badly shaken by yesterday's injury to resume command of his division, which was to remain in reserve today under Pettigrew, the senior brigadier. Hood rode up soon afterwards, ahead of his men. As he watched the bluecoats cluster thicker on the ridge across the mile-wide valley, Lee told him what he had told his corps commander earlier. "The enemy is here," he said, "and if we do not whip him, he will whip us." Hood interpreted this to mean that Lee intended to take the offensive as soon as possible, but Longstreet took him aside and explained in private: "The general is a little nervous this morning. He wishes me to attack. I do not wish to do so without Pickett. I never like to go into battle with one boot off."

Hood could see that both men were under a strain; but whatever its cause, it was mild compared to what followed presently. As the sun climbed swiftly clear of the horizon, Lee worked out a plan whereby he would extend his right down Seminary Ridge to a point beyond the enemy left, then attack northeast up the Emmitsburg Road, which ran diagonally across the intervening valley, to strike and crumple the Union flank on Cemetery Ridge. Though he said nothing of this to Longstreet, who had expressed his disapproval in advance, he explained it in some detail to McLaws when he rode up shortly after 8 o'clock.

"I wish you to place your division across this road," Lee told him, pointing it out on the map and on the ground. "I wish you to get there if possible without being seen by the enemy. Can you do it?" McLaws said he thought he could, but added that he would prefer to take a close-up look at the terrain in order to make certain. Lee replied that a staff engineer had been ordered to do just that, "and I expect he is about ready." He meant that the officer was probably about ready to report, but McLaws understood him to mean that he was about ready to set out. "I will go with him," he said.

Before Lee could explain, Longstreet broke in, having overheard the conversation as he paced up and down. "No, sir," he said emphatically, "I do not wish you to leave your division." As he spoke he leaned forward and traced a line on the map, perpendicular to the one Lee had indicated earlier. "I wish your division placed so," he said. Quietly but in measured tones Lee replied: "No, General, I wish it placed just opposite." When the embarrassed McLaws repeated that he would like to go forward for a look at the ground his division was going to occupy, Longstreet once more refused to permit it and Lee declined to intervene further. So McLaws retired in some bewilderment to rejoin his troops and await the outcome of this unfamiliar clash of wills.

Presently the staff engineer, S. R. Johnston, returned from his early-morning reconnaissance on the right, and his report was everything Lee could have hoped for. According to him, the Federals had left the southern portion of Cemetery Ridge unoccupied, along with both of the Round Tops. When Lee asked pointedly, "Did you get there?"—for the information was too vital to be accepted as mere hearsay—Johnston replied that his report was based entirely on what he had seen with his own eyes. Lee's pulse quickened. This confirmed the practicality of his plan, which was for Longstreet to launch an oblique attack up the Emmitsburg Road, get astride Cemetery Ridge, and then sweep northward along it, rolling up the Union flank in order to get at the rear of the force on Cemetery Hill, kept under pressure all this time by Ewell, who was to attack on the left, fixing the bluecoats in position and setting them up for the kill, as soon as he heard the guns open fire to the south. Moreover, while Lee was considering this welcome intelligence, Longstreet received a report that his reserve artillery, eight batteries which were to lend the weight of their metal to the assault, had just arrived.

It was now about 9 o'clock. Except for Pickett's division and Evander Law's brigade, on the march respectively from Chambersburg and New Guilford, the whole First Corps was at hand. Still, Lee did not issue a final order for the attack, wanting first to confer with Ewell and thus make certain that the Second Corps understood its share in the revised plan for the destruction of "those people" across the way.

Leaving Hill and Longstreet on Seminary Ridge, he rode to Ewell's headquarters north of Gettysburg, only to find that the general was off on a tour of inspection. Trimble was there, however, serving in the capacity of a high-ranking aide and advisor, and while they waited for Ewell to return he conducted Lee to the cupola of a nearby almshouse, which afforded a good view of the crests of Culp's and Cemetery hills, above and beyond the rooftops of the town below. Observing that the defenses on the two heights had been greatly strengthened in the course of the sixteen hours that had elapsed since Ewell first declined to attack the rallying Federals there, Lee said regretfully: "The enemy have the advantage of us in a short and inside line, and we are too much extended. We did not or could not pursue our advantage of yesterday, and now the enemy are in a good position." When Ewell at last returned, Lee repeated what he had told Trimble, stressing the words, "We did not or could not pursue our advantage," as if to impress Ewell with his desire that the Second Corps would neglect no such opportunity today. Though it was plain that the Union stronghold had been rendered almost impregnable to attack from this direction, he explained his overall plan in detail, making it clear that all three divisions here on

the left were to menace both heights as soon as
Longstreet's guns began to roar, and he added that the
demonstration was to be converted into a full-scale
assault if events disclosed a fair chance of success.

This done, he rode back toward Seminary Ridge,
along whose eastern slope two of Hill's divisions were
already posted, well south of the Chambersburg Pike.
Anderson's, which had not arrived in time for a share in
yesterday's fight, was farthest south, under orders to join
Longstreet's attack as it came abreast, rolling northward,
and Pender's was to do the same in turn, simultaneously
extending its left to make contact with the Second
Corps southwest of Gettysburg. Heth's division, which
was in about as shaken a state as its shell-shocked commander, would remain in reserve on the far side of
Willoughby Run, not to be called for except in the event
of the threat of a disaster.

It was just past 11 o'clock when Lee returned to Seminary Ridge, suffering en route from what an officer who
rode with him called "more impatience than I ever saw
him exhibit upon any other occasion," and gave
Longstreet orders to move out. Observing his chief's
disappointment at finding the two First Corps divisions
still occupying the standby positions in which he had left
them two hours earlier, Longstreet did not presume to
suggest that he wait for Pickett—as he had told Hood he
preferred to do, even though this would have postponed
the attack until sundown at the soonest—but he did
request a half-hour delay to allow for the arrival of Law,
whose brigade was reported close at hand by now. Lee
agreed, although regretfully, and when Law came up
shortly before noon, completing a 24-mile speed march
from New Guilford in less than nine hours, the two
divisions lurched into motion, headed south under cover

of Herr Ridge, which screened them from observation by enemy lookouts on the Round Tops.

Apparently Meade had begun to rectify his neglect of those bastions, for signal flags were flapping busily from the summit of the nearer of the two. Lee was not disturbed by this, however. Now that the march was under way, his calm and confidence were restored. "Ah, well, that was to be expected," he said when scouts reported that the enemy left was being extended southward along Cemetery Ridge. "But General Meade might as well have saved himself the trouble, for we'll have it in our possession before night."

Longstreet's veterans agreed. The march was far from an easy one, the day being hot and water scarce, but they were accustomed to such hardships, which were to be endured as prelude to the delivery of the assault that would determine the outcome of the battle. Moreover, they considered it standard procedure that theirs was the corps selected for that purpose. "There was a kind of intuition, an apparent settled fact," one of its members later declared, "that after all the other troops had made their long marches, tugged at the flanks of the enemy, threatened his rear, and all the display of strategy and generalship had been exhausted in the dislodgment of the foe, and all these failed, then when the hard, stubborn, decisive blow was to be struck, the troops of the First Corps were called on to strike it."

As it turned out, however, the march was a good deal harder and longer than they or anyone else, including Lee and Longstreet, had expected when they began it. The crow-flight distance of three miles, from their starting point near Lee's headquarters to their jump-off position astride the Emmitsburg Road just opposite the Round Tops, would be doubled by the necessity for tak-

ing a roundabout covered route in order to stay hidden
from Meade, who would be able to hurry reinforcements to any portion of his line within minutes of being
warned that it was threatened. Nor was that all. This
estimated distance of six miles had to be redoubled in
turn, at least for some of the marchers, when it was discovered that the movement eastward would be disclosed
to the enemy if the butternut column passed over the
crest of Herr Ridge here to the south where the woods
were thin.

Plainly upset by this sign of the guide's incompe-
tence—but no more so than the guide himself, a lowly
captain on Lee's staff, who had neither sought nor
wanted the assignment, who had not reconnoitered west
of Seminary Ridge at all, and who later protested that he
"had no idea that I had the confidence of the great General Lee to such an extent that he would entrust me with
the conduct of an army corps moving within two miles
of the enemy line"—Longstreet halted the column and
reversed its direction of march, back northward to a
point near the Chambersburg Pike again, where the
ridge could be crossed under cover of heavy woods.
Some time was saved by giving the lead to Hood, who
had followed McLaws till then, but nearly two full hours
had been wasted in marching and countermarching,
only to return to the approximate starting point.
Longstreet's anger soon gave way to sadness. A soldier
who watched him ride past, "his eyes cast to the ground,
as if in deep study, his mind disturbed," recorded afterwards that Old Peter today had "more the look of
gloom" than he had ever seen him wear before.

Southward the march continued, under cover of
McPherson's Ridge, then around its lower end, eastward
across Pitzer's Run and through the woods to Seminary

Ridge, which here approached the Emmitsburg Road at the point desired. The head of the column—Law's brigade, which by now had spent twelve blistering hours on the march—got there shortly after 3 o'clock. This was not bad time for the distance hiked, but the better part of another hour would be required to mass the two divisions for attack. Worst of all, as Hood's men filed in on the far right, confronting the rocky loom of Little Round Top, they saw bluecoats clustered thickly in a peach orchard half a mile to the north, roughly that same distance in advance of the main Federal line on Cemetery Ridge and directly across the road from the position McLaws had been assigned. This came as a considerable surprise. They were not supposed to be there at all, or at any rate their presence was not something that had been covered by Lee's instructions.

★ ★ ★

Neither was their presence in the orchard covered by any instructions from their own commander. In fact, at the time Hood's men first spotted them, Meade did not even know they were there, but supposed instead that they were still back on the ridge, in the position he had assigned to them that morning.

Since 9 o'clock—six hours ago, and within six hours of his arrival—his dispositions for defense had been virtually complete. Slocum's two divisions, reunited by shifting Geary north from Little Round Top, occupied the southeast extremity of Culp's Hill, while Wadsworth's I Corps division was posted on the summit and along the saddle leading west to Cemetery Hill. There Howard's three divisions held the broad plateau, supported by the other two divisions of the First Corps, now under Vir-

ginia-born John Newton, whom Meade had ordered
forward from Sedgwick's corps because he mistrusted
Doubleday. Thus eight of the sixteen available divisions
were concentrated to defend the barb and bend of the
fishhook, with Sykes's three in general reserve, available
too if needed. South of there, along the nearly two miles
of shank, the five divisions under Hancock and Sickles
extended the line down Cemetery Ridge to the vicinity
of Little Round Top, though the height itself remained
unoccupied after Geary's early-morning departure.
Buford's cavalry guarded the left flank, Gregg's the
right, and Kilpatrick's the rear, coming west from
Hanover.

Meade had established headquarters in a small house
beside the Taneytown Road, half a mile south of Cemetery Hill and thus near the center of his curved, three-
mile line. Here, once the posting of his men and guns
had been completed, he busied himself with attempts to
divine his opponent's intentions. With Ewell's three
divisions in more or less plain view to the north, he
expected the rebel attack to come from that direction
and he had massed his troops accordingly. However, as
the sun climbed swiftly up the sky, the apparent inactiv-
ity of the other two enemy corps disturbed him, knowing as he did that Lee was seldom one to bide his time.
It seemed to him that the Virginian must have something up his sleeve—something as violent and bloody,
no doubt, as Chancellorsville, where Hooker had been
unhorsed—and the more he considered this possibility,
the less he liked the present look of things.

At 9.30, thinking perhaps the proper move would be
to beat his old friend to the punch, he asked Slocum to
report from Culp's Hill on "the practicability of attacking the enemy in that quarter." When Slocum replied an

hour later that the terrain on the right, though excellent for defense, was not favorable for attack, Meade abandoned the notion of taking the offensive when Sedgwick arrived. In point of fact, he already had his chief of staff at work in the low-ceilinged garret of his headquarters cottage, preparing an order for retirement. Not that he meant to use it unless he had to, he explained later; but with so large a portion of Lee's army on the prowl, or at any rate out of sight, he thought it best to be prepared for almost anything, including a sudden necessity for retreat. At 3 o'clock, still with no substantial information as to his adversary's intentions, he wrote Halleck that he had his army in "a strong position for defensive." He was hoping to attack, he said, but: "If I find it hazardous to do so, or am satisfied the enemy is endeavoring to move by my rear and interpose between me and Washington, I shall fall back to my supplies at Westminster. . . . I feel fully the responsibility resting upon me," he added, "and will endeavor to act with caution."

At least one of his corps commanders—Sickles, whose two divisions were on the extreme left of the line—had serious reservations about the defensive strength of the position, at least so far as his own portion of it was concerned. Cemetery Ridge lost height as it extended southward, until finally, just short of Little Round Top, it dwindled to comparatively low and even somewhat marshy ground. Three quarters of a mile due west, moreover, the Emmitsburg Road crossed a broad knoll which seemed to Sickles, though its crest was in fact no more than twelve feet higher than the lowest point of the ridge, to dominate the sector Meade had assigned him. The only cover out there was afforded by the scant foliage of a peach orchard in the southeast corner of a junction formed by a dirt road leading back across the ridge; artillery from either side could bludgeon, more or less at will, that otherwise bald hump of earth and everything on it. But to Sickles, gazing uphill at it from his post on the low-lying far left of the army, the situation resembled the one that had obtained when his enforced abandonment of Hazel Grove caused the Union line to come unhinged at Chancellorsville, and he reasoned that the same thing would happen here at Gettysburg unless something more than skirmishers were advanced to deny the Confederates access to that dominant ground directly to his front. As the morning wore on and Meade did not arrive to inspect the dispositions on the left, Sickles sent word that he was grievously exposed. Meade, concerned exclusively with the threat to his right and having little respect anyhow for the former Tammany politician's military judgment, dismissed the warning with the remark: "Oh, generals are apt to look for the attack to be made where they are."

To Sickles this sounded more than ever like Hooker, and at midmorning he went in person to headquarters to ask if he was or was not authorized to post his troops as he thought best. "Certainly," Meade replied, "within the limits of the general instructions I have given you. Any ground within those limits you choose to occupy I leave to you." So Sickles rode back, accompanied by Henry Hunt, whom Meade sent along to look into the complaint, and though the artillerist rather agreed that it was valid, he also pointed out the danger of establishing a salient—for that was what it would amount to—so far in advance of the main line, so open to interdictory fire, and so extensive that the available troops would have to be spread thin in order to occupy it. In short, he declined to authorize the proposed adjustment, though

ing another of those savage attacks that had won fame for him and his scarecrow infantry.

★ ★ ★

Although Lee's ready acceptance of the role of attacker seemed to indicate otherwise, the odds were decidedly with Meade. Sedgwick's arrival completed the concentration of the Army of the Potomac, which remained some 80,000 strong after deductions for stragglers and yesterday's casualties. Lee, on the other hand, with Pickett's division and six of the seven cavalry brigades still absent, had fewer than 50,000 effectives on the field after similar deductions. Moreover, the tactical deployment of the two forces extended these eight-to-five odds considerably. Meade's 51 brigades of infantry and seven of cavalry were available for the occupation of three miles of line, which gave him an average of 27,000 men per mile, or better than fifteen to the yard—roughly twice as heavy a concentration as the Confederates had enjoyed at Fredericksburg—whereas Lee's 34 brigades of infantry and one of cavalry were distributed along a five-mile semicircle for an average of 10,000 men to the mile, or fewer than six per yard. As for artillery, Meade had 354 guns and Lee 272, or 118 to the mile, as compared to 54.

Nor were numbers the whole story. If the attacker enjoyed the advantage of being able to mass his troops for a sudden strike from a point of his choice along the extended arc, this was largely offset by the defender's advantage of being able to rush his ample reserves along the chord of that arc, first to bolster the threatened point and then to counterattack; so that the problem for Lee was not only to achieve a penetration, but also to

he promised to discuss it further with the army commander and send back a final decision. As the sun went past the overhead and no word came from headquarters, Sickles continued to fume and fret. Learning finally that Buford's cavalry had been relieved from its duty of patrolling the left flank, which he believed exposed him to assault from that direction, he could bear it no longer. If Meade was blind to obvious portents of disaster, Sickles certainly was not. He decided to move out on his own.

At 3 o'clock, while Meade was writing Halleck that his position was a strong one "for defensive," the veterans of Hancock's corps, playing cards and boiling coffee along the northern half of Cemetery Ridge, taking it easy as the long hot day wore on and no attack developed, were surprised to hear drums rolling and throbbing, off to the left, and when they looked in that direction they saw Sickles' two divisions of better than 10,000 men advancing westward across the open fields in formal battle order, bugles blaring and flags aflutter, lines carefully dressed behind a swarm of skirmishers all across the front. "How splendidly they march!" one of the watchers cried, and another remarked in round-eyed admiration: "It looks like a dress parade, a review."

The movement was so deliberate, so methodical in execution, that John Gibbon, sitting his horse alongside Hancock, who had dismounted, wondered if the II Corps had somehow failed to receive an order for a general advance. Hancock knew better. Leaning on his sword and resting one knee on the ground, he tempered his surprise with amusement at the sight of Old Dan Sickles leading his soldiers to the war. "Wait a moment," he said, and he smiled grimly as he spoke, "you'll see them tumbling back."

Some among Sickles' own officers were inclined to agree with this prediction: especially after they had reached and examined their new position, half a mile and more in front of the rest of the army. In ordering the maneuver, one brigadier observed, the corps commander had shown "more ardor to advance and meet the fight than a nice appreciation of the means to sustain it." Old soldiers reviewing the situation down the years expressed the same thought in simpler terms when they said that Sickles "stuck out like a sore thumb."

Not only was there little cover or means of concealment, out here on the broad low hump of earth; there was also a half-mile gap between the extreme right of the salient and the left of Hancock's corps, back on the ridge. Moreover, Hunt's theoretical objection that Sickles did not have enough troops for the operation he proposed was sustained by the fact that his new line—extending from near the Cordori house, well up the Emmitsburg Road, to the peach orchard, where it bent sharply back to form an angle, and then across the southwest corner of a large wheat field, to end rather inconclusively in front of a mean-looking jumble of boulders known appropriately as the Devil's Den, just west of Little Round Top—was about twice the length of the mile-long stretch of ridge which now lay vacant in its rear. As a result, the position had little depth, practically no reserves or physical feature to fall back on, and was unsupported on both ends. To some, it seemed an outright invitation to disaster: an impression that was strengthened considerably, within half an hour of the march out, by a full-scale bombardment from rebel guns across the way, in the woods along the eastern slope of Seminary Ridge.

Riding down at last in response to the sudden uproar,

Meade was appalled to see what Sickles had improvised here on the left. "General, I am afraid you are too far out," he said, understating the case in an attempt to keep control of his hair-trigger temper. Still in disagreement, Sickles insisted that he could maintain his position if he were given adequate support: a stipulation he had not made before. "However, I will withdraw if you wish, sir," he added. Meade shook his head as the guns continued to growl and rumble in the woods beyond the Emmitsburg Road. "I think it is too late," he said. "The enemy will not allow you."

He was calculating his chances as he spoke. The situation had been greatly improved by the arrival of Sedgwick, whose three divisions now were filing up the Baltimore Pike, across Rock Creek, and onto the field, ending on schedule their long march from Manchester. They could replace Sykes in general reserve and thus free those three well-rested divisions to move in support of Sickles. "If you need more artillery, call on the reserve!" Meade shouted above the thunder of the bombardment. "The V Corps and a division of Hancock's will support you—"

But that was as far as he got. His horse reared in terror at the roar of a nearby gun and suddenly bolted, the bit in his teeth. For a moment all Meade's attention was on the fear-crazed animal, which seemed as likely to carry him into the enemy lines as to remain within his own, but presently he got him under control again and galloped off to order up supports for Sickles in the salient.

It was clear by now that they would be needed soon; for behind him, as he rode, he could hear above the uproar of the guns the unnerving quaver of the rebel yell, which signified all too clearly that Lee was launch-

maintain it afterwards in order to exploit it, which might prove an even greater difficulty. What was more, as he had warned Ewell the evening before, any thinning of the circumferential line to provide a striking force elsewhere would expose the weakened sector to being swamped and broken by the kind of powerful assault Meade could launch, more or less at will, from his interior lines. In short, if Sickles had exposed his two divisions to possible destruction by his occupation of the salient, the same might be said of Lee, in the light of all this, with regard to his whole army and the manner in which he had disposed it.

Longstreet had discerned a good deal of this at first glance; at any rate he had recognized the potentials of disaster, even though he had no access to figures comparing the tactical strengths of the two armies. The two positions were there to look at, Meade's and Lee's, and the only thing he liked about the latter was that it could be abandoned without much trouble. When Lee declined his suggestion that the Confederates move around the Federal left and take up a similar position of their own, thus reversing the present assignment of roles, Old Peter was dismayed. Failure by Hill and Ewell to complete the victory by driving the blue fugitives from the heights they had fallen back on, which was his second choice as a proper course of action, only increased his despondency. "It would have been better had we not fought at all than to have left undone what we did," he had said the night before, in response to a staff officer's exuberance over the day's success. Renewing his plea for a withdrawal this morning, the burly Georgian had been rebuffed again: whereupon he turned sulky. Though he had of course obeyed all orders given him, he had not anticipated them in the best tradition of the Army of Northern Virginia, with the result that he was partly to blame for the delays encountered in the course of the unreconnoitered flank march. As it approached its close, however, his spirits rose—as they always did in proximity to the enemy. Above all, by a sort of extension if not reversal of his native stubbornness, he was determined to carry out Lee's orders to the letter.

Just how determined Longstreet was in this respect was demonstrated to McLaws and Hood shortly after they halted their divisions in wooded jump-off positions due west of the Peach Orchard and the Devil's Den. McLaws rode forward, then dismounted and walked to the edge of the woods, about a quarter of a mile from the Emmitsburg Road, for a look at the ground over which his troops would be advancing. There in plain sight he saw two blue divisions, one posted north along the road and the other southeast in the direction of the Round Tops. "The view presented astonished me," he later recalled, "as the enemy was massed in my front, and extended to my right and left as far as I could see."

Whatever validity they might have had when they were conceived, two miles away and something over five hours ago, Lee's plans for an attack up the Emmitsburg Road, in order to get astride the upper end of Cemetery Ridge, were obviously no longer practicable. Not only was the Union left not overlapped, as had been presupposed, but McLaws would be exposing his flank to end-on fire if he attacked in accordance with instructions. He notified Longstreet of this turn of events, only to be told that the orders were not subject to alteration. "There is no one in your front but a regiment of infantry and a battery of artillery," the staff man who brought this message informed him. McLaws replied that he knew better, having seen with his own eyes what was out there. But this had no effect. Three times he protested, and three times he was told to attack as ordered.

The same was true of Hood. Never in his military life had the sad-eyed blond young giant requested a modification of an order to attack, but he took one look at the situation and reacted much as McLaws was doing, half a mile to the north. Before protesting, however, he sent out scouts to search for an alternative to what appeared to him to be a suicidal venture. They promptly found one. All the country south of the Round Tops was unoccupied, they reported; Meade's far left was wide open to just such an attack as Lee had contemplated. So Hood sent word to Longstreet that it was "unwise to attack up the Emmitsburg Road, as ordered," and requested instead that he be allowed "to turn Round Top and attack the enemy in flank and rear."

Longstreet's reply—based, as he said later, on Lee's repeated earlier refusal to permit any maneuver around the enemy left—was brief and to the point: "General Lee's orders are to attack up the Emmitsburg Road." Supposing there must have been some misunderstanding, Hood repeated his request, and again his chief replied with that one sentence: "General Lee's orders are to attack up the Emmitsburg Road." By now Hood had been in position for nearly an hour, confronting the fissured tangle of the Devil's Den and the rocky frown of Little Round Top, and the longer he looked at what his men were being required to face, the more he became convinced that they were doomed. "In fact," he declared afterwards, "it seemed to me that the enemy occupied a position so strong—I may say impregnable—that, independently of their flank fire, they could easily repel our attack by merely throwing or rolling stones down the mountain side as we approached." Once more he urged Longstreet to grant him freedom to maneuver, only to have Old Peter deny him for still a third time: "General Lee's orders are to attack up the Emmitsburg Road." All that was lacking to complete the symbolism was a cock-crow.

What came instead was a staff officer with peremptory instructions for him to go forward without delay, and while Hood was making last-minute adjustments in the alignment of his brigades, the corps commander himself rode up. It was 4 o'clock. With his troops already in motion, Hood made a fourth and final appeal for permission to maneuver around Round Top for a strike at the open flank and rear of the blue army. Longstreet still would not agree, though he did at least change the wording of his one-sentence reply. "We must obey the orders of General Lee," he said.

Lee's instructions called for the attack to be launched in echelon, from right to left, not only by divisions—first Hood, then McLaws, and finally Anderson, with Pender alerted to strike in turn if additional pressure was needed—but also by the brigades within those divisions, so that the attack would gather strength as it rolled northward.

This meant that Law, on Hood's and therefore the army's right, would be the first to step off. And so he did, promptly at 4 o'clock: but not as ordered. If Longstreet would not disregard or modify Lee's instructions, nor Hood Longstreet's, Law—a month short of his twenty-seventh birthday and next to the youngest of Lee's generals—had no intention of exposing first the flank and then the rear of his troops to the destructive fire of the Yankees in the Devil's Den, as would necessarily be the

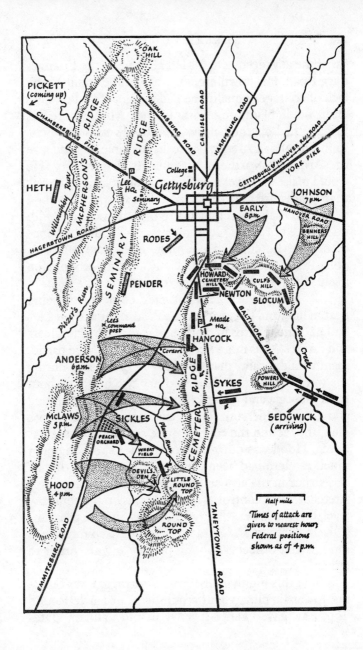

case if he advanced with his left aligned on the Emmitsburg Road. His unwillingness was not the result of any
lack of courage, a quality he had demonstrated on field
after field, beginning with Gaines Mill, where his
brigade had charged alongside Hood's to break Fitz-
John Porter's apparently unbreakable triple line and give
the Army of Northern Virginia its first victory. He
would make whatever sacrifice was called for, but he saw
that to advance as ordered would be to spill the blood
of his five Alabama regiments to little purpose and with
no chance of return. Consequently, in flat disobedience
of orders, he charged due east, in a frontal not an
oblique attack on the Devil's Den and Little Round Top
itself, which he saw as the key to control of the field.

J. B. Robertson's Texas brigade conformed, being
next in line, and the result, as Lee's far right and Meade's
far left came to grips in that vine-laced maze of boulders
and ravines, "was more like Indian fighting," one partic-
ipant would recall, "than anything I experienced during
the war." By the time Hood's other two brigades, both
from Georgia and under Georgians, Henry L. Benning
and G. T. Anderson, joined the melee in the Devil's
Den, they found the conflict quite as confused as it was
fierce. Hood was down, unhorsed by a shell fragment
much as Heth had been the day before, except that he
was struck in the arm and carried out of the battle on a
stretcher. Such control as remained was on the company
level, or even lower. "Every fellow was his own general,"
a Texan later wrote. "Private soldiers gave commands as
loud as the officers; nobody paying any attention to
either."

While this highly individualistic struggle was building toward a climax half a mile west of Little Round
Top, Law gave twenty-seven-year-old William Oates

instructions to veer southward with two regiments and flush a troublesome detachment of Union sharpshooters out of some woods at the foot of the steep northwest slope of Round Top. It was done in short order, though not without galling casualties; after which the five hundred survivors continued their uphill charge, scrambling hand over hand around and across huge boulders and through heavy underbrush, to call a halt at last on the lofty summit, panting for breath and wishing fervently that they had not sent their canteens off to be filled just before they received the order to advance.

Unlike the lower conical hill immediately to the north, which had been cleared of timber in the fall and thus afforded an excellent all-round view of the country-side, this tallest of all the heights in Adams County— sometimes called Sugarloaf by the natives—was heavily wooded from base to crown, a condition detracting considerably from its tactical usefulness. Through the trees due north, however, just over a hundred feet below and less than half a beeline mile away, Oates could see the barren, craggy dome of Little Round Top, deserted except for a handful of enemy signalmen busily wagging their long-handled flags, while off to the left, on lower ground, smoke boiled furiously out of the rocks where the fight for the Devil's Den was raging at the tip of the left arm of the spraddled V drawn by Sickles, its apex in the Peach Orchard and its right arm extended for the better part of a mile up the Emmitsburg Road, south and west of the main Federal position along the upper end of Cemetery Ridge and on the dominant heights to the north and east, bend and barb of the fishhook Meade had chosen to defend.

All this lay before and below the young Alabama colonel, who continued to look it over while his troops

were catching their breath on the crest of Round Top.
Victory seemed as clear to him, in his mind's eye, as the
town of Gettysburg itself, which he could see through
the drifting smoke, and the green fields rolling northward out of sight. He believed that with his present
force he could hold this hilltop stronghold against the
whole Yankee army, if necessary, so steep were the
approaches on all sides, and if a battery of rifled guns
could somehow be manhandled up here, piece by piece
and part by part if need be, not a cranny of Meade's fishhook line would be tenable any longer than it would
take a detail of axmen to clear a narrow field of fire. So
he believed. But just then a courier arrived from Law
with instructions for him to push on and capture Little
Round Top. Oates protested briefly, to no avail, then got
his parched and weary men to their feet—feet that had
covered no less than thirty miles of road and mountain-
side since 3 o'clock that morning at New Guilford—and
started them down the northern face of Round Top,
intent on carrying out the order.

It did not seem to him that this would be too difficult,
particularly after he crossed the wooded valley between
the Round Tops and was joined by a third regiment of
Alabamians and two of Texans who had fought their way
eastward through the lower fringes of the Devil's Den.
Earlier, looking down from the taller of the two peaks,
he had seen that the lower was not only undefended but
also unoccupied, except by a handful of signalmen, and
the confidence he derived from this was strengthened
as the uphill march began and then continued without
an indication that a single enemy rifleman stood or
crouched among the rocks ahead. Two thirds of the way
up, however, as the butternut skirmishers approached a
ledge that formed a natural bastion around the south-

west face of the hill, a heavy volley of musketry exploded in their faces.

Oates knew at once, from the volume of fire—he afterwards described it as the most destructive he had ever encountered—that it had been delivered by nothing less than a brigade, and probably a veteran one at that. This meant that he had a fight on his hands, against troops in a position that afforded the same advantages he had contemplated enjoying in defense of the hilltop he had just abandoned under protest that he could hold it against all comers with two regiments of about 500 badly winded men and no artillery at all. It was obvious here on Little Round Top, though, that a good many more men than that were shooting at him from the rocky ledge ahead, and what was more they had artillery, two guns spraying canister from the crest above and beyond them. As soon as he could establish a firing line of his own, the three Alabama regiments on the right and the two Texas regiments on the left, Oates gave the order for an all-out uphill charge to drive the Federals back on their guns and off the mountaintop.

That the blue defenders had taken position on Little Round Top, even as Oates was on his way down from the companion height to seize it, was due to the vigilance and perception of one man, a staff brigadier who, strictly speaking, had no direct command over troops at all. Gouverneur K. Warren, the army's thirty-three-year-old chief engineer, a frail-looking New Yorker, thin-faced and clean-shaven except for a drooped mustache and a tuft of beard just below his lower lip, had ridden over to inspect the hill's defenses at about the same time Meade's brief talk with Sickles was being interrupted by his horse's antic reaction to the rebel cannonade. Disturbed to find the high ground all but unoc-

cupied, despite its obvious tactical value, Warren told
the signalmen to keep up their wigwag activity, simply as
a pretense of alertness, whether they had any real messages to transmit or not—which was why Oates had
found them so busy when he looked down at them from
across the valley—and quickly notified Meade of the
grave danger to his left. Meade passed the word to
Sykes, whose corps by now was in motion to reinforce
Sickles, and Sykes passed it along to Barnes.

Barnes, who at sixty-two was one of the two oldest
division commanders in the army, was not with his
troops at the time, but Strong Vincent, who at twenty-
six was the army's youngest brigade commander,
responded by marching at once to occupy the hill.
Arriving less than a quarter of an hour before the Texans
and Alabamians, he advanced his brigade—four regiments from as many different states, Pennsylvania, New
York, Maine, and Michigan—to the far side of the crest,
well downhill in order to leave room for reinforcements,
and took up a stout position in which to wait for what
was not long in coming.

Warren meanwhile had ordered up two guns from
Charles Hazlett's battery, helping to manhandle them
up the rocky incline and onto the summit. This done, he
went in search of infantry supports, which he could see
were about to be needed badly, and found Stephen H.
Weed's brigade of Ayres's division marching west on the
road leading out to the Peach Orchard. When the commander of the rear regiment, Patrick O'Rorke—by
coincidence it was the 140th New York, which Warren
himself had commanded before he moved up to staff—
protested that he and his men were under orders to join
Sickles, Warren did not waste time riding to the head
of the column to find Weed. "Never mind that, Paddy,"

he said. "Bring them up on the double-quick, and don't stop for aligning. I'll take the responsibility." O'Rorke did as Warren directed, and Weed soon followed with his other three regiments, double-timing them as best he could up the steep, boulder-clogged incline and over the crest, to find the struggle raging furiously below him on the equally steep and rocky southwest face of the fuming hill.

Vincent by then had fallen, shot through the heart as he ranged up and down the firing line. "Don't yield an inch!" was his last command, and though his men tried their hardest to do as he said, one officer was to recall that, under the influence of no less than five charges and countercharges, "the edge of the fight swayed back and forward like a wave." The conflict was particularly desperate on the far left, where the 20th Maine, made up of lumberjacks and fishermen under Joshua Chamberlain, a former minister and Bowdoin professor, opposed the 15th Alabama, Oates's own regiment, composed for the most part of farmers. Equally far from home—Presque Isle and Talladega were each 650 crowflight miles from Little Round Top, which lay practically on the line connecting them—the men of these two outfits fought as if the outcome of the battle, and with it the war, depended on their valor: as indeed perhaps it did, since whoever had possession of this craggy height on the Union left would dominate the whole fishhook position. "The blood stood in puddles in some places on the rocks," Oates said later.

Losses were especially heavy among Federals of rank. O'Rorke, who was barely twenty-three and an officer of much promise, having been top man in the West Point class of '61, was killed along with more than two dozen of his men in the first blast of musketry that greeted his arrival. Weed, coming up behind him with the rest of the brigade, was shot in the head by a sniper down in the Devil's Den, and as Hazlett, who was standing beside him directing the fire of his two guns, bent forward to catch any last words the twenty-nine-year-old brigadier might utter, he too was dropped, probably by the same long-range marksman, and fell dead across Weed's body.

Casualties on the Confederate side were as heavy, if not heavier, and increased steadily as blue reinforcements continued to come up, unmatched by any on the downhill side. With all but one of the field officers killed or wounded in the Texas regiments, and no replacements anywhere in sight, Major J. C. Rogers, who had succeeded to leadership of the 5th Texas by elimination, might have thought he had been forgotten by the high command, except that presently a courier from division came up the hillside, dodging from boulder to boulder among the twittering bullets and screaming ricochets. He brought no expected word of reinforcements, but he did have a message from the wounded Hood's successor. "General Law presents his compliments," he told Rogers, "and says to hold the place at all hazards." This was altogether too much for the hard-pressed major. "Compliments, hell!" he roared above the clatter of battle. "Who wants compliments in such a damned place as this? Go back and ask General Law if he expects me to hold the world in check with the 5th Texas regiment!"

Oates could see that the struggle could have but one end if it continued at this rate, five regiments fighting uphill against eight who were supported by artillery in defense of a position he had judged to be nearly impregnable in the first place. So long as there was a hope of reinforcements he would fight—"Return to your companies; we will sell out as dearly as possible," he had told his captains—but presently, after the courier arrived with nothing more substantial than Law's compliments, he ordered a withdrawal. Just as the word was passed, the Maine men launched a bayonet attack. "When the signal was given we ran like a herd of wild cattle," Oates later admitted.

Near the base of the hill they rallied, being joined by the rest of Law's and Robertson's brigades, together with those of Anderson and Benning, who had succeeded by now in driving the Federals out of the Devil's Den, capturing three guns in the process. Not that the fighting had abated; Sykes had brought up two of his divisions in support of Sickles, with the result that the odds were as long down here as they had been above. There on the lower western slopes of Little Round Top the survivors began collecting rocks of all shapes and sizes, constructing a barricade to fight behind, and all the while the soldiers of both armies kept up a hot fire, banging away at whatever showed itself or perhaps at nothing at all. "Both sides were whipped," a Texas private explained afterwards, "and all were mad about it."

McLaws was also engaged by now, in part at least, and though this finally helped to relieve the pressure on the men who were fighting for their lives at the base of the rocky hill, the wait had been a long one, Longstreet having held him back in hopes that when he went forward at last he would find the enemy line greatly weakened by the shift of troops to meet Hood's attack on Little Round Top, which after all was not the assigned objective. Such withholding tactics had made possible the one-punch knockout Old Peter had scored at Second Manassas, a year ago next month, and he planned to repeat that coup today. If this was hard on Hood, whose men were thus required to absorb the single-minded attention of the entire Federal left wing for more than an hour, it was not easy on McLaws and his four brigade commanders, who were burning to advance: particularly William Barksdale, whose thirst for glory was as sharp in Pennsylvania as it had been on his great day at Fredericksburg, where Lee to his delight had let him challenge the whole Yankee army.

From the eastern fringe of the woods in which his troops awaited the signal to move out, the Mississippian could see bluecoats milling about in the Peach Orchard, as if they had it in mind to advance against him, and a battery posted temptingly at the apex of the salient, less than six hundred yards away. "General, let me go; General, let me charge," he kept begging McLaws, who declined, being under orders to wait for corps to inform him when the time was ripe. Soon Longstreet came riding northward through the woods and drew rein to talk with McLaws. Born within a week of each other, forty-two years ago, the two Georgians had been classmates at West Point. Equally burly of form and shaggy of hair and beard, they even resembled one another, not only in looks but also in their deliberative manner. Barksdale approached them and renewed his plea. "I wish you would let me go in, General," he appealed to the corps commander; "I will take that battery in five minutes." Longstreet looked out at the guns in the orchard, then back at the tall, white-maned Mississippian, who was trembling with excitement. Old Peter liked Barksdale, who was half a year his junior but looked older because of the prematurely gray hair worn shoulder-length, and greatly admired his spirit; but he would not be hurried. "Wait a little," he said in a calm, deep voice. "We are all going in presently."

It was near 5.30 before he gave the signal that opened the secondary attack. McLaws went in as Hood had done, his brigades committed in echelon from the right, which meant that Barksdale had some more waiting to do, being stationed on the left. South Carolinians under J. B. Kershaw—one of the five generals the town of Camden was to contribute to the Confederacy before the war was over—went forward with a shout, headed straight for the big wheat field north of the Devil's Den, about midway between Little Round Top and the Peach Orchard. Longstreet walked out with them as far as the Emmitsburg Road, where he stopped and waved them on with his hat, adding his own deep-throated version of the rebel yell to the tumult. They struck the center of Birney's division, which was posted behind a low stone wall along the near edge of the shimmering field of wheat, with Barnes's two remaining brigades in close support. As the fighting mounted swiftly toward a climax, Paul J. Semmes—younger brother of the *Alabama*'s captain—brought his Georgians out to join the stand-up fight, and behind them came the third brigade, still more Georgians, under W. T. Wofford, who had led them since the death of Tom Cobb in the sunken road at Fredericksburg. The Union line began to crumble under this added pressure, men dropping all along it and others scrambling rearward to get a head start in the race for safety.

Just then Semmes fell mortally wounded, which resulted in some confusion among his troops; but the loss was overbalanced at this critical point by one on the other side. Sickles was riding his line, erect on horseback, ignoring the whistle of bullets and the scream of shells, until one of the latter came along that could not be ignored because it struck his right leg, just above the knee, and left it hanging in shreds. He fell heavily to the ground, but kept cool enough to save his life by ordering a tourniquet improvised from a saddle strap. As he lay there, pale from the sudden loss of blood, his thigh bone protruding stark white against the red of mangled flesh, a staff officer rode up and asked solicitously, if superfluously: "General, are you hurt?"

Normally, Sickles would have laughed at the simplicity of the question, but not now. "Tell General Birney he must take command," he replied. Lifted onto a stretcher, he heard through the waves of pain and shock that a rumor was being spread that he was dead; so he called the bearers to a halt while one of them lit a cigar for him, then rode the rest of the way to the aid station with it clenched at a jaunty angle between his teeth, puffing industriously at it by way of disproving the rumor that he had stopped breathing. Thus did Old Dan Sickles leave the war, to proceed in time to other fields of endeavor, including a well-publicized liaison with the deposed nymphomaniac Queen of Spain.

There was to be a great deal of discussion, beginning tonight and continuing down the years, as to whether his occupation of the salient, half a mile and more in front of the main Union line, had been a colossal blunder or a tactically sound maneuver. Whatever else it was or wasn't—and entirely aside from the fact that it helped to discourage Longstreet's men from attacking as Lee had ordered, straight up the Emmitsburg Road, which probably would have meant utter destruction for them if Sickles had stayed back on the ridge to tear their flank as they went by—the movement resulted at any rate in the wrecking of his corps, whose two divisions, formerly under Phil Kearny and Joe Hooker and therefore among the most famous in the army, were to suffer well over four thousand casualties in the two hours before sunset.

The worst of the damage occurred when the line gave way at the western rim of the wheat field. "It is too hot; my men cannot stand it!" Barnes cried, and he ordered a retreat. Birney's were quick to follow, despite his efforts to stop them. But as the elated Confederates started forward, in close and hot pursuit, they were met by a fresh division under Caldwell, whom Hancock had alerted to stand by for trouble after predicting—quite accurately, as it turned out—that Sickles' troops would "come tumbling back" from the salient. Caldwell struck with all his strength, holding nothing in reserve. And now, though he lost three of his four brigade commanders, two of them killed on contact, it was the rebels who fell back through the trampled grain, the steam gone out of their drive.

From Little Round Top to the northern edge of the wheat field, the fighting degenerated into a bloody squabble as regiment fought regiment, alternately driving and being driven. "What a hell is there down in that valley!" a Federal lieutenant exclaimed after viewing the carnage from up on Cemetery Ridge. Birney's men were out of it by then, such as remained uncaptured and alive, and now the turn had come of those with Humphreys in the orchard and strung out along the road northeast of there.

Longstreet's "presently" had begun to seem interminable to Barksdale and his soldiers, held under cover and straining at the leash all the time the other three brigades were taking on most of Birney's and Barnes's divisions and finally all of Caldwell's, which came in fresh to stop them short of the ridge. Though opinion was divided as to the distinguishing characteristics of

these troops from the Deep South—a Virginia artilleryman, for example, having learned to feel secure whenever his battery had the support of the Mississippians,
was to say that theirs was the brigade "I knew and loved
best of all in Lee's army"; whereas a Chambersburg
civilian, observing the various rebel outfits that passed
through his town, decided quite to the contrary that
"those from Mississippi and Texas were more vicious
and defiant" than the rest—the men themselves not only
would have considered both of these remarks compli-
mentary, but also would have been hard put to say which
compliment they preferred. Certainly their viciousness
and defiance were apparent to the Federals in the
orchard, just over a quarter-mile away, as they came running eastward out of the woods, unleashed at last and
eager to come to grips.

Barksdale was out in front of the whole line, his face
"radiant with joy," as one observer remarked, to be leading what a Confederate lieutenant and a Union colonel
referred to afterwards, respectively, as "the most magnificent charge I witnessed during the war" and "the
grandest charge that was ever made by mortal man." His
earlier assurance that he could "take that battery in five
minutes" had sounded overconfident at the time, mainly
because the stout rail fences on both sides of the
Emmitsburg Road seemed likely to slow his advance
while they were being torn down or climbed over. As it
turned out, however, the fences were no deterrent at all.
They simply vanished under the impact of the charging
Mississippians, who reached the Peach Orchard even
sooner than their general had predicted, whooping with
delight as they swarmed over the battery and such of its
defenders as had resisted the impulse to get out of the
path of that savage assault. Four of the guns and close

to a thousand prisoners were taken in one swoop, but that was only a part of what Barksdale was after. Still out front, hatless so that his long white hair streamed behind him as he ran, he shouted: "Forward, men! Forward!" pointing with his sword at the blue line half a mile ahead on Cemetery Ridge.

He did not make it that far, nor did any of his men. A Federal brigadier, watching the conspicuous figure draw nearer across the stony floor of the valley, assigned a whole company of riflemen the task of bringing him down; which they did. As for his men, the vigilant Hunt had prepared a reception for them by massing forty guns along the crest and down the slope of the ridge. Meade had seen to it that these batteries had infantry support by shifting troops southward from his overcrowded right, but the guns themselves, blasting the attackers wholesale as they came within easy range, turned out to be enough. Still they came on, overrunning the first line of artillery on the slope, where the cannoneers fought them with pistols and rammer staffs and whatever came to hand, and all the while the guns on the crest flung canister point-blank at them, mangling blue and gray alike. Finally, unsupported on the left or right, Barksdale's men fell back westward to a line along Plum Run, midway between the road and the ridge, leaving half their number dead or wounded on the field, including their commander. Scouts from a Vermont regiment were to bring him into their lines that night, shot through both legs and the breast, and he would die by morning, his thirst for glory slaked at last.

Hood and McLaws had done their worst, and the 15,000 men in their eight brigades, having taken on six full enemy divisions, together with major portions of three others—a total of 22 Federal brigades, disposed with all the advantages of the defensive and containing better than twice as many troops as came against them—were fought to a standstill along an irregular line stretching northwest from the Round Tops to the Peach Orchard, anywhere from half a mile to a mile beyond the Emmitsburg Road, which had marked the line of departure. Proud of what his soldiers had accomplished against the odds, though he knew it was less than Lee had hoped for, Longstreet was to say: "I do not hesitate to pronounce this the best three hours' fighting ever done by any troops on any battlefield."

The cost had been great—more than a third of the men in the two divisions had been hit; Hood would be out of combat for some time, a grievous loss, and Semmes and Barksdale forever—but so had been the gain: not so much in actual ground, though that had been considerable, as in its effect of setting the bluecoats up for the kill. Meade had been stripping his center, along with his right, to reinforce his left. And now the offensive passed to Hill, or more specifically to Richard Anderson, whose division was on the right, adjoining McLaws, and who now took up his portion of the eche-lon attack from a position directly opposite the weak-ened Union center.

In this as in the other two divisional attacks the brigades were to be committed in sequence from the right, and it opened with all the precision of a maneuver on the drill field. Nor was there any such delay as there had been in the case of McLaws, held in check by Longstreet while Hood's men were storming the Devil's Den and fighting for their lives on Little Round Top. At 6.20, when Barksdale's survivors began their withdrawal from the shell-swept western slope of Cemetery Ridge,

Anderson sent Cadmus Wilcox and his Alabamians driving hard for a section of the ridge just north of where the Mississippians had struck and been repulsed. Next in line, David Lang's small brigade of three Florida regiments followed promptly, supported in turn by Ambrose Wright's Georgians, who came forward on the left.

But that was where the breakdown of the echelon plan began. Carnot Posey, having already committed three of his four Mississippi regiments as skirmishers, had not understood that he was to charge with the fourth, and his doubts became even graver when he discovered that his left would not be covered by William Mahone, who could not be persuaded that his Virginia brigade, posted all day in reserve, was intended to have a share in the attack. Wilcox by now had sent his adjutant back to ask for reinforcements, and Anderson had sent him on to Mahone with full approval of the request. But Mahone refused to budge. "I have my orders from General Anderson himself to stay here," he kept insisting, despite the staff man's protest that it was the division commander who had sent him. As a result, Posey advanced his single regiment only as far as the Emmitsburg Road, where he came under heavy artillery fire, and Wright, after pausing briefly to give the two laggard brigades a chance to catch up and cover his left, went on alone when he saw that the Mississippians would come no farther and that the Virginians had no intention of advancing at all.

The fault was primarily Anderson's. Missing the firm if sometimes heavy hand of Longstreet, under whom he had always fought before—except at Chancellorsville, where Lee himself had taken him in charge—he was unaccustomed to Hill's comparatively light touch, which allowed him to be less attentive to preparatory details.

Furthermore, Hill had understood that his right division was more or less detached to Longstreet, whereas Longstreet had interpreted Lee's instructions merely to mean that Hill would be in support and therefore still in command of his own troops. Consequently, neither exercised any control over Anderson, who followed suit by leaving the conduct of the attack to his subordinates, with the result that it broke down in midcareer.

At this point, however, with Wilcox, Lang, and Wright driving hard for Cemetery Ridge, the question of blame seemed highly inappropriate. A more likely question seemed to concern a proper distribution of praise among the three attacking brigades for having pierced the Union center. Hancock certainly saw it in that light, and with good cause. Meade having placed him in command of the III Corps as well as his own when Sickles fell, he had sent one of his three divisions to reinforce the left an hour ago, and since then he had been using elements of the two remaining divisions to bolster the line along Plum Run, where McLaws was keeping up the pressure. As a result, he had found neither the time nor the means to fill the gap on his left, where Caldwell had been posted until his departure, and the even larger gap that had yawned beyond it ever since Sickles moved out to occupy the salient. To his horror, Hancock now saw that Wilcox was headed directly for this soft spot, driving the remnant of Humphreys' division pell-mell before him as he advanced, with Lang on his left and Wright on the left of Lang. Gambling that no simultaneous attack would be launched against his right, just below Cemetery Hill, Hancock ordered Gibbon and Hays to double-time southward along the ridge and use what was left of their commands to plug the gap the rebels were about to strike.

He hurried in that direction, ahead of his troops, and arrived in time to witness the final rout of Humphreys, whose men were in full flight by now, with Wilcox close on their heels and driving hard for the scantly defended ridge beyond. As he himself climbed back up the slope on horseback, under heavy fire from the attackers, Hancock wondered how he was going to stop or even delay them long enough for a substantial line of defense to be formed on the high ground. Gibbon and Hays "had been ordered up and were coming on the run," he later explained, "but I saw that in some way five minutes must be gained or we were lost." Just then the lead regiment of Gibbon's first brigade came over the crest in a column of fours, and Hancock saw a chance to gain those five minutes, though at a cruel price.

"What regiment is this?" he asked the officer at the head of the column moving toward him down the slope.

"First Minnesota," its commander William Colvill replied.

Hancock nodded. "Colonel, do you see those colors?" As he spoke he pointed at the Alabama flag in the front rank of the charging rebels. Colvill said he did. "Then take them," Hancock told him.

Quickly, although scarcely a man among them could have failed to see what was being asked of him, the Minnesotans deployed on the slope—eight companies of them, at any rate; three others had been detached as skirmishers, leaving 262 men present for duty—and charging headlong down it, bayonets fixed, struck the center of the long gray line. Already in some disorder as a result of their run of nearly a mile over stony ground and against such resistance as Humphreys had managed to offer, the Confederates recoiled briefly, then came on again, yelling fiercely as they concentrated

their fire on this one undersized blue regiment. The
result was devastating. Colvill and all but three of his
officers were killed or wounded, together with 215 of his
men. A captain brought the 47 survivors back up the
ridge, less than one fifth as many as had charged down
it. They had not taken the Alabama flag, but they had
held onto their own. And they had given Hancock his
five minutes, plus five more for good measure.

Those ten minutes were enough. By the time Wilcox
reached the foot of the ridge, with Lang bringing up his
three regiments on the left, Gibbon's division had taken
position on the crest and was pouring heavy volleys of
musketry into the ranks of both brigades from dead
ahead. Staggered by this, and torn on his unprotected
right by fire from the massed batteries that had repulsed
Barksdale half an hour before, Wilcox looked back
across the valley and saw that his appeal for reinforcements had not been answered. Regretfully he ordered a
retreat. So did Lang at the same time. And as the
Alabamians and Floridians began their withdrawal from
the base of the ridge, Wright's Georgians struck with
irresistible force, some four hundred yards to the north.
"On they came like the fury of a whirlwind," a Pennsylvania captain later recalled.

The impetus of their drive carried them swiftly up the
slope and into the breaking ranks of the defenders, then
through the line of guns, whose cannoneers scattered,
and onto the crest. They did not stay there long—Gibbon and Hays had them greatly outnumbered, as well
as outflanked on the right and left, and Meade had
already ordered another three divisions to converge on
the threatened point from Cemetery Hill, three quarters
of a mile to the north, and Culp's Hill, about the same
distance across the eastern valley—but while they were

there Wright believed that he had victory within his reach. On the reverse slope, bluecoats were streaming rearward across the Taneytown Road, and half a mile beyond it the Baltimore Pike was crowded with fugitives. Yet these were only the backwash of the battle. Nearer at hand, on the left and right, he saw heavy blue columns bearing down on him, and he saw too—like Wilcox and Lang before him, though they had achieved no such penetration of the main Union line—that to stay where he was, unsupported, meant capture or annihilation.

He ordered a withdrawal, which was achieved only by charging a body of Federals who had gained his rear by now, and then fell back across the Emmitsburg Road, taking punishment all the way from the two dozen guns he had captured and then abandoned. Like Wilcox and Lang, Wright had lost nearly half his men in that one charge, and he found this a steep price to pay for one quick look at the Union rear, even though he believed ever after that the end of the war had been within his reach if only he had been supported while he was astride the crest of Cemetery Ridge, midway of the Yankee line and within plain sight of the cottage Meade was using as headquarters for his army.

The hard fact that no supports were at hand when the Georgians crested the ridge and stood poised there, silhouetted against the eastern sky for one brief fall of time as they pierced the enemy center, did not mean that none had been available. Though Posey and Mahone had hung back, declining for whatever reasons to go forward—the former calling a halt halfway across the valley and the latter refusing to budge from the shade of the trees on Seminary Ridge, directly behind Lee's command post—there still was Pender, whose division was to the Third Corps what Hood's and Johnson's were to the First and Second, the hardest-hitting and fiercest of the three. And yet Pender was not there after all: not Pender in person. Like Heth and Hood, at about the same time yesterday and earlier today, he had been unhorsed by a casual fragment of shell while riding his line to inspect and steady his men for their possible share in the attack then rolling northward. The wound in his leg, though ugly enough, was not thought to be very serious, or at any rate not fatal. But it was. Two weeks later the leg was taken off, infection having set in during the long ambulance ride back to Virginia, and he did not survive the amputation. "Tell my wife I do not fear to die," the twenty-nine-year-old North Carolinian said in the course of his suffering, which was intense. "I can confidently resign my soul to God, trusting in the atonement of our Lord Jesus Christ. My only regret is to leave her and our children." If this had the tone of Stonewall Jackson, under whom Pender had developed into one of the best of all Lee's generals despite his youth, his last words sounded even more like his dead chief: "I have always tried to do my duty in every sphere of life in which Providence has placed me."

Few doubted afterwards that he would have done that duty here today at Gettysburg by leading his four brigades across the valley to assault the ridge just north of where Wright had struck it. There was in fact little to stop him once he got there. Not only had Hancock shifted his two divisions south to counter Anderson's attack; Meade had also moved Newton's two in that direction from their position supporting Howard on Cemetery Hill. But that was beside the point, as it turned out. The decision whether to join the charge had been discretionary anyhow, according to Lee's orders, and when Pender was hit and carried off the field, his temporary successor James Lane, having watched Anderson's two adjoining brigades falter, decided that it was no longer advisable for his troops to advance, since they would not be supported on the right. Moreover, A. P. Hill was not there at the time, having ridden northward to confer with Rodes, and did not urge Lane on.

With that, the three-hour-long assault on Cemetery Ridge broke down completely. Hood, McLaws, and Anderson—some 22,000 men in all, including the cannoneers—had tried their hands in sequence against a total of no less than 40,000 blue defenders. Better than 7000 of the attackers had fallen in the attempt, and all they had to show for this loss of one third of the force engaged was the Devil's Den, plus the Peach Orchard, which had been proved to be practically indefensible in the first place, and a few acres of stony ground on the floor of the valley between the ridges. "The whole affair was disjointed," a member of Lee's staff admitted later. "There was an utter absence of accord in the movements of the several commands."

The truth was, the army had slipped back to the disorganization of the Seven Days, except that here at Gettysburg there was no hard-core tactical plan to carry it through the bungling. There was in fact scarcely any plan at all, Lee's instructions for an attack up the Emmitsburg Road having been rejected out of necessity at the start. This, together with the refusal of the Federals to panic under pressure, as they had done so often before when the graybacks came screaming at them, had stood in the way of victory.

And yet, in light of the fact that each of the three attacking divisions in turn had come close to carrying the day, there was more to it than that. Specifically, there was

Warren and there was Hancock, both of whom had
served their commander in a way that none of Lee's chief
lieutenants had served him. Warren had acted on his own
to save Little Round Top and the battle, and Hancock
had done the same to prevent a breakthrough, first at the
lower end and then at the center of Cemetery Ridge; but
no one above the rank of colonel—Oates, the exception,
lacked the authority to make it count—had acted with
any corresponding initiative on the other side. There
was, as always, no lack of Confederate bravery, and the
army's combat skill had been demonstrated amply by the
fact that, despite its role as the attacker, it had inflicted
even more casualties than it had suffered; yet these qualities could not make up for the crippling lack of direction
from above and the equally disadvantageous lack of initiative just below the top.

Longstreet sensed a good part of this—perhaps even
his own share of the blame, at least to a degree—but
once more his reaction was a strange one. Though he
was saddened by the wounding of Hood and the death
or capture of Barksdale, which he believed were the
main reasons he had failed to break Meade's line, he was
by no means as gloomy as he had been in the course of
the roundabout march into position. "We have not been
so successful as we wished," he told an inquirer, and that
was all he said. He seemed glad, for once, that his share
of the fighting was over. If Hill had broken down, it was
not his fault; he had small use for Little Powell anyhow.
And now the battle passed to Ewell.

Stung by Lee's complaint that he had failed to "pursue
our advantage of yesterday," Ewell was eager to make a
redemptive showing today, despite the difficulties of terrain on this northern quarter of the field. After Lee

departed he had kept busy, all through what was left of the morning and most of the afternoon, inspecting his three divisions, which were disposed along a convex arc on three sides of Gettysburg, Rodes to the west, Early just south, and Johnson to the east, confronting the two dominant heights at the bend and barb of the Union fishhook. His instructions required him to guard the Confederate left, keeping as many bluecoats occupied there as possible, and to stage a vigorous demonstration, by way of insuring that effect, when Longstreet's guns began to roar at the far end of the line. Moreover—and this was the prospect he found most attractive, in connection with his desire to make a showing—if Ewell decided that he could strike with a fair chance of success, he was to convert the demonstration into a real attack, driving the enemy from Cemetery and Culp's hills, which commanded the Taneytown Road and the Baltimore Pike, both vital to the Federals if they were thrown into retreat from these two northern heights and the ridge leading southward to the Round Tops. The wait was a long one, anxious as Ewell was, and some time after 4 o'clock, when the distant booming at last informed him that Longstreet's artillery preparation had begun, he decided to respond in the same fashion.

Six batteries, held under cover till then by Joseph Latimer, Johnson's twenty-year-old chief of artillery, were sent to the crest of Benner's Hill, a solitary eminence one mile east of town, with orders to pummel Culp's Hill, half a mile southwest across the valley of Rock Creek. Ewell felt that this would not only serve as a "vigorous demonstration," fixing the blue defenders in position as required, but would also afford him an opportunity to study their reaction and thus determine the advisability of launching an all-out uphill infantry assault.

The answer was both sudden and emphatic, as might have been expected if a proper reconnaissance had been made. Benner's Hill was not only fifty feet lower than the height across the way; it was also bald, which meant that the two dozen guns found neither cover nor concealment when they went into action there, whereas the Federal cannoneers had spent the past twenty hours digging lunettes and piling up embankments to add to the security of their densely wooded battery positions. Lashing their teams up the reverse slope of the isolated hill, the Confederates opened fire from its crest soon after 5 o'clock, and within a few minutes of the prompt and wrathful response by the heavier guns directly across the valley, as well as by those a mile away on Cemetery Hill, it was obvious that there could be no doubt as to the outcome of the duel, but only as to how long it could be sustained against the odds. Starkly exposed on the naked summit, the gray gunners stood to their work under a deluge of hot metal and amid sudden pillars of smoke and flame reared by exploding caissons.

After about an hour of this, Latimer, who was known as the "Boy Major" and was said to be developing fast into another Pelham, felt compelled to send word that his position was untenable, a thing he had never done before in the two years since he had interrupted his sophomore year at VMI to join the army. Johnson at once authorized him to withdraw all but four of the guns, which were to remain there in support of the attack Ewell had just ordered all three of his divisions to make, despite this graphic evidence of the fury they were likely to encounter as they approached the hilltop objectives he assigned them. Latimer's withdrawal was necessarily slow, his crews having been reduced to skeletons by the counterbattery fire, and he himself was mortally wounded before it was completed, a high price to pay for confirming what should have been apparent before the one-sided contest even began.

On the face of it, the infantry attempt seemed equally doomed. Actually this was not the case, however, for the paradoxical reason that Ewell had failed in his primary mission of holding the blue forces in position on his front. By 6 o'clock, when the attack order was issued, Meade had taken thorough alarm at the series of threats to his left and center, and by 7 o'clock, when the advance began against his right, he had shifted two of Newton's three divisions southward, together with all but a single brigade from the two divisions in Slocum's corps. All that remained by then on Cemetery Hill, which Early and Rodes were to assault in sequence from the north and the northwest, were the three battered divisions under Howard, while Culp's Hill was even more scantly held by Wadsworth's division of the I Corps, down to half its normal strength after yesterday's drubbing on Seminary Ridge, and the one brigade Slocum had left behind. That was where the paradox came in. If Ewell had succeeded in holding the departed bluecoats in position, as Lee had instructed him to do, the attack would have been as suicidal as any ever attempted by either army in the whole course of the war; but as it was, with the defenses manned only by Howard's jumpy Dutchmen, Wadsworth's thin line of survivors from the rout of the day before, and the single brigade from Geary's division, the chances of a Confederate breakthrough here on the north were considerably better than fair, despite the obvious difficulties of the terrain. For one thing, thanks to Meade's alarm at the unrelenting fury of the three-hour-long assault on the Round Tops and Cemetery Ridge, Ewell's troops outnumbered the defenders to their front, an advantage no other attacking force had enjoyed on any portion of the field today.

Johnson's division, which had arrived too late for a share in the battle yesterday, had remained in the same position for nearly twenty-four hours, a mile east of Gettysburg and north of the Hanover Road, its four brigades posted from right to left under J. M. Williams, John M. Jones, George H. Steuart, and James A. Walker. The men of the first were Louisianians, and the rest were nearly all Virginians, like Old Clubby himself, who took them forward at 7 o'clock, brandishing the post-thick hickory stick from which his nickname was derived. That left half an hour till sunset, but they had more than a mile to go and armpit-deep Rock Creek to cross before they came within musket range of their Culp's Hill objective. As a result, the sun was well down behind it by the time they came surging up the northeast slope, yelling fiercely as they approached the crest.

They did not make it all the way; Wadsworth's troops, including the remnant of the Iron Brigade, were well dug in and quite as determined as they had been when they shattered Heth's attack the day before. Jones was wounded early in the fight, and his and Williams' men, unsupported because Walker and his famed Stonewall Brigade remained in reserve on the far side of the creek, had all they could do to keep from being driven off the hillside.

Around to the left, Steuart had better luck, the trenches down the southern nose of the hill having yawned vacant ever since Slocum's departure, half an hour before the rebel advance got under way. The gray attackers swarmed into and along them, whooping as they swung northward in the twilight, apparently unopposed, only to strike a new line of fortifications, drawn at right angles to the old and occupied by the brigade Slocum had left behind. The struggle here was as bitter as on the right, and the defenders—five regiments of upstate New Yorkers under George S. Greene—fought with a determination every bit as grim as Wadsworth's.

Rhode Island–born, with a seagoing son who had served as executive officer on the *Monitor*, Greene was sixty-two, a few months older than the ineffectual Barnes and therefore the oldest Federal on the field. "Old Man Greene," his soldiers called him, or sometimes merely "Pop," for though he had finished second in his class at West Point forty years ago, he affected an easy style of dress that made him look more like a farmer than a regular army man. What he was, in fact, was a civil engineer; he had left the service early to build railroads and design municipal sewage and water systems for Washington, Detroit, and several other cities, including New York, whose Central Park reservoir was his handiwork, along with the enlarged High Bridge across the Harlem River. Such experience, as he applied it now to laying out intrenchments, stood him and his 1300 men in good stead this evening on Culp's Hill. Rather than attempt to hold the empty trenches on his right with his one brigade, which would have stretched it beyond the breaking point, he had dug a traverse, midway of the line and facing south behind a five-foot-thick embankment of earth and logs. Here his troops fought savagely, holding their own against Steuart's frantic lunges, and were reinforced at last by two regiments Wadsworth was able to spare when the pressure eased on the north end of the hill. When the comman-

der of the first of these reported to him on the firing
line, the battle racket was so terrific that Greene had to
give up trying to shout above the uproar, and instead
wrote his name on a card which he handed to the
colonel by way of identification.

For two hours, from twilight well into darkness, the
firing hardly slacked. Then gradually it did, dying away
to a sputter of individual shots, as if by mutual agreement that the blind slaughter had grown pointless: as
indeed it had. Johnson was forced to content himself
with what was after all a substantial lodgment on the far
Union right, and Greene was more or less satisfied that
he had been able to keep it from being enlarged, though
it was clear to the fighters on both sides that the lull
would not last past daylight.

Although it started later and ended sooner, Early's
attack on Cemetery Hill, launched when he heard Johnson open fire on the far left, not only accomplished a
deeper penetration but also came even closer than
Wright's had done, two hours ago, to achieving a complete breakthrough and the consequent disruption of
Meade's whole fishhook system of defense. His four
brigades were from four different states, Virginia,
Louisiana, North Carolina, and Georgia; Gordon commanded the last of these, and the other three were
respectively under William Smith, Harry T. Hays, and
Isaac Avery. Smith had no share in the assault, having
been posted two miles out the York Pike to fend off a
rumored threat to the rear. Nor did Gordon, as the
thing turned out; Early held him in reserve. But the
North Carolinians and Louisianians did all they could,
in fury and hard-handed determination, to make up for
these subtractions. Hays advanced on the right and
Avery on the left, headed straight for the steep northeast

face of the hundred-foot hill, and neither brigade would be stopped. Avery fell at the outset, mortally wounded, but his men kept going, over and past three successive lines of bluecoats disposed behind stone walls, defying the frantic overhead fire of infantry and artillery massed on the summit. Hays, a Tennessee-born and Mississippi-raised New Orleans lawyer whose brigade had first won fame under Richard Taylor in the Shenandoah Valley, refused to be outdone, though he too had to contend with three successive blue lines, the first along the far side of a ravine at the foot of the hill, the second behind a stone wall halfway up, and the third in well-dug rifle pits just short of the crest, protected by an abatis of felled trees.

Losses were surprisingly light, partly because the downhill-firing Federals tended to overshoot the climbing graybacks, but mostly, as Hays said later, because of "the darkness of the evening, now verging into night, and the deep obscurity afforded by the smoke." Another reason was that the defenders here were Howard's men, who had yesterday's disaster fresh in mind. Hays called no names, merely reporting that his troops, having taken the third Yankee line at small cost to themselves, "found many of the enemy who had not fled hiding in the pits for protection." While these were being rousted out and told to make their own way to the rear as prisoners, the two rebel brigades surged over the lip of the plateau, in hot pursuit of the fugitive survivors. One-armed Howard was there, again the unhappy witness of a scene that by now was becoming familiar. "Almost before I could tell where the assault was made," he afterwards declared, "our men and the Confederates came tumbling back together."

Once more, having failed to stem the rout, he was left

with a choice of joining it or exposing himself to capture, along with the guns his cannoneers had abandoned when the attackers reached point-blank range. "At that time," Hays noted proudly, "every piece of artillery which had been firing upon us was silent." The Louisianians and Tarheels swarmed among them, in full possession of the Union stronghold at the bend of the three-mile fishhook. Like Wright before him, a mile to the south, though darkness permitted him no such view of the enemy rear, Hays experienced a feeling of elation as he looked about the plateau for the reinforcements he had been told to expect.

For a moment he thought he saw them; heavy masses of infantry were coming up from the southwest in the gloom. He could not be sure they were not Federals, in which case he would take them under fire, but he had been "cautioned to expect friends" from that direction, either Longstreet or Hill, or Rodes from his own corps. Even when they fired at him, dropping a number of his men, he did not shoot back, not wanting to compound the error if they were Confederates. They fired again and kept coming on through the darkness; still he held his fire, perhaps remembering the fall of Jackson in the Wilderness, two months ago tonight. A third volley crashed, much nearer now, and he saw by the fitful glare of the muzzle flashes that the uniforms were blue. A close look even showed the trefoil insignia of the II Corps on the flat-top forage caps of the still advancing Federals, whose "Clubs Are Trumps" motto Hays and his men knew only too well from hard experience.

They were, in fact, S.S. Carroll's brigade of Hancock's third division, and Hancock himself had sent them. He had been talking just now with Gibbon in the twilight, gazing westward from the point on Cemetery

Ridge where Wright's breach had been sealed, when the racket of Early's attack erupted on the north slope of Cemetery Hill. "We ought to send some help over there," he told Gibbon, who was acting as corps commander while his chief undertook the larger duties Meade had assigned him. As the uproar drew nearer, signifying the progress of the attackers, Hancock added with rapid decision: "Send a brigade. Send Carroll."

Carroll it was. And Hays, already staggered by the three unanswered volleys—the third had been especially destructive, delivered as it was at such close range—gave the order at last for his men to return the fire. This they did, glad to be released from hard restraint, and kept it up as fast as they could ram cartridges and draw triggers, bringing the blue mass to a stumbling halt. Beyond it, however, Hays could see other such masses forming in the flame-stabbed darkness; Howard's fugitives were rallying to support the troops who had opened ranks to let them through and then gone on to stop the rebels in their tracks. Looking back over his shoulder for some sign that Gordon was advancing, and wishing fervently that at any moment he would see Rodes and his five brigades come charging across the plateau from the west, Hays held his own for a time against the odds, but then, abandoning all hope of support, gave the necessary commands for a withdrawal. Unpursued past the line of abandoned guns, the two brigades fell back in good order, firing as they went, and called a halt at the bottom of the hill, angry that neither Gordon nor Rodes had mounted the slope to help them exploit the greatest opportunity of the day.

This lack of support—which, if supplied, might well have made up for all the miscalculations and fumbled chances of the past two days—resulted from a series of interrelated hesitations and downright failures of nerve on the part of several men. Early had withheld Gordon because he saw at the last moment that Rodes was not advancing on his right, and Rodes had called off his attack for the same reason, with regard to Lane. In a sense, it all went back to the fall of Pender and the curious defection of Mahone; or perhaps it went even further back than that, to the near escape from disaster Rodes had experienced yesterday. Restrained at first by a fear of being involved in another fiasco if he charged unsupported up Cemetery Hill, he now was prodded by a desire to retrieve what his restraint had cost him. When he heard the clatter of gunfire on the overhead plateau, which signified unmistakably that the blue defenses had been breached, he repented his inaction and decided to go forward anyhow, with or without support. But by the time he got his troops in position to advance—most of them had been waiting all day in Gettysburg itself, which meant that they had to be disentangled from the complex of streets and houses before they could form for attack—the hilltop clatter had subsided; Hays had brought his two brigades back down the northeast slope.

Rodes took a careful, close-up look at the objective, which bristled with guns, and decided—no doubt wisely, at this late hour—that "it would be a useless sacrifice of life to go on." However, instead of bringing his five brigades back to their various starting points, he put them in line along the hollow of an old roadbed southwest of town, a position, he later reported, "from which I could readily attack without confusion." He did not explain why he had not done this sooner, in order to be able to move promptly in support of Hays, but he added: "Everything was gotten ready to attack at daybreak."

So he said. But for now the fighting was over, all but the final stages of Johnson's blind assault on Old Man Greene's well-engineered intrenchments, a mile across the way. Presently this too sputtered into silence, and moonlight glistened eerily on the corpse-strewn valleys and hillsides, its refulgence no longer broken by the fitful and ubiquitous pinkish-yellow stabs of muzzle flashes. Here and there, the wounded troubled the stillness with their cries for water and assistance, but for the most part the veterans of both armies were inured to this by now; they slept to rest their minds and bodies for tomorrow.

Thus ended the second day of what was already the bloodiest battle of the war to date, with no one knew how much more blood still to be shed on this same field.

★ ★ ★

Their lines drawn helter-skelter in the darkness, the soldiers could sleep; but not the two commanders and their staffs, who had the task of assessing what had been done today, or left undone, in order to plan for tomorrow. In this, the two reacted so literally in accordance with their native predilections—Lee's for daring, Meade's for caution—that afterwards, when their separate decisions were examined down the tunnel of the years—which provides a diminished clarity not unlike that afforded by a reversed telescope—both would be condemned for having been extreme in these two different respects.

Lee had spent the battle hours at his command post on Seminary Ridge, midway of that portion of the line occupied by Hill's two divisions, and though this gave him a clear view of most of the fighting in the valley below and on the ridge across the way, he had made no

attempt to control or even influence the action once the
opening attack had been launched on the far right. An
observer who was with him recorded that he sent only
one message and received only one all afternoon,
despite what another witness described as "an expression of painful anxiety" on his face as the assault rolled
north toward its breakdown—just at the point where he
stood, between Anderson and Pender, with Mahone's
brigade taking it easy in the woods directly behind the
command post—then shifted across to Culp's Hill and
moved back toward him through the gathering dusk,
only to stall again when it got to Rodes. Both break-
downs were particularly untimely, since in each case
they had occurred at the moment when the echeloned
build-up of pressure resulted at last in a penetration of
the enemy defenses, hard by the point that had been
scheduled to be struck next.

If there was bitter mockery in these two near-suc-
cesses, which had had to be abandoned for lack of support, there was also much encouragement in the over-all
results of the five-hour contest. All that had been lacking, Lee perceived and later reported, was "proper concert of action." Substantial lodgments had been effected
and maintained by Hood and Johnson, on the far right
and far left; Meade was clamped as in a vise. Moreover,
high ground along the Emmitsburg Road had been
taken by McLaws in the vicinity of the Peach Orchard,
which afforded good positions for the massing of
artillery to support an attack on the enemy center or left
center. It was just at that point, shortly before sundown
and directly opposite the command post, that Lee had
focused his binoculars to watch Wright's Georgians
storm Cemetery Ridge, driving off the defending
infantry and cannoneers, and then stand poised on the

crest for a long moment, as if balanced on a knife blade, before they had to fall back for want of support. What had almost been achieved today could be achieved tomorrow, Lee believed, with "proper concert of action" and artillery support.

Basically, what he intended was a continuation of the tactics employed today. Longstreet and Ewell would strike simultaneously on the right and left, driving for the Taneytown Road and the Baltimore Pike, just in rear of their primary objectives, while Hill stood by to assist either or both in exploiting whatever opportunities proceeded from the exertion of this double pressure on an enemy Lee presumed was badly shaken by the headlong routs and heavy losses of the last two days. Not that there was no room for doubt or occasion for hesitation. There was indeed. If the fighting today had shown nothing else, it certainly had shown that this was a difficult undertaking. However, the situation was not without its compensations and attractions from the Confederate point of view. In at least one sense, the very strength of the close-knit Federal position worked to the disadvantage of the men who occupied it, and this was that any collapse at all was likely to be total and disastrous. Lee could never forget the breakthrough Hood and Law had scored a year ago at Gaines Mill, where they had launched a frontal assault on Turkey Hill under conditions not unlike those the army faced at Gettysburg. What he hoped for, in short, was a repetition of that exploit tomorrow: by Pickett.

That general had marched his three Virginia brigades to within three miles of the field by 6 o'clock, an hour and a half before sunset; but when he notified Lee of his arrival and asked if he was to press on and join the battle he could hear raging toward its climax just ahead,

Lee had sent him instructions to go into bivouac where he was, apparently wanting the men to be fully rested for the work he already had in mind for them tomorrow. These 5000 soldiers would come a good deal short of making up for the nearly 9000 who had fallen here today, not to mention the nearly 8000 who had fallen or been captured the day before, but there were others to be taken into account in comparing the force of the blow he planned to strike with the one he had struck already, which had failed. In addition to Pickett, whose newly arrived division would supply the extra power Lee believed would insure an initial breakthrough, two of Hill's divisions and one of Ewell's had taken little or no part in the fighting today, and the same could be said of two of Anderson's brigades, two of Early's, and one of Johnson's; Longstreet alone had put in all the men he had on hand. In point of fact, only 16 of the army's 37 infantry brigades had been seriously engaged today, which left 21 presumably well rested for tomorrow. Moreover, Stuart's three veteran brigades of cavalry would also be available—two had arrived by sundown and the third was expected before sunrise—to harry the retreat of whatever remnant of the blue army survived the collapse that would attend the rapid exploitation of Pickett's breakthrough.

Such then were the factors that contributed to Lee's decision to renew the attack next morning. All this seemed not only possible but persuasive to a man who had determined to stake everything on one blow and whose confidence in his troops—"They will go any-where and do anything, if properly led"—had been strengthened by the sight of what they had accom-plished, rather than weakened by the thought of what they had failed to accomplish because of a lack of "concert" on the part of their commanders. Just as yesterday's successes had led to a continuation of the offensive today, so did today's successes—such as they were —lead to a continuation of the offensive tomorrow. And both were a part of what would be meant, in the years ahead, when it came to be said of Lee that the stars had fought against him in Pennsylvania.

By midnight, when he retired to his tent to get some sleep, his plans had been developed in considerable detail. A message had gone to Ewell, instructing him to open the action on the left at daybreak, and another to Hill, directing him to detach two brigades from Rodes to reinforce Johnson on Culp's Hill for that purpose, while Pendleton had been told to advance the artillery, under cover of darkness, into positions from which to support the attack on the left and right and center. No orders reached Longstreet, however; nor was Pickett alerted for the night march he would have to make if he was to have any share in the daybreak assault. Perhaps this was an oversight, or perhaps Lee had decided by then to attack at a later hour and thus give his troops more rest, though if so he neglected to inform Ewell of the change. In any event, none of the three corps commanders visited headquarters that evening to discuss their assignments for tomorrow; Lee neither summoned them nor rode out to see them, and though he sent instructions to Ewell and Hill, he did not get in touch with Longstreet at all, apparently being satisfied that the man he called his old warhorse would know what was expected of him without being told.

Across the way, on Cemetery Ridge, the northern leader was taking no such chances. An hour before Lee retired for the night, Meade assembled his corps com-

manders for a council of war in the headquarters cottage
beside the Taneytown Road. He sent for them not only
because he wanted to make sure they understood their
duties for tomorrow, but also because he wanted to confer with them as to what those duties should be. Moreover, he wanted their help in solving a dilemma in which
he had placed himself earlier that evening, the
unguarded victim of his own enthusiasm. Elated by Warren's success in holding Little Round Top, as well as by
Hancock's subsequent ejection of the rebels who pierced
his center near sundown, he had gotten off an exultant
message to Halleck. "The enemy attacked me about 4
p.m. this day," he wrote, "and, after one of the severest
contests of the war, was repulsed at all points." This last
was untrue and he knew it, though he might contend
that, strictly speaking, neither the Devil's Den nor the
Peach Orchard was an integral part of his fishhook system of defense. In any case, he closed the dispatch with
a flat assurance: "I shall remain in my present position
tomorrow, but am not prepared to say, until better
advised of the condition of the army, whether my operations will be of an offensive or defensive character."

The courier had scarcely left with the message—it was
headed 8 p.m.—when Johnson's attack exploded on the
right. His troops swarmed into and along the trenches
Slocum had vacated half an hour before, and while their
advance was being challenged by Wadsworth and
Greene, Early struck hard at Cemetery Hill, driving
Howard's panicky troops from the intrenchments on the
summit. Thanks to Hancock, the nearer of these two
dangers was repulsed, at least for the time, but the graybacks maintained the lodgment they had effected at the
far end of the line. To Meade, this meant that his position—already penetrated twice today, however briefly,

first left, then right of center—was gravely menaced at both extremities: from the Devil's Den, hard against Little Round Top, and on Culp's Hill itself. The inherent possibilities were unnerving. Though he ordered Slocum to return to the far right with all his troops and prepare to oust the rebels at first light, Meade now began to regret the flat assurance he had given Halleck that he would not budge from where he was.

He foresaw disaster, and not without cause. Five days in command, he already had suffered about as many casualties as the bungling Hooker had lost in five whole months, and it appeared fairly certain that he was going to suffer a good many more tomorrow. In fact, considering what Lee must have learned today from his exploratory probes of the Union fishhook, it was by no means improbable that he had plans for breaking it entirely. And if that happened, the chances were strong that the Army of the Potomac would be abolished right here in its new commander's own home state. The more he thought about it, the more it seemed to Meade that the best way to avoid that catastrophe would be to pull out before morning and retire to the Pipe Creek line, which had seemed to him much superior in the first place. By now, moreover, his chief of staff Daniel Butterfield had completed the formal orders for withdrawal; they could be issued without delay. As for his untimely assurance to Washington—"I shall remain in my present position tomorrow"—it occurred to him that a negative vote on the matter by his corps commanders would release him from his promise. Accordingly, he sent word for them to come to headquarters at once for a council of war.

All seven came, and more. Pleasanton was off on cavalry business—he later testified that he had been ordered to prepare for covering the withdrawal—but since Hancock and Slocum had brought Gibbon and Williams along, nine generals were present in addition to Meade and two staff advisors, Butterfield and Warren. A dozen men made quite a crowd in the little parlor, which measured barely ten feet by twelve and whose furnishings included a deal table in the center, with a cedar water bucket, a tin cup, and a pair of lighted candles on it, a somewhat rickety bed in one corner, and five or six chairs. These last were soon filled, as was the bed, which served as a couch, leaving three or four of the late arrivers, or their juniors, with nothing to sit on but the floor. A witness remarked afterwards that, for all their rank, those in attendance were "as modest and unpretentious as their surroundings" and "as calm, as mild-mannered, and as free from flurry or excitement as a board of commissioners met to discuss a street improvement."

By 11 o'clock all were there. Meade opened the council by announcing that he intended to follow whatever line of action was favored by a majority of those present. Then he submitted three questions for a formal vote: "1. Under existing circumstances, is it advisable for this army to remain in its present position, or to retire to another nearer its base of supplies? 2. It being determined to remain in present position, shall the army attack or wait the attack of the enemy? 3. If we wait attack, how long?" As was the custom in such matters, the junior officer voted first, the senior last. From Gibbon through Slocum, with Butterfield keeping tally, all nine agreed that the army should neither retreat nor attack. Only on the third question was there any difference of opinion, and this varied from Slocum's "Stay and fight it out" to Hancock's "Can't wait long," which perhaps was some measure of how much fighting each had done already. At any rate, Meade had his answer. His lieutenants having declined to take him off the hook, the assurance he had given Halleck remained in effect. "Well, gentlemen," he said when all the votes were in, "the question is settled. We will remain here."

By now it was midnight. On the far side of the valley, Lee had retired, and on this side the Union council of war was breaking up. As the generals were departing to rejoin their commands, along and behind the three-mile curve of line, Meade stopped Gibbon, whose troops were posted on the nearby crest of Cemetery Ridge, due west of the headquarters cottage. "If Lee attacks tomorrow, it will be in your front," he told him. Gibbon asked why he thought so. "Because he has made attacks on both our flanks and failed," Meade said, "and if he concludes to try it again it will be on our center." Nearly a quarter-century later Gibbon recalled his reaction to this warning that it was his portion of the fishhook line that Lee would strike at: "I expressed the hope that he would, and told General Meade, with confidence, that if he did we would defeat him."

July 3; Lee rose by starlight, as he had done the previous morning, with equally fervent hopes of bringing this bloodiest of all his battles to a victorious conclusion before sunset. Two months ago today, Chancellorsville had thundered to its climax, fulfilling just such hopes against longer odds, and one month ago today, hard on the heels of a top-to-bottom reorganization occasioned by the death of Stonewall Jackson, the Army of Northern Virginia had begun its movement from the Rappahannock, northward to where an even greater triumph had seemed to be within its reach throughout the past forty-odd hours of savage fighting. Today would settle the outcome, he believed, not only of the battle—that went without saying; flesh and blood, bone and sinew and nerve could only stand so much— but also, perhaps, of the war; which, after all, was why he had come up here to Pennsylvania in the first place.

He woke to a stillness so profound that one of Gibbon's officers, rolled in his blankets near a small clump of trees on Cemetery Ridge, two thirds of the way up the shank of the Union fishhook, heard the courthouse clock a mile away in Gettysburg strike three. Lee emerged from his tent soon afterwards, fully dressed for the fight, and shared a frugal breakfast with his staff. Three miles northwest, Pickett's men were stirring, too, in a grove of oaks where they had made camp beside the Chambersburg Pike at sundown. Well rested though still a little stiff from yesterday's long march, which had ended not in battle, as they had expected, but in bivouac, they were the shock troops Lee would employ today in an ultimate attempt to achieve the breakthrough he had been trying for all along. It was for this reason, this purpose, that he had withheld them from the carnage they might otherwise have arrived in time to share the day before.

With sunrise only an hour away, however, it was obvious that he had abandoned his plan for a dawn attack. A good two hours would be required for Pickett to move his three brigades from their present bivouac area and mass them in a jump-off position well down Seminary Ridge. For them to have any share in an attack at dawn, they had to have been in motion at least an hour ago, and Lee not only had not sent Pickett or his corps commander any word of his intentions; he did not even do so now. Perhaps, on second thought, he had reasoned that more deliberate preparations were required for so desperate an effort, including another daylight look at the objective, which the enemy might have reinforced or otherwise rendered impregnable overnight. Besides, the assault would necessarily be a one-shot endeavor; late was as good as early, and maybe better, since it not only would permit a more careful study of all the problems, but also would lessen the time allowed the Federals for mounting and launching a counterattack in event of a Confederate repulse. Or perhaps it was even simpler than that. Perhaps Lee merely wanted time for one more talk with the man he called his warhorse, whose three divisions he had decided to use in the assault. At any rate, it was Longstreet he set out to find as soon as he mounted Traveller in the predawn darkness and rode eastward up the reverse slope of Seminary Ridge, delaying only long enough to send a courier to Ewell with word that the proposed attack, though still designed as a simultaneous effort on the right and the far left, would be delayed until 10 o'clock or later.

From the crest of the ridge, as he gazed southeast to where the first pale streaks of dawn had just begun to glimmer, he was greeted by a sudden eruption of noise that seemed to have its source in the masked valley beyond Cemetery Hill. It was gunfire, unmistakably, a cannonade mounting quickly to a sustained crescendo; but whose? In the absence of reports, Lee could not tell,

but he knew at once that one of two regrettable things
had happened. Either his message had failed to reach
Ewell in time, in which case his plan for the synchro-
nization of the two attacks had gone awry, or else Meade
had gotten the jump on him in that direction, leaving
Ewell no choice whatsoever in the matter of when to
fight.

In point of fact, it was something of both. The
courier had not yet reached Second Corps headquarters
(indeed, he had not had time to) and Meade *had* seized
the initiative. Slocum, returning to the Federal right
with both of his divisions before midnight, had massed
them along the Baltimore Pike for the purpose of driving the Confederates from the lower end of Culp's Hill,
where they had effected a lodgment soon after his sundown departure. Half an hour before dawn, accordingly,
he opened with four batteries he had posted along the
northern slope of Powers Hill, blasting away at the
rebels crouched in the trenches his own men had dug
the day before. For fifteen minutes he kept up the fire,
taking care that the guns did not overshoot and drop
their shells on Greene's troops just beyond, then paused
briefly to survey the damage as best he could in the dim
light. Apparently unsatisfied, he resumed the cannonade, joined now by a battery firing southeast from
Cemetery Hill, and continued it for the better part of an
hour, after which he intended to launch an infantry
assault.

This time, though, it was the Confederates who got
the jump on their opponents in this struggle for possession of the barb of the Union fishhook. Unable to bring
artillery over Rock Creek and the rough ground he had
crossed to gain the position he now held, Johnson had
his men lie low among the rocks and in the trenches

while the shells burst all around them. Then, as soon as the hour-long bombardment ended, he sent them surging forward, determined to gain control of the Baltimore Pike in accordance with last night's orders from Lee and Ewell. In this he was unsuccessful, though he gave it everything he had, including the added strength of the two brigades from Rodes, under Junius Daniel and Edward O'Neal. Slocum's troops refused to yield, and now that the graybacks were out of their holes the guns resumed their firing on the left and on the right, their targets clearly defined for them against the risen sun.

Presently word arrived from Ewell that Lee had ordered a postponement of the attack here on the left so that it might be coordinated with Longstreet's on the right, which had been delayed; but Old Clubby, fighting less by now in hope of gain than for survival—to attempt to disengage would be to invite destruction—no longer had any say-so in the matter. Unrelentingly severe, the contest degenerated into a series of brief advances and sudden repulses, first by one side, then the other. For better than five hours this continued, Slocum being reinforced by a brigade from Sedgwick's corps and Johnson adding William Smith's brigade of Early's division to his ranks, but neither could gain a decided advantage over the other, except in the weight of metal thrown. The unopposed Federal guns made the real difference, and they were what told in the end.

By 10.30 the Confederates had been driven off Culp's Hill, approximately back to the line at its eastern base along Rock Creek, from which they had launched their attack the day before. Slocum, having recovered his lost trenches, was content to hold them, and Johnson was obliged to forgo any attempt to retake them. All he could do today he had done already, for the casualties in his seven brigades had been heavy and the survivors were fought to a frazzle. Whatever Longstreet was going to accomplish, around on the far side of the fishhook, would have to be accomplished on his own.

Lee had already taken this into account, however, and he had not seen in it any cause for cancellation of his plans. Ewell's share in them had been secondary anyhow, a diversionary effort designed to mislead his opponent into withholding reinforcements from that portion of the Federal line assigned to Longstreet for a breakthrough, with consequent disruption of the whole. If Meade had taken the offensive against Ewell, Lee's purpose might be served even better in that regard, since this would require the northern commander to employ more troops at the far end of his position than if he had remained on the defensive there. A more serious question was whether he could be prevented from turning the tables on the Confederates by scoring a breakthrough of his own, but Lee was no more inclined to worry about the possibility of such a mishap here at Gettysburg than Jackson had been at Fredericksburg, when he remarked of the soldiers now under fire on Culp's Hill, "My men have sometimes failed to take a position, but to defend one, never!" Lee might have said the same thing now, and he also might have added on Ewell's behalf, as Jackson had done on his own, "I am glad the Yankees are coming." At any rate, after pausing on the crest of Seminary Ridge to listen to the cannonade two miles across the way, he turned Traveller's head southward, noting with pleasure by the spreading light of dawn that Meade did not seem to have strengthened his center overnight, and continued his ride in search of Longstreet.

He found him shortly after sunrise, three miles down

the line, in a field just west of Round Top. The burly Georgian had emerged at last from the gloom into which his heavy losses, following hard upon the rejection of his counsel, had plunged him the previous evening. Moreover, his first words showed the reason for this recovery of his spirits. "General," he greeted Lee, "I have had my scouts out all night, and I find that you still have an excellent opportunity to move around to the right of Meade's army and maneuver him into attacking us."

Apparently he believed that yesterday's experience must have proved to the southern commander the folly of attempting to storm a position of great natural strength, occupied by a numerically superior foe who had demonstrated forcefully his ability to maintain it against the most violent attempts at dislodgment. But Lee was as quick to set Old Peter straight today as he had been the day before, and he did so with nearly the same words. "The enemy is there," he said, pointing northeast as he spoke, "and I am going to strike him."

Longstreet's spirits took a sudden drop. He knew from Lee's tone and manner that his mind was quite made up, that no argument could persuade him not to continue the struggle on this same field. Accordingly, after giving instructions canceling the intended shift around the south end of the Federal line, Old Peter turned again to his chief to receive his orders for the continuation of the battle he did not want to fight, at least not here.

These orders only served to deepen his gloom still further. What Lee proposed was that Longstreet strike north of the Round Tops with his whole corps, now that Pickett was at hand, in an attempt to break the Union line on Cemetery Ridge. Essentially, this was what Old

Peter had tried and failed to do the day before, after
protesting to no avail, and he did not believe that his
chances for success had been improved by the repulse
already suffered, especially in view of the fact that all
three of the attacking divisions had been fresh and up
to full strength when they were committed yesterday,
whereas two of the three Lee intended to employ today
were near exhaustion and had lost no less than a third
of their men by way of demonstrating that the attempt
had been unwise in the first place. In opposing the selec-
tion of troops for the assault, Longstreet pointed out
that to withdraw his two committed divisions from the
vicinity of the Devil's Den and the Wheat Field would
be to expose the right flank of the attacking column to
assault by the bluecoats now being held in check in that
direction.

Lee thought this over briefly, then agreed. McLaws
and Law would hold their ground; Pickett would be
supported instead by two of Hill's divisions, and the
point of attack would be shifted northward, from the left
center to the right center of the enemy ridge, though
this would afford the attackers less cover and a greater
distance to march before they came to grips with the
defenders on the far side of the nearly mile-wide valley.

Longstreet did some rapid calculations. Pickett had
just under 5000 men, his division being the smallest in
the army, and the chances were that Hill's would be no
larger, if as large, after his losses of the past two days.
That gave a rough total of 15,000 or less, and Longstreet
did not believe this would be enough to do the job Lee
had in mind. Perhaps he had reproached himself the
night before for not having made a firmer protest yesterday against what he had believed to be an unwise assignment. If so, he made sure now, at the risk of being

considered insubordinate, that he would have no occasion for self-reproach on that account tonight. "General," he told Lee in a last face-to-face endeavor to dissuade him from extending what he believed was an invitation to disaster, "I have been a soldier all my life. I have been with soldiers engaged in fights by couples, by squads, companies, regiments, divisions, and armies, and should know as well as anyone what soldiers can do. It is my opinion that no 15,000 men ever arrayed for battle can take that position."

Lee's reply to this was an order for Pickett to be summoned. He was to post his three brigades behind Seminary Ridge, just south of the army command post near the center of the line, and there await the signal to attack. Two of Anderson's brigades, those of Lang and Wilcox, already posted in the woods adjoining Pickett's assembly area, would be on call for his support if needed. On his left, north of the command post and also under cover of the ridge, Heth's four brigades— under Pettigrew, for Heth was still too jangled to resume command—would be massed for the same purpose, supported in turn by two brigades from Pender, who was also incapacitated. Longstreet was to be in over-all command of the attack, despite his impassioned protest that it was bound to fail, and would give the signal that would launch it, though only three of the eleven brigades involved were from his corps. The plan itself, as Lee explained it to his lieutenant while they rode northward for an inspection of the terrain and the units selected to cross it, had at least the virtue of simplicity.

The objective was clearly defined against the skyline: a little clump of umbrella-shaped trees, four fifths of a mile away on Cemetery Ridge, just opposite the Confederate command post. Pickett and Pettigrew, each with two brigades in support, would align on each other as they emerged from cover and advanced, guiding on the distinctive landmark directly across the shallow valley from the point where their interior flanks would come together. By way of softening up the objective, the assault would be preceded by a brief but furious bombardment from more than 140 guns of various calibers: 80 from the First Corps, disposed along a mile-long arc extending from the Peach Orchard to the command post back on Seminary Ridge, and 63 from the Third Corps, strung out north of the command post, along the east slope of the ridge. This would be the greatest concentration of artillery ever assembled for a single purpose on the continent, and Lee appeared to have no doubt that it would pave the way for the infantry by pulverizing or driving off the batteries posted in support of the Union center.

Longstreet displayed considerably less confidence than did his chief as they rode north along the line McLaws had fallen back to in the darkness, after charging eastward across the wheat field and part way up the western slope of Cemetery Ridge. "Never was I so depressed as upon that day," Old Peter declared years later. Presently they came to Wofford, who proudly reported to Lee that his brigade had nearly reached the crest of the ridge the day before, just north of Little Round Top, in pursuit of the troops Dan Sickles had exposed. But when the army commander inquired if he could not go there again, the Georgian's jubilation left him.

"No, General, I think not," he said.

"Why not?" Lee asked, and Wofford replied:

"Because, General, the enemy have had all night to

intrench and reinforce. I had been pursuing a broken enemy, and the situation now is very different."

Longstreet looked at Lee to see what effect this might have on him, but apparently it had none at all. The two men continued their ride northward, all the way to the sunken lane where Rodes's three remaining brigades were posted on the outskirts of Gettysburg, and then back south again. Twice they rode the full length of the critical front, and all this time Lee refused to be distracted by the clatter of Ewell's desperate back-and-forth struggle across the way, smoke from which kept boiling out of the hidden valley in rear of Lee's prime objective on Cemetery Ridge. He was leaving as little as possible to chance, including the posting of individual batteries for the preliminary bombardment.

Only once, in the three hours required for this careful examination of the ground over which the attack would pass, did he admit the possibility that it might not be successful, and this was when A. P. Hill, who joined him and Longstreet in the course of the reconnaissance, suggested that instead of using only eight of his thirteen brigades, as instructed, he be allowed to send his whole corps forward. Lee would not agree. "What remains of your corps will be my only reserve," he said, "and it will be needed if General Longstreet's attack should fail."

By now it was 9 o'clock; Pickett's three brigades of fifteen veteran regiments—4600 men in all, and every one a Virginian, from the division commander down—were filing into position behind Seminary Ridge, there to await the signal which Longstreet, who would give it, believed would summon them to slaughter. Pickett himself took no such view of the matter. He saw it, rather, as his first real chance for distinction in this war, and he welcomed it accordingly, his hunger in that regard being as great as that of any man on the field, on either side. This was not only because he had missed the first two days of battle, marking time at Chambersburg, then eating road dust on the long march toward the rumble of guns beyond the horizon, but also because it had begun to appear to him, less than two years short of forty and therefore approaching what must have seemed the down slope of life, that he was in danger of missing the whole war. That came hard; for he had already had one taste of glory, sixteen years ago in Mexico, and he had found it sweet.

After a worse than undistinguished record at West Point—the class of 1846 had had fifty-nine members, including George McClellan and T. J. Jackson, and Pickett had ranked fifty-ninth—he went to war, within a year of graduation, and was the first American to scale the ramparts at Chapultepec, an exploit noted in official reports as well as in all the papers. Twelve years later he made news again, this time by defying a British squadron off San Juan Island in Puget Sound; "We'll make a Bunker Hill of it," he told his scant command; for which he was commended by his government and applauded by the press. Then came secession, and Pickett resigned his commission and headed home from Oregon. Arriving too late for First Manassas, he was wounded in the shoulder at Gaines Mill, just too early for a part in the charge that carried the day. That was a year ago this week, and he had seen no large-scale fighting since, not having returned to duty till after Second Manassas and Sharpsburg. At Fredericksburg his division had been posted in reserve, with scarcely a glimpse of the action and no share at all in the glory; after which, by way of capping the anticlimax, as it were, the Suffolk excursion had caused him to miss Chancellorsville entirely. But now there was Gettysburg, albeit the contest was two thirds over before he reached the field, and when he was offered this opportunity to deliver what Lee had designed as the climactic blow of the greatest battle of them all, he perceived at last what fate had kept in store for him through all these tantalizing months of blank denial. He grasped it eagerly, not only for his own sake, but also for the sake of the girl he called "the charming Sally," his letters to whom were always signed "Your Soldier."

So eager was he, indeed, that an English observer who saw him for the first time here today, just after Pickett learned of his assignment, described him as a "desperate-looking character." But the fact was he might have given that impression almost anywhere, on or off the field of battle, if only because of his clothes and his coiffure. Jaunty on a sleek black horse, he wore a small blue cap, buff gauntlets, and matching blue cuffs on the sleeves of his well-tailored uniform. Mounted or afoot, he carried an elegant riding crop. His boots were brightly polished and his gold spurs glinted sunlight, rivaling the sparkle of the double row of fire-gilt buttons on his breast. Of middle height, slender, graceful of carriage—"dapper and alert," a more familiar witness termed him, while another spoke of his "marvelous pulchritude"—he sported a curly chin-beard and a mustache that drooped beyond the corners of his mouth and then turned upward at the ends. To add to the swashbuckling effect, his dark-brown hair hung shoulder-length in ringlets which he anointed with perfume. There were those who alleged that he owed his rapid advancement to his friendship with the corps commander, which dated back to the peacetime army, rather than to any native ability, which in fact he had had little chance to prove. "Taking Longstreet's orders in emergencies," the corps adjutant would recall, "I could always see how he looked after Pickett, and made us give him things very fully; indeed, sometimes stay with him to make sure he did not go astray."

His three brigadiers were all his seniors in years, and one had been his senior in rank as well, until Pickett's October promotion to major general. James L. Kemper, the youngest, was just past his fortieth birthday. A former Piedmont lawyer and politician, twice elected speaker of the House of Delegates, he was the only non-professional soldier of the lot, and though he retained a fondness for high-flown oratory—"Judging by manner and conversation alone," an associate observed, "he would have been classed as a Bombastes Furioso"—his combat record was a good one, as was that of his troops, whose three previous commanders now commanded the three corps of the army. Kemper had been with the brigade from the outset, first at the head of a regiment, and had fought in all its battles, from First Manassas on. He and his men shared another proud distinction, dating back to what Southerners liked to refer to as the "earlier" Revolution; one of the five regiments was a descendant of George Washington's first command, and Kemper's grandfather had served as a colonel on the future President's staff.

By contrast, though he too was of a distinguished Old Dominion family—one that had given the Confederacy the first of its seventy-seven general officers who would die of wounds received in action—Richard B. Garnett was a comparative newcomer to the division and had never led his present brigade in a large-scale battle. Forty-five years old, strikingly handsome, a West Pointer and a regular army man, he had advanced

rapidly in the early months of the war and had succeeded Jackson as commander of the Stonewall Brigade.
Then at Kernstown, where he ordered a withdrawal to
avoid annihilation, had come tragedy; Jackson removed
him from his post and put him in arrest for retreating
without permission. Garnett promptly demanded a
court-martial, convinced that it would clear him of the
charge, but the case dragged on for months, interrupted
by battle after battle—all of which he missed—until Lee
took a hand in the matter, immediately after Sharpsburg, and transferred him to Longstreet's corps to take
command of Pickett's brigade when that general, whom
he had previously outranked, was promoted to command of the division. Neither Fredericksburg nor Suffolk brought Garnett the opportunity by which he
hoped to clear his record of the Kernstown stain, and
now in Pennsylvania he was not only limping painfully
from an injury lately suffered when he was kicked in the
knee by a horse; he was also sick with chills and fever.
Medically speaking, he should have been in bed, not in
the field, but he was determined to refute—with blood,
if need be—the accusations Jackson had leveled against
his reputation.

The third and oldest of the three brigadiers, forty-six-
year-old Lewis Armistead, was also something of a
romantic figure, though less by circumstance than by
inclination. A widower, twice brevetted for gallantry in
Mexico, he was a great admirer of the ladies and enjoyed
posing as a swain. This had earned him the nickname
"Lo," an abbreviation of Lothario, which was scarcely in
keeping with his close-cropped, grizzled beard or receding hairline. He had, however, a sentimental turn of
mind and fond memories of life in the old army. For
example, he and Hancock, who was waiting for him now

across the way though neither knew it, had been friends. "Hancock, goodbye," he had said in parting, two years ago on the West Coast as he prepared to cross the continent with Albert Sidney Johnston; "you can never know what this has cost me." As he spoke he put both hands on his friend's shoulders, and tears stood in his eyes.

Now he and Dick Garnett stood together on the crest of Seminary Ridge, looking out across the gently rolling valley toward the little clump of umbrella-shaped trees which had been pointed out to them as their objective, just under a mile away on Cemetery Ridge. Both men were experienced soldiers, and both knew at a glance the ordeal they and their brigades would be exposed to when the signal came for them to advance. Finally Garnett broke the silence. "This is a desperate thing to attempt," he said. Armistead agreed. "It is," he replied. "But the issue is with the Almighty, and we must leave it in His hands."

Completing what was described as "a shady, quiet march" of about five miles, southeast along the turnpike, then due south through the woods along the far bank of a stream called Pitzer's Run, Pickett's men were unaware of what awaited them beyond the screening ridge; or as one among the marchers later put it, "No gloomy forebodings hovered over our ranks." Not since Sharpsburg, nearly ten months ago, had the troops in these fifteen regiments been involved in heavy fighting, and this encouraged them to believe—quite erroneously, but after the custom of young men everywhere—that they were going to live forever. Near the confluence of Pitzer's and Willoughby runs, they were halted and permitted to break formation for a rest in the shade of the trees. The sun had burned the early morning clouds away, and though the lack of breeze gave promise of a sultry afternoon, the impression here in this unscarred valley behind Seminary Ridge was of an ideal summer day, no different from any other except in its perfection. "Never was sky or earth more serene, more harmonious, more aglow with light and life," one among the loungers afterwards wrote.

Presently they were called back into ranks, told to leave their extra gear in the care of a single guard from each regiment, and marched eastward over the crest of the ridge, then down its opposite slope and into a wooded swale a couple of hundred yards beyond, where they were halted. Here too they were shielded from hostile observers by the low bulge of earth extending northward from the Peach Orchard, along which they could see the corps artillery disposed in a slow curve from the right, the cannoneers silhouetted against the skyline directly in their front. Two brigades of infantry were up there, too, under Wilcox, but Pickett's orders were for his own troops to take it easy here in the swale, doing nothing that might attract the enemy's attention.

Soon after they were in position, Lee arrived and began to ride along the lines of reclining men. Mindful of their instructions not to give away their presence, they refrained from cheering; but as the general drew abreast of each company, riding slowly, gravely past, the men rose and took off their hats in silent salute. Lee returned it in the same manner, the sunlight in his gray hair making a glory about his head.

If he seemed graver than usual this morning, he had cause. He had just come from making a similar inspection of the troops disposed northward along the densely wooded eastern slope of Seminary Ridge, where they too were waiting under cover for the signal to move out, and he had noticed that a good number of them wore bandages about their heads and limbs. "Many of these poor boys should go to the rear; they are not able for duty," he remarked. Drawing rein before one hard-hit unit, he looked more closely and realized, apparently for the first time, how few of its officers had survived the earlier fighting. "I miss in this brigade the faces of many dear friends," he said quietly. Riding away, he looked back once and muttered to himself, as if to fend off such tactical doubts as were provoked by personal sorrow: "The attack must succeed."

His choice of the half-dozen brigades that made up the left wing of the assault force—Heth's four, plus two from Pender—was doubly logical, in that all the troops so chosen were handy to the jump-off position and had not been engaged the day before, which not only lessened the chance of disclosing his intention to the enemy by their preliminary movements, but also was presumed to mean that they were fresh, or at any rate well rested, for the long advance across the valley and the subsequent task of driving the bluecoats off the ridge on the far side. What had not been taken into account, however—at least not until Lee saw for himself the thinned ranks and the bandaged wounds of the survivors—was the additional and highly pertinent fact that five of the six had suffered cruelly in the first day's fighting. Both division commanders were out of action, and only two of the six brigades were still under the leaders who had brought them onto the field. The one exception on both counts was Lane's brigade, which had not been heavily engaged and still had its original commander; but this was offset by the misfortune of the other brigade from Pender's division, which had lost its leader, Alfred Scales, together with all but two of its officers above the rank of captain and more than half of those of that rank or below. This was the unit Lee had paused in front of this morning to remark that he missed "the faces of many dear friends," and it was led now by William Lowrance, who never before had commanded anything larger than a regiment. Moreover, because Lee did not consider Lane experienced enough to succeed the wounded Pender, he had summoned old Isaac Trimble over from Ewell and put him in charge of the two brigades, though he too had never served in such a capacity before, despite his recent promotion to major general, and had had no previous acquaintance, on or off the field of battle, with the troops he was about to lead across the valley in support of the four brigades under Pettigrew.

These last made up the first wave of the attack, here on the left, and they too had been more severely mauled in the earlier fighting than the army commander or his staff took into account. "They were terribly mistaken about Heth's division in the planning," Lee's chief aide declared afterwards. "It had not recovered, having suffered more than was reported on the first day." In point of fact, whether the planners knew it or not, the division had lost no less than forty percent of its officers and men. Ordinarily, this would have ruled out its employment as a fighting force, particularly on the offensive, until it had been reorganized and brought back up to strength; but in this case it had been selected to play a major role in the delivery of an attack designed as the climax of the army's bloodiest battle. Whether the choice proceeded from ignorance, indifference, or desperation (there was evidence of all three; Longstreet, while admitting his own profound depression, later said flatly that Lee had been "excited and off his balance") some measure of the condition of the division should have been perceived from the fact that only one of the original four commanders remained at the head of his brigade, and this was the inexperienced Davis, whose troops had lost so heavily when he led them into an ambush on the opening day. The captured Archer had been replaced by B. D. Fry, John M. Brockenbrough by Joseph Mayo, and Pettigrew by J. K. Marshall. All three colonels were thus as new to command of their brigades as Pettigrew was to command of the division, which in turn had not been organized till after Chancellorsville and had gone into its first fight as a unit less than fifty hours ago. It had in all, after the cooks, the extra-duty men, and the lightly wounded were given rifles and brought forward into its ranks, about the same number of troops as Pickett had; that is, about 4600. Trimble had 1750 in the second line. If Wilcox and Lang added their 1400 to the assault, this Pickett-Pettigrew-Trimble total of just under 11,000 would be increased to roughly 12,500 effectives, a figure well below the 15,000 which the man in over-all command of the attack had already said would not be enough to afford him even the possibility of success.

In addition to Armistead and Garnett, who agreed that the maneuver was "a desperate thing to attempt," a good many other high-ranking officers had had a look at the ground in front by now, and their impressions were much the same. To a staff major, on a midmorning visit to the command post near the center, the long approach to the Union position across the shallow valley—more than half a mile out to the Emmitsburg Road, past a blue skirmish line "almost as heavy as a single line of battle," then another quarter-mile up the gradual slope of Cemetery Ridge, where the main enemy line was supported from the crest above by guns that could take the attackers under fire throughout most of their advance—resembled "a passage to the valley of death."

Impressions mainly agreed, but reactions varied. For example, an artillerist observed that Pickett was "entirely sanguine of success in the charge, and was only congratulating himself on the opportunity," whereas Pettigrew seemed more determined than elated. Tomorrow would be his thirty-fifth birthday, and though his intellectual accomplishments were perhaps the highest of any man on the field—a scholar in Greek and Hebrew, fluent as well in most of the modern languages of Europe, he had made the best grades ever recorded at the University of North Carolina, where he had also excelled in fencing, boxing, and the single stick, then had traveled on the continent and written a book on what he had seen before returning to settle down to a brilliant legal career, only to have it interrupted by the war and the experience of being left for dead on the field of Seven Pines—he now was devoting his abilities to the fulfillment of his military duties. Slender and lithe of figure, with a neatly barbered beard, a spike mustache, and a dark complexion denoting his Gallic ancestry, Pettigrew was quite as eager as Pickett for distinction, but his eagerness was tempered by a sounder appreciation of the difficulties, since he had fought on this same field two days ago, against this newest version of the Army of the Potomac. Perhaps he recalled today what he had written after a visit to Solferino: "The invention of the Minié ball and the rifled cannon would, it was thought, abolish cavalry and reduce infantry charges within a small compass." On the other hand, if he was remembering his comments on that battle, fought four years ago in Italy, he might have drawn encouragement from the fact that in it the French had crushed the Austrian center, much as Lee intended to crush the Union center here today, with a frontal assault delivered hard on the heels of an intense bombardment.

The men themselves, though few of them had the chance to examine the terrain over which they would be advancing, knew only too well what lay before them; Lee and Longstreet had directed that they be told, and they had been, in considerable detail. "No disguises were used," one wrote afterwards, "nor was there any underrating of the difficult work at hand." They were told of the opportunities, as well as of the dangers, and it was stressed that the breaking of the Federal line might mean the end of the war. However, there were conflicting reports of their reaction. One declared that the men of Garnett's brigade "were in splendid spirits and confident of sweeping everything before them," while another recalled that when Mayo's troops, who were also Virginians, were informed of their share in the coming attack, "from being unusually merry and hilarious they on a sudden had become as still and thoughtful as Quakers at a love feast."

Some managed to steal a look at the ground ahead, and like their officers they were sobered by what they saw. One such, a Tennessee sergeant from Fry's brigade, walked forward to the edge of the woods, looked across the wide open valley at the bluecoats standing toylike in the distance on their ridge, and was so startled by the realization of what was about to be required of him that he spoke aloud, asking himself the question: "June Kimble, are you going to do your duty?" The answer, too, was audible. "I'll do it, so help me God," he told himself. He felt better then. The dread passed from him, he said later. When he returned to his company, friends asked him how it looked out there, and Kimble replied: "Boys, if we have to go it will be hot for us, and we will have to do our best."

All this time, the waiting soldiers had been hearing the clatter of Ewell's fight beyond the ridge. By 10.30 it had diminished to a sputter and withdrawn eastward, indicating only too plainly how he had fared; Lee knew unmistakably, before any such admission reached him from the left, that what he had designed as a two-pronged effort had been reduced, by Ewell's failure, to a single thrust which the enemy would be able to oppose with a similar concentration of attention and reserves. However, he did not cancel or revise his plans in mid-career. That was not his way. Like Winfield Scott, on whose staff he had served in Mexico, he believed it "would do more harm than good," once the selected units were in position, for him to attempt to interfere. "It would be a bad thing if I could not rely on my brigade and division commanders," he told a Prussian observer three days later. "I plan and work with all my might to bring the troops to the right place at the right time. With that, I have done my duty."

The same rule applied to a brisk skirmish that broke out, at 11 o'clock, around a house and barn on the floor of the valley, half a mile east-northeast of the command post and about midway between the lines. Confederate sharpshooters posted in the loft of the barn had been dropping Federal officers on the opposing ridge all morning, and finally two blue regiments moved out and drove the snipers back; whereupon Hill's guns opened thunderously with a half-hour bombardment. This in turn made the house and barn untenable for the new occupants, who set them afire and withdrew to their own lines, having solved the problem they had been sent to deal with. Lee watched from the command post and made no protest, either at the expenditure of ammunition, which was considerable, or at the resultant disclosure of the battery positions, which up to now the crews had been so careful to conceal. "I strive to make my plans as good as human skill allows," he told the Prussian inquirer, in further explanation of the hands-off policy he practiced here today, "but on the day of battle I lay the fate of my army in the hands of God."

By now it was noon, and a great stillness came down over the field and over the two armies on their ridges. Between them, the burning house and barn loosed a long plume of smoke that stood upright in the hot and windless air. From time to time some itchy-fingered picket would fire a shot, distinct as a single handclap, but for the most part the silence was profound. For the 11,000 Confederates maintaining their mile-wide formation along the wooded slope and in the swale, the heat was oppressive. They sweated and waited, knowing that they were about to be launched on a desperate undertaking from which many of them would not be coming back, and since it had to be, they were of one accord in wanting to get it over with as soon as possible.

"It is said, that to the condemned, in going to execution, the moments fly," a member of Pickett's staff wrote some years later, recalling the strain of the long wait. "To the good soldier, about to go into action, I am sure the moments linger. Let us not dare say, that with him, either individually or collectively, it is that 'mythical love of fighting,' poetical but fabulous; but rather, that it is nervous anxiety to solve the great issue as speedily as possible, without stopping to count the cost. The Macbeth principle—*'Twere well it were done quickly*—holds quite as good in heroic action as in crime."

* * *

E. P. Alexander, a twenty-eight-year-old Georgian and West Pointer, had been up all night and hard at work all morning, supervising the movement into position of the 80 guns of the First Corps. By noon the job had been completed; the batteries were disposed along their mile-long arc, southward from the command post to the Peach Orchard and beyond, and the colonel, having taken time to breakfast on a crust of cornbread and a cup of sweet-potato coffee, was awaiting notification to fire the prearranged two-gun signal that would open the 143-gun bombardment. Young as he was, he had been given vital assignments from the outset of the war and had fought in all the army's major battles, first as Beauregard's signal officer, then as Johnston's chief of ordnance, and later as commander of an artillery battalion under Longstreet. Serving in these various capacities, he had contributed largely to the curtain-raising victory at Manassas, as well as to the subsequent effectiveness of Confederate firepower, and since his transfer from staff to line he had been winning a reputation as perhaps the best artillerist in Lee's army, despite the flashier performances of men like Latimer and Pelham. His had been the guns that defended Marye's Heights at Fredericksburg and accompanied Jackson on the flank march at Chancellorsville.

However, his most challenging assignment came today from Longstreet, who instructed him to prepare and conduct the First Corps' share of the bombardment preceding the infantry attack. When the objective was shifted northward along Cemetery Ridge, after the early morning conference between Lee and Longstreet, Alexander rearranged his dispositions "as inoffensively as possible," seeking to hide his intentions from enemy lookouts on the heights, and took care to keep his crews from "getting into bunches." He listened with disapproval as Hill's 60-odd guns began their premature cannonade, northward along Seminary Ridge, and would not allow his own to join the action, lest they give away the positions he had taken such pains to conceal.

As the uproar subsided and was followed by the silence that came over the field at noon, he received an even greater shock from his own corps commander, who informed him that he would be required to make the decision, not only as to when the infantry attack was to begin, but also as to whether it was to be launched at all. "If the artillery fire does not have the effect to drive off the enemy or greatly demoralize him, so as to make our effort pretty certain," Longstreet wrote in a message delivered by an aide, "I would prefer that you should not advise Pickett to make the charge. I shall rely a great deal upon your judgment to determine the matter and shall expect you to let General Pickett know when the moment offers."

Alexander experienced a violent reaction to this sudden descent of command responsibility. "Until that moment, though I fully recognized the strength of the enemy's position," he recalled years later, "I had not doubted that we would carry it, in my confidence that Lee was ordering it. But here was a proposition that *I* should decide the question. Overwhelming reasons against the assault at once seemed to stare me in the face." He replied at some length, declining the heavy burden Old Peter appeared to be attempting to unload.

"General," he protested, "I will only be able to judge of the effect of our fire on the enemy by his return fire, for his infantry is but little exposed to view and the smoke will obscure the whole field. If, as I infer from your note, there is any alternative to this attack, it should be carefully considered before opening our fire, for it will take all the artillery ammunition we have left to test this one thoroughly, and if the result is unfavorable, we will have none left for another effort. And even if this is entirely successful it can only be so at a very bloody cost."

Longstreet's answer was not long in coming. Having failed to persuade the colonel to join him in resubmitting his protest that the charge was bound to fail—which was what he had been suggesting between the lines of his rather turgid note—he merely rephrased the essential portion of what he had said before. "Colonel," he wrote, "The intention is to advance the infantry if the artillery has the desired effect of driving the enemy's off, or having other effect such as to warrant us in making the attack. When that moment arrives advise General P., and of course advance such artillery as you can use in aiding the attack."

This left one small loophole—"*if* the artillery has the desired effect"—and Alexander saw it. No cannonade had ever driven Union batteries from a prepared position, and he certainly had no confidence that this one would accomplish that result. But before he replied this second time he decided to confer with two men of higher authority than his own. The first was his fellow Georgian Ambrose Wright, who had stormed the enemy ridge the day before, achieving at least a temporary penetration, and could therefore testify as to the difficulty involved. "What do you think of it?" Alexander asked him. "Is it as hard to get there as it looks?" Wright spoke frankly. "The trouble is not in going there," he said. "I was there with my brigade yesterday. There is a place where you can get breath and re-form. The trouble is to stay there after you get there, for the whole Yankee army is there in a bunch."

Alexander took this to mean that the attack would succeed if it was heavily supported, and he assumed that Lee had seen to that. Thus reassured, he went to see how Pickett was reacting to the assignment. He not only found him calm and confident, but also gathered that the ringleted Virginian "thought himself in luck to have the chance." So the colonel returned to his post, just north of the Peach Orchard, and got off a reply to Old Peter's second message. "When our fire is at its best," he wrote briefly, even curtly, "I will advise General Pickett to advance."

Word came soon afterwards from Longstreet: "Let the batteries open. Order great care and precision in firing."

By prearrangement, the two-gun signal was given by a battery near the center. According to a Gettysburg civilian, a professor of mathematics and an inveterate taker of notes, the first shot broke the stillness at exactly 1.07, following which there was an unpropitious pause, occasioned by a misfire. Nettled, the battery officer signaled the third of his four pieces and the second shot rang out.

"As suddenly as an organ strikes up in church," Alexander would recall, "the grand roar followed from all the guns."

★ ★ ★

The firing was by salvos, for deliberate precision, and as the two-mile curve of metal came alive in response to the long-awaited signal, the individual pieces bucking and fuming in rapid sequence from right to left, a Federal cannoneer across the valley was "reminded of the 'powder snakes' we boys used to touch off on the Fourth of

July." To a man, the lounging bluecoats, whose only concern up to then had been their hunger and the heat, both of which were oppressive, knew what the uproar meant as soon as it began. "Down! Down!" they shouted, diving for whatever cover they could find on the rocky forward slope of Cemetery Ridge. By now the rebel fire was general, though still by salvos within the four-gun units, and to Hunt, who was up on Little Round Top at the time, the sight was "indescribably grand. All their batteries were soon covered with smoke, through which the flames were incessant, whilst the air seemed filled with shells, whose sharp explosions, with the hurtling of their fragments, formed a running accompaniment to the deep roar of the guns."

That was how it looked and sounded to a coldly professional eye and ear, sited well above the conflict, so to speak. But to Gibbon, down on the ridge where the shots were landing, the bombardment was "the most infernal pandemonium it has ever been my fortune to look upon." One of his soldiers, caught like him in the sudden deluge of fire and whining splinters, put it simpler. "The air was all murderous iron," he declared years later, apparently still somewhat surprised at finding that he had survived it.

In point of fact, despite the gaudiness of what might be called the fireworks aspect of the thing, casualties were few among the infantry. For the most part they had stone walls to crouch behind; moreover, they were disposed well down the slope, and this, as it turned out, afforded them the best protection of all. At first the fire was highly accurate, but as it continued, both the ridge and the batteries at opposite ends of the trajectory were blanketed in smoke, so that the rebel gunners were firing blind, just as Alexander had foretold. As the trails

dug in, the tubes gained elevation and the shellbursts
crept uphill, until finally almost all of the projectiles
were either landing on the crest, where most of the
close-support artillery was posted, or grazing it to
explode in the rearward valley. "Quartermaster
hunters," the crouching front-line soldiers called these
last, deriving much satisfaction from the thought that
what was meant for them was making havoc among the
normally easy-living men of the rear echelon.

Havoc was by no means too strong a word, especially
in reference to what was occurring around and in army
headquarters. The small white cottage Meade had com-
mandeered, immediately in rear of that portion of the
ridge on which the rebels had been told to mass their
hottest fire, became untenable in short order. Its steps
were carried away by a direct hit at the outset, along
with the supports of the porch, which then collapsed.
Inside the house, a solid shot crashed through a door
and barely missed the commanding general himself,
while another plowed through the roof and garret, fill-
ing the lower rooms with flying splinters. Meade and his
staff retired to the yard, where sixteen of their horses lay
horribly mangled, still tethered to a fence; then moved
into a nearby barn, where Butterfield was nicked by a
shell fragment; and finally transferred in a body all the
way to Powers Hill, where Slocum had set up the night
before. Here at last they found a measure of the safety
they had been seeking, but they were about as effectively
removed from what was happening back on Cemetery
Ridge, or was about to happen, as if they had taken
refuge on one of the mountains of the moon.

Meanwhile, other rear-area elements had been catching it nearly as hard. Down and across both the Taneytown Road and the Baltimore Pike, fugitives of all

kinds—clerks and orderlies, ambulance drivers and mess personnel, supernumeraries and just plain skulkers—were streaming east and south to escape the holocaust, adding greatly to the panic in their haste and disregard for order. Nor were such noncombatants the only ones involved in the confusion and the bloodshed. Returning to its post on the left, the VI Corps brigade that had been lent to Slocum that morning to assist in the retaking of Culp's Hill—he had not had to use it, after all—was caught on the road and lost 23 killed and wounded before it cleared the zone of fire. More important still, tactically speaking, the parked guns of the reserve artillery and the wagons of the ammunition train, drawn up in assumed safety on the lee side of the ridge, came under heavy bombardment, losing men and horses and caissons in the fury of the shellbursts, and had to be shifted half a mile southward, away from the point where they would be needed later. All in all, though it was more or less clear already that the gray artillerists were going to fail in their attempt to drive the blue defenders from the ridge, they had accomplished much with their faulty gunnery, including the disruption of army headquarters, the wounding of the chief of staff, and the displacement of the artillery reserve, not to mention a good deal of incidental slaughter among the rearward fugitives who had not intended to take any part in the fighting anyhow. Unwittingly, and in fact through carelessness and error, the Confederates had invented the box barrage of World War One, still fifty-odd years in the future, whereby a chosen sector of the enemy line was isolated for attack.

Awaiting that attack, crouched beneath what seemed a low, impenetrable dome of screaming metal overarching the forward slope of their isolated thousand yards of ridge, were three depleted divisions under Hancock, six brigades containing some 5700 infantry effectives, or roughly half the number about to be sent against them. This disparity of forces, occupying or aimed at the intended point of contact, was largely the fault of Meade, whose over-all numerical superiority was offset by the fact that his anticipations did not include the threat which this small segment of his army was about to be exposed to. Despite his midnight prediction to Gibbon that today's main rebel effort would be made against "your front," he not only had sent him no reinforcements; he had not even taken the precaution of seeing that any were made immediately available by posting them in proximity to that portion of the line.

Daylight had brought a change of mind, a change of fears. He no longer considered that the point of danger, partly because his artillery enjoyed an unobstructed field of fire from there, but mostly because he recollected that his opponent was not partial to attacks against the center. As the morning wore on and Ewell failed to make headway on the right, Meade began to be convinced that Lee was planning to assault his left, and he kept his largely unused reserve, the big VI Corps, massed in the direction of the Round Tops. At 12.20, when Slocum sent word that he had "gained a decided advantage on my front, and hope to be able to spare one or two brigades to help you on some other part of the line," the northern commander was gratified by the evidence of staunchness, but he took no advantage of the offer. Then presently, under the distractive fury of the Confederate bombardment, which drove him in rapid, headlong sequence from house to yard, from yard to barn, and then from barn to hilltop, he apparently forgot it. Whatever defense of that critical thousand yards of ridge was going to be made would have to be made by the men who occupied it.

They amounted in all to 26 regiments, including two advanced as skirmishers, and their line ran half a mile due south from Ziegler's Grove, where Cemetery Hill fell off and Cemetery Ridge began. Gibbon held the center with three brigades, flanked on the left and right by Doubleday and Hays, respectively with one and two brigades; Gibbon had just over and Hays just under 2000 infantry apiece, while Doubleday had about 1700. For most of the long waiting time preceding the full-scale Confederate bombardment, these 5700 defenders had been hearing the Slocum-Johnson struggle for Culp's Hill, barely a mile away. At first it made them edgy, occurring as it did almost directly in their rear, but as it gradually receded and diminished they gained confidence. Finally it sputtered to a stop and was succeeded by a lull, which in turn was interrupted by the brief but lively skirmish for possession of the house and barn down on the floor of the western valley. The half-hour rebel cannonade that followed accomplished nothing, one way or the other, except perhaps as a bellow of protest at the outcome of the fight.

By contrast, hard on the heels of this, the midday silence was profound. "At noon it became as still as the Sabbath day," a blue observer later wrote. He and his fellows scarcely knew what to make of this abrupt cessation, in which even the querulous skirmishers held their fire. "It was a queer sight to see men look at each other without speaking," another would recall; "the change was so great men seemed to go on tiptoe, not knowing how to act."

This lasted a full hour, during which they tried to improvise shelter from the rays of the sun and sought

relief from the pangs of hunger. There was precious little of either shade or food, there on the naked ridge, but
shortly after 1 o'clock, when the curtain of silence was
suddenly ripped to tatters by the roar of what seemed
to be all the guns in the world, they forgot the discom-
forts of heat and hunger, acute as these had been, and
concentrated instead on a scramble for cover behind the
low stone walls. However, as the pattern of shellbursts
moved up the slope and stayed there—except for an
occasional round, that is, that tumbled and fell short—
they found that, once they grew accustomed to the
whoosh and flutter of metal just overhead, the bombardment was not nearly so bad as it seemed. "All we
had to do was flatten out a little thinner," one of the
earth-hugging soldiers afterwards explained, "and our
empty stomachs did not prevent that."

Despite the feeling of security that came from lying
low, it seemed to another crouching there "that nothing four feet from the ground could live." Presently,
however, he and his companions all along that blasted
thousand yards of front were given unmistakable proof
that such was not the case, at least so far as one man was
concerned. As the bombardment thundered toward
crescendo, they were startled to see Hancock, mounted
on a fine black horse and trailed by most of his staff, riding the full length of his line amid the hiss and thud of
plunging shells and solids. He rode slowly, a mounted
orderly beside him displaying the swallow-tailed corps
guidon. Resisting the impulse to weave or bob when he
felt the breath of near misses on his face, the general
only stopped once in the course of his excursion, and
that was when his horse, with less concern for show than
for survival, became unmanageable and forced him to
take over the more tractable mount of an aide, who per-

haps was not unhappy at the exchange since it permitted him to retire from the procession.

Hancock resumed his ride at the same deliberate pace, combining a ramrod stiffness of backbone with that otherwise easy grace of manner expected of top-ranking officers under fire—a highly improbable mixture of contempt and disregard, for and of the rebel attempt to snuff out the one life he had—whereby the men under him, as one of them rather floridly explained, "found courage to endure the pelting of the pitiless gale." Intent on giving an exemplary performance, he would no more be deterred by friendly counsel than he would swerve to avoid the enemy shells that whooshed around him. When a brigadier ventured a protest: "General, the corps commander ought not to risk his life that way," Hancock replied curtly: "There are times when a corp commander's life does not count," and continued his ride along the line of admiring soldiers, who cheered him lustily from behind their low stone walls, but were careful, all the same, to remain in prone or kneeling positions while they did so.

Another high-ranking Federal was riding better than three times that length of line at the same time, but he did so less by way of staging a general show, as Hancock was doing to bolster the spirits of the men along his portion of the front, than by way of assuring conformity with Army Regulations. "In the attack," these regulations stated, "the artillery is employed to silence the batteries that protect the [enemy] position. In the defense, it is better to direct its fire on the advancing troops." It was the second of these two statements that here applied, and no one knew this better than Henry Hunt, who had been an artillery instructor at West Point and had spent the past two years in practical application, on the field of battle, of the theories he had expounded in the classroom. On Cemetery Hill, on Little Round Top, and along the ridge that ran between them, he had twenty batteries in position, just over one hundred guns that could be brought to bear on the shallow western valley and the ridge at its far rim. Just now there were no "advancing troops" for the long line of Union metal "to direct its fire on," but Hunt was convinced there soon would be, and his first concern—after observing, from his lofty perch at the south end of the line, the "indescribably grand" beginning of the Confederate bombardment—was that his cannoneers not burn up too much of their long-range ammunition in counterbattery fire, lest they run short before the rebel infantry made its appearance.

Accordingly, after instructing B. F. Rittenhouse to keep up a deliberate fire with his six-gun battery on Little Round Top, Hunt rode down onto the lower end of Cemetery Ridge and ordered Freeman McGilvery, commanding seven batteries of 37 guns from the artillery reserve, to refrain from taking up the enemy challenge until the proper time. The same instructions went to John G. Hazard, commanding the six II Corps batteries whose 29 guns were posted north of there, above and below the little umbrella-shaped clump of trees. On Cemetery Hill, completing the two-mile ride from Little Round Top, Hunt repeated what he had told Rittenhouse at the outset; T. W. Osborn was to keep up a deliberate counterbattery fire with the 29 guns of his six XI Corps batteries. By this arrangement, one third of the 101 guns were to do what they could to disconcert the rebel gunners by maintaining a crossfire from the high-sited extremities of the Federal position, while the remaining two thirds kept silent along the comparatively low-lying ridge that ran between them.

However, it did not work out that way entirely. Completing his slow ride along his thousand-yard portion of the front, Hancock observed that his cannoneers were idle (if idle was quite the word for men who were hugging the earth amid a deluge of shells) and promptly countermanded Hunt's instructions. He did so, he explained afterwards, because he believed that his infantry needed the deep-voiced encouragement of the guns posted in close support on the crest of the ridge directly in their rear. Whatever comfort the blue foot soldiers derived from the roar and rumble in response to the fire of the rebel guns down in the valley, Hunt watched with disapproval as the half-dozen II Corps batteries came alive, but there was nothing he could do about it, since the corps commander had every right to do as he thought best with his own guns, no matter what any and all staff specialists might advise.

All this time the Confederates kept firing, exploding caissons, dismounting guns, and maiming so many cannoneers—particularly in those batteries adjacent to the little clump of trees—that replacements had to be furnished from nearby infantry outfits, supposedly on a volunteer basis, but actually by a hard-handed form of conscription. "Volunteers are wanted to man the battery," a Massachusetts captain told his company. "Every man is to go of his own free will and accord. Come out here, John Dougherty, McGivern, and you Corrigan, and work those guns." For a solid hour the bombardment did not slacken, and when another half hour was added to this, still with no abatement, McGilvery ordered his seven batteries to open fire at last, convinced that by now the rebels must be getting low on ammunition and would have to launch their infantry attack, if they were going to launch it at all, before his own supply ran low.

That was about 2.30; all the surviving Union guns were in action, bucking and roaring along the whole two miles of line. From down in the valley, Alexander peered through the billowing smoke and it seemed to him that both enemy heights and the connecting ridge were "blazing like a volcano." On Cemetery Hill, where he availed himself of the excellent observation post established by the XI Corps chief of artillery, Hunt watched with gratification this tangible proof that, for all its prolonged fury, the rebel cannonade had failed to drive his gun crews from their pieces or the guns themselves from their assigned positions.

It occurred to him, however, that in the light of this evidence, as plain from below as from above, the Confederates might not attempt their infantry assault at all, and he considered this regrettable. Standing beside him, Osborn suddenly asked: "Does Meade consider an attack of the enemy desirable?" When Hunt replied that the army commander had expressed a fervent hope that the rebels would try just that, "and he had no fear of the result," the major added: "If this is so, why not let them out while we are all in good condition? I would cease fire at once, and the enemy could reach but one conclusion, that of our being driven from the hill."

Hunt thought this over briefly, then agreed. Moreover, while the batteries on the hill fell silent one by one, he rode down onto Cemetery Ridge to increase the effectiveness of the ruse by passing the word along to the remaining two thirds of his guns. At closer range, however, he found the II Corps batteries so badly mauled by the rebel cannonade and so low on ammunition that he decided they might as well use up what few long-range rounds were still on hand. For example, Alonzo Cushing's battery, posted just north of the clump of trees, had only three of its six guns still in working order and only two of these in action, casualties having reduced the number of cannoneers to barely enough for two slim crews; Cushing himself, a twenty-two-year-old West Pointer from Wisconsin, had twice been hit by fragments of exploding shells, one of which had struck him in the crotch and groin. Despite the pain, he refused to leave the field or relinquish his command, and Hunt let him stay, together with his handful of survivors.

A Rhode Island battery just south of the clump was in even worse shape, its ammunition practically exhausted, all of its officers dead or wounded, and barely enough men left to serve the three remaining guns; Hunt took a quick look at the wreckage and gave the survivors permission to withdraw, which they did in a rather helter-skelter fashion, being leaderless, but took their three guns with them. Riding on south, Hunt passed the cease-firing order along to McGilvery, down near the far end of the ridge, and finally to Rittenhouse, whose six guns had been firing all the while from Little Round Top. When the weary and badly cut-up batteries of the II Corps had gotten off their few remaining rounds, thus adding to the effectiveness of the pretense by giving the impression that the guns were being knocked out group by group, spasmodically, the whole Union line fell silent under the continuing rain of rebel projectiles.

That was about 2.45, and it soon became apparent that the ruse had worked, at least in part. Within another five or ten minutes, the Confederates also stopped firing, and what Osborn later referred to as "a singularly depressing silence" settled over the field. Whether the ruse had worked entirely would not be known until the enemy infantry started forward across the valley, but the Federal cannoneers were taking no chances that it had failed. The cooling tubes were swabbed to remove the gritty residue of powder and thus prepare them for the rapid-fire work that lay ahead, while in those batteries that had used up all their long-range ammunition, the pieces were carefully loaded with canister. Forty-four-year-old Alex Hays, a Pennsylvanian like his corps and army commanders, was certain that the rebs would soon be coming through the screening smoke. "Now, boys, look out; you will see some fun!" he called to the men of his two brigades, posted north of the clump of trees.

In confirmation of his prediction, shortly after 3 o'clock, Warren wigwagged a message from the Little Round Top signal station, which afforded a clear view beyond the hump of earth that Sickles had claimed and lost the day before: "They are moving out to attack." Presently, all along the bend and shank of the Union fishhook, the waiting troops could see for themselves, through or below the rifting, lifting smoke, that what Warren had signaled was true. "Here they come!" men exclaimed as they caught sight of the long gray lines moving toward them across the shallow basin inclosed by the two ridges.

Reactions to this confrontation varied. "Thank God! Here comes the infantry!" one exuberant bluecoat cried. Though it was obvious at a glance that the attackers, moving steadily forward under their red and blue flags, outnumbered the defenders by no less than two to one, he and others like him looked forward to the slaughter, anticipating a Fredericksburg in reverse. A New Yorker, on the other hand, remembering the sight two days later, wrote in a home letter: "Beautiful, gloriously beautiful, did that vast array appear in the lovely little valley." Then he and his fellows—first the cannoneers, who took up their work with a will, and then the foot soldiers, no less eager—settled down to the task of transforming those well-dressed long gray lines into something far from beautiful.

There they came. And for them, advancing eastward over the gently undulating floor of the shallow valley, the relief of tension was as great as it was for the men awaiting their arrival on the ridge just under a mile across the way. In fact, if a comparison of losses was any measure of the strain, it was probably greater. The Federal infantry had suffered a good deal less from the bombardment than the Federal artillery had done, but for the Confederates, whose infantry was posted behind instead of in front of their fuming line of metal, it was the other way around. Both sides were overshooting, with the unequal result that the eastbound "overs" spared the bluecoats on the forward slope of their ridge, whereas a high proportion of their long shots landed squarely in the ranks of the gray soldiers drawn up to await the order to advance. Fewer than 200 of the former were hit, while the latter suffered approximately twice that number of casualties in the course of the nearly two-hour-long exchange.

"Such a tornado of projectiles it has seldom been the fortune or misfortune of anyone to see," one of Pickett's veterans declared. It seemed to go on forever, he recalled, under a high hard hot blue sky that soon became "lurid with flame and murky with smoke," until presently the sun was in a red eclipse, "shadowing the earth as with a funeral pall," though this gave little relief from the heat, which was even more oppressive here in the swale than it was for the blue soldiers on the high

ground in the distance. "Many a poor fellow thought his
time had come," another grayback wrote. "Great big,
stouthearted men prayed—loudly, too." Stretcher-bearers were kept on the run, answering the sudden, high-
pitched yells of the wounded up and down the sweaty,
mile-long formation. One of Kemper's men, attempting later to describe what he had been through, finally
gave it up and contented himself with a four-word
description of his ordeal by fire: "It was simply awful."
Even so, not all the accustomed butternut risibility was
suppressed. Near one badly pounded company, when a
rabbit suddenly broke from a clump of bushes and went
bounding for the rear: "Run, old hare," a man called
after him. "If I was a old hare, I'd run too."

Officers of rank, commanders of the nine brigades
and three divisions, kept moving among the waiting
troops, seeking to encourage them by example, much as
Hancock was doing at the same time across the way.
However, the response was somewhat different on this
side of the valley. When Longstreet rode along the front
of Pickett's division and a round shot plowed the ground
immediately under his horse's nose, the general kept the
startled animal under control, "as quiet as an old farmer
riding over his plantation on a Sunday morning, and
looked neither to the right or left." Thus an admiring
captain described the scene; but the men themselves,
apparently resentful of the implication that they needed
steadying, had a different reaction. "You'll get your old
fool head knocked off!" one of them called out to him,
while others shouted angrily: "We'll fight without you
leading us!"

Similarly, in Armistead's brigade, where the troops
had been instructed to remain prone throughout the
bombardment, there was resentment that their com-

mander felt it necessary to move erect among them with encouraging remarks and a showy disregard for the projectiles whooshing past him. One soldier rose in protest, and when Armistead ordered him to lie back down, pointed out that he was only following his general's example. Armistead, however—like his friend Hancock, on the ridge across the valley—had a ready answer. "Yes, but never mind me," he said. "We want men with guns in their hands."

Out front, on the low bulge of earth crowned by the Peach Orchard Barksdale's men had seized the day before, Alexander had been watching all this time for evidence that the cannonade was accomplishing its mission, which was to wreck the enemy batteries or drive them from the ridge that was the infantry's objective. So far, although an hour had elapsed since his guns first opened, the young colonel had seen little that encouraged him to believe that he was going to succeed in his assignment. Volcano-like, the enemy ridge and its two flanking heights not only continued to return the fire directed at them, but presently that return fire grew more furious than ever, despite an occasional burst of flame and the sudden resultant erection of a pillar of smoke whose base marked the former location of a caisson. Earlier, Wright and Pickett had persuaded him that all Lee intended would be accomplished in short order. After more than an hour of steady firing, however, Alexander's doubts returned in strength. Moreover, the pressure of command responsibility grew heavier by the minute, until at last, as he wrote later, "It seemed madness to order a column in the middle of a hot July day to undertake an advance of three fourths of a mile over open ground against the center of that line." What was worse, another half hour reduced the ammu-

nition supply to the point where the attack would have
to be launched without delay if it was to have artillery
support.

Shortly after 2.30, with the counterbattery fire approaching crescendo, Alexander dispatched a courier with
a note informing Pickett of the situation. "If you are to
come at all, you must come at once," he told him, "or we
will not be able to support you as we ought. But the
enemy's fire has not slackened materially and there are
still 18 guns firing from the cemetery." This last had reference to the little clump of trees, which the colonel had
been told was a cemetery, and though he was mistaken
in this, his estimate as to the number of guns still active
in that vicinity was accurate enough. And presently, as
he kept peering through the smoke to catch the slightest
encouraging reaction by the blue gunners in the distance, he observed with gratification that the Federals
had ceased firing on the hill to the left, and soon afterwards he spotted a rearward displacement by some guns
near the critical center. It was the battered Rhode
Islanders, whom Hunt had given permission to withdraw their three surviving pieces, but in his elation—for
the enemy fire continued to slacken all along the ridge
and on both adjoining heights—Alexander persuaded
himself that the withdrawal had been considerably more
substantial than it was in fact. In other words, the blue
ruse had worked far better than its authors would have
any way of knowing until they saw the long gray lines
of infantry advancing.

He got off a second note to Pickett, hard on the heels
of the first: "For God's sake come quick. The 18 guns
have gone. Come quick or my ammunition will not let
me support you properly."

Pickett by then had already acted on the first of the

two dispatches. Glad to receive anything that might end
the strain of waiting, he mounted his horse and rode at
once to Longstreet, whom he found sitting on a snake
rail fence out front, observing the bombardment. Dismounting, he handed him the note. Old Peter read it
deliberately, but said nothing. "General, shall I
advance?" Pickett asked eagerly. Longstreet, who later
explained: "My feelings had so overcome me that I could
not speak, for fear of betraying my want of confidence,"
responded with a silent nod. That was enough for the
jaunty long-haired Virginian. "I am going to move forward, sir," he said. Then he saluted, remounted, and rode
back to join his men.

Front and center of his division, he delivered from
horseback what one of his officers called "a brief, ani-
mated address" which only those soldiers nearest him
could hear but which ended on a ringing note: "Up,
men, and to your posts! Don't forget today that you are
from old Virginia!" There was, however, no disconcert-
ing haste as the troops were placed in attack formation.
For the most part, they simply rose to their feet and
began to dress their regimental lines while their
colonels passed among them repeating the instructions
received from above: "Advance slowly, with arms at
will. No cheering, no firing, no breaking from common
to quick step. Dress on the center." In at least one outfit, a survivor would recall, one of the captains led in the
singing of a hymn and a white-haired chaplain offered
prayer.

Nor was the step-off itself unduly precipitate. Pettigrew gave the signal on the left to the new leader of his
old brigade: "Now, Colonel, for the honor of the good
Old North State, forward!" The advance was somewhat
ragged at first, as if the Virginians, Mississippians,

Alabamians, and Tennesseans of his division supposed
that the spoken order only applied to the Carolinians,
but the laggard brigades soon restored the alignment by
double-timing to catch up.

Meanwhile, in the wooded swale to the south, others
had taken up the cry. Armistead, whose brigade comprised the supporting line on the right, as Trimble's two
did on the left, did not neglect the opportunity afforded
for another display of determination. "Sergeant, are you
going to plant those colors on the enemy works today?"
he asked a nearby color-bearer, and when the sergeant
gave the staunch expected answer, "I will try, sir, and if
mortal man can do it, it shall be done," the general
removed his wide-brimmed black felt hat, placed it on
the point of his sword, and raised it high for all to see,
shouting in a voice that carried from flank to flank of
his brigade: "Attention, 2d Battalion, the battalion of
direction! Forward, guide centerrr, *march*!" and led the
way.

Beyond the left, within the lower limits of the town
of Gettysburg, onlookers from Rodes's division, seeing
Pettigrew's troops emerge from the woods and begin
their downhill march into the valley, called out to the
Federal surgeons who had remained behind to tend the
captured wounded of their army: "There go the men
who will go through your damned Yankee line for
you!"

Longstreet had preceded them out to the line of guns
and was conferring with Alexander. Pleased though he
had been at seeing the enemy artillery first slack then
cease its fire, he was anything but pleased when he saw
his own guns follow suit immediately after he gave Pickett the nod that would send him forth to what he himself
had predicted would be slaughter. But his greatest sur-

prise was at Alexander's explanation that he had suspended firing in order to save ammunition, being doubtful whether enough remained on hand for proper support of the infantry on its way across the valley. Old Peter was plainly horrified, despite the colonel's earlier statement that the supply was limited.

"Go and stop Pickett right where he is, and replenish your ammunition!" he exclaimed. Now it was Alexander's turn to be surprised. "We can't do that, sir," he protested. "The train has but little. It would take an hour to distribute it, and meanwhile the enemy would improve the time." Longstreet made no reply to this. For a long moment he stood there saying nothing. Then he spoke, slowly and with deep emotion. "I do not want to make this charge," he said; "I do not see how it can succeed. I would not make it now but that General Lee has ordered it and expects it."

With that he stopped, gripped by indecision and regret, though in point of fact he had been given no authority to halt the attack even if he had so chosen. The young artillerist volunteered nothing further. Just then, however, the issue was settled for once and all by the appearance of Garnett's and Kemper's brigades from the swale behind the guns. Garnett was mounted, having been granted special permission to ride because of his injured knee and feverish condition, and Alexander went back to meet him; they had been friends out on the plains in the old army. Apparently the Virginian was experiencing a chill just now, for he wore an old blue overcoat buttoned close to his throat despite the July heat. Alexander walked beside the horse until they reached the slope leading down to the Emmitsburg Road and the Union ridge beyond. There he stopped and watched his friend ride on.

"Goodbye," he called across the widening gap, and he added, as if by afterthought: "Good luck."

★ ★ ★

By now—some twenty or thirty minutes after the Union guns stopped firing, and consequently about half that long since Alexander followed suit—much of the smoke had been diffused or had drifted off, so that for the attackers, many of whom had stepped at a stride from the dense shade of their wooded assembly areas into the brilliant sunlight that dappled the floor of the valley, the result was not only dazzling to their eyes but also added to their feeling of elation and release. "Before us lay bright fields and fair landscape," one among them would recall.

It was not until the effect of this began to wear off, coincidental with the contraction of their pupils, that they saw at last the enormity of what was being required of them, and by then, although the vista afforded absolute confirmation of their direst apprehensions, the pattern of exhilaration had been set. Under the double influence of secondary inertia and terrific deliberation, the long gray lines came on, three brigades to the south under Pickett and six to the north under Pettigrew and Trimble, with a quarter-mile gap between the interior flanks of the two formations, the former composed of fifteen and the latter of twenty-seven regiments, all with their colors flying at more or less regular intervals along the rows of nearly 11,000 striding men.

Harvey Hill was to say of the individual Confederate, as he had observed him in offensive action: "Of shoulder-to-shoulder courage, spirit of drill and discipline, he knew nothing and cared less. Hence, on the battlefield, he was more of a free-lance than a machine. Whoever saw a Confederate line advancing that was not crooked as a ram's horn? Each ragged rebel yelling on his own hook and aligning on himself." But Hill, though he was to see about as much combat as any general on either side before the war was over, was not at Gettysburg. If he had been, he would have had to cite it as the exception.

Forbidden to step up the cadence or fire their rifles or even give the high-pitched yell that served at once to steady their own nerves and jangle their opponents', the marchers concentrated instead on maintaining their alignment, as if this in itself might serve to awe the waiting bluecoats and frighten them into retreat. And in point of fact, according to one among the watchers on the ridge across the way—a colonel commanding a brigade adjacent to the little clump of trees—it did at least produce the lesser of these two reactions. For him, the advancing graybacks had "the appearance of being fearfully irresistible," while a foreign observer, whose point of vantage was on the near side of the valley, used the same adjective to communicate the impression the attackers made on him: "They seemed impelled by some irresistible force." Out front with the rebel skirmishers, a captain had a closer view of the troops as they strode down the slope toward where he crouched, and he remembered ever afterwards the "glittering forest of bayonets," the two half-mile-wide formations bearing down "in superb alignment," the "murmur and jingle" of trouser-legs and equipment, and the "rustle of thousands of feet amid the stubble," which stirred up dust and chaff beneath and before them "like the dash of spray at the prow of a vessel."

They came on at a steady rate of about one hundred

yards a minute, and before they had been three minutes
in the open—barely clear of the line of friendly guns,
whose cannoneers raised their hats in salute and wished
them luck as they passed through—the Union batteries,
as if in quick recovery from the shock of seeing them
appear thus, massed for slaughter, began to roar. The
gray lines dribbled rag-doll shapes, each of which left a
gap where it had been while still in motion. Flags
plunged with sudden flutters in the windless air, only to
be taken up at once as the fallen color-bearers were
replaced. This happened especially often in the regiments on the flanks, which came under galling long-
range fire delivered in enfilade from the two heights,
Cemetery Hill on the left and Little Round Top on the
right.

Pettigrew's troops had farther to go, since they had
begun their march from Seminary Ridge itself, but this
had been foreseen and allowed for; Pickett had been
charged with closing the quarter-mile interval between
the two formations, which would lengthen the distance
his three brigades would have to cover in the course of
their advance. Accordingly, once they were clear of the
line of guns, in plain view of the little clump of trees just
over half a mile ahead, he gave his troops the order,
"Left oblique!" They obeyed it neatly, executing in midstride a half-face to the north, which, at every full step of
their own, brought them half a step closer to the flank of
the undeviating marchers on their left. All this time,
both groups were taking losses, a more or less steady
leakage of killed and wounded, who lay motionless
where they fell or turned and hobbled painfully up the
slope they had descended.

Coming presently to a slight dip, about midway of
the valley—a swale not deep enough to hide them from

the enemy gunners, but conveniently parallel to the ridge that was their objective—Pickett's men received their second order, which was to halt, close up the gaps their casualties had left, and dress the line. They did so, once more with the deliberate precision of the drill field, but with the difference that such gaps continued to appear at an even more alarming rate as the Union gunners, delighted with this sudden transformation of a moving into a stationary target, stepped up their rate of fire. The result was the first evidence of confusion in the Confederate ranks. A soldier would look toward the comrade on his right, feeling meanwhile with his extended hand for the shoulder of the comrade on his left, and there would be a constant sidling motion in the latter direction, as men continued to fall all down the line, leaving additional gaps that had to be closed. This might have gone on indefinitely, or at any rate until there were no survivors left to dress or dress on, but at last the order came for them to continue the advance, still on the oblique.

This they did, to the considerable relief of most of the bluecoats on the ridge ahead, whose reaction to the maneuver was one of outrage, as if they had been exposed to a blatant indecency, such as the thumbing of a nose, though for others the feeling of revulsion was tempered by awe and incredulity. "My God, they're dressing the line!" some among the waiting infantry exclaimed, more by way of protest than applause.

In the course of the ten- or fifteen-minute lull allowed by the enemy guns before the attackers first appeared on the far side of the valley, the defenders had improved the time by repairing what little damage had been done to their improvised earthworks by the rebel cannonade. Now there was nothing left to do but wait, and in some ways that was the hardest thing of all. In fact, some among them found it downright impossible. Despite the renewed Confederate bombardment, they stood up behind their low stone walls or their meager scooped-up mounds of dirt and began to shoot at the graybacks half a mile away, only to have their officers tell them gruffly to hold their fire until the Johnnies came within decent range. Hays, who was jumpy enough himself, being of an excitable nature, found a way to pass the time for the men of his two brigades; he put them through a few stiff minutes of drill in the manual of arms, despite the overhead hiss and flutter of going and coming projectiles. Meanwhile the Union cannoneers kept busy, at any rate those who had husbanded their long-range ammunition for the opportunity now at hand, including the men in a six-gun battery that came up with full limbers just as the lull was ending and replaced the departed Rhode Islanders in the position directly south of the clump of trees. Rittenhouse and Osborn had the best of it in this respect, slamming their shells in at angles that caught the advancing lines almost end-on, but others were by no means idle. "We had a splendid chance at them," one of McGilvery's captains later testified, "and we made the most of it."

Watching the effects of this—the gnawed flanks and the plunging flags, the constantly recurring gaps all up and down the long gray front—the bluecoats cheered, and from time to time a man would holler "Fredericksburg!" elated by the thought that he was seeing, or was about to see, a repetition of that fiasco, though with certain welcome differences. On that field, for example, only the last four hundred yards of the attack had been made in full view of the defenders behind their wall of stone and dirt, yet not a single one of the attackers had come within twenty yards of the objective. Here the critical distance was more than three times as great, and the waiting soldiers took much consolation in the fact that the respective roles of the two armies, as attackers and defenders, had been reversed. "Come on, Blue Belly!" the rebs had yelled, but now it was the other way around; now it was the Federals who were yelling, "Come on, Johnny! Keep on coming!" even though the Confederates were bringing no blankets or overcoats along and their worn-out shoes would not be worth stripping from their corpses.

On Pickett's right, Kemper's brigade was taking cruel punishment from the half-dozen guns on Little Round Top, whose gunners tracked their victims with the cool precision of marksmen in a monstrous shooting gallery, except that in this case the targets were displayed in depth, which greatly increased the likelihood of hits. Moreover, the slightest excess in elevation landed their shots in Garnett's ranks "with fearful effect," as one of his officers would report, "sometimes as many as ten men being killed [or] wounded by the bursting of a single shell."

But worse by far was the predicament of the troops on Pettigrew's left. Here Mayo's brigade—Virginians too, but fewer by half in number; their heavy losses at Chancellorsville had never been made up, and they had been under a series of temporary commanders for nearly a year, with the result that their morale had been known to be shaky even before the bloody action two days ago had taken its further toll—caught the end-on fire, not of six but of 29 high-sited guns, with correspondingly greater suffering and disruption. As they tottered forward under the merciless pounding from the batteries on Cemetery Hill, these unfortunates had all they could do

to maintain their alignment and keep their four flags flying. Whereupon, about two hundred yards short of the
Emmitsburg Road, having passed the still-hot ashes of
the house and barn set afire by the forenoon bombardment, they were struck on the flank by a regiment of
Ohioans from the Union skirmish line, whose colonel
massed and launched them in an assault as unexpected
as it was bold. The reaction of the Virginians—it was
they who "on a sudden had become as still and thoughtful as Quakers at a love feast" when they first learned that
the attack was to be made and that they were to have a
share in it—was immediate and decisive. Despite their
four-to-one numerical advantage and their well-earned
heritage of valor, they took off rearward at a run, flags
and all, to the considerable dismay of the onlookers who
had told the Federal surgeons, "There go the men who
will go through your damned Yankee line for you," and
did not stop until they regained the cover of Seminary
Ridge. By quick subtraction, four of Pettigrew's regiments, nearly one fourth of the total in his division,
thus were removed from his calculations as effectively
as if they had stepped into bottomless quicksand.
Osborn's gunners, observing the flight of the brigade
which up to now had been their sole concern, cheered
lustily and swung their muzzles without delay along a
short arc to the left. Their first shell burst in the midst
of Davis's brigade, killing five men in one of his Mississippi regiments.

Nothing quite like this abrupt defection had ever happened before, at least not in Lee's army, though the sight
had been fairly common in the ranks of its opponents
over the past two years, beginning at First Manassas and
continuing through Second Winchester. Most Confederate witnesses reacted first with unbelief and then with

consternation; but not Longstreet, who had steeled himself at the outset by expecting the very worst. Still seated on the snake rail fence at the far end of the field, he moved at once to counteract what he had seen through the shellbursts to the north, sending word for Anderson to commit his three remaining brigades—Wright's and Posey's and Mahone's; Lang and Wilcox had already been instructed to furnish such help for Pickett if it was needed—in support of the line thus weakened. No one could know whether the sudden collapse of this one brigade was indicative of what the others would do when the pressure intensified, but there was always the danger, even in quite sound units, that when a flank started to crumble, as this one had done, the reaction would continue all down the line. And in fact it did continue in one regiment under Davis, some of whose green troops took off rearward in the wake of the Virginians, but the other three held steady, taking in turn the end-on pounding from the batteries on the height as they kept up their steady progress across the valley.

By now the interior flanks of Pettigrew and Pickett had come together on the near side of the fence-lined Emmitsburg Road, beyond which the blue skirmishers fired a volley or two before hurrying back to their own line, some four hundred yards up the slope behind them. The resultant crowding of Fry's and Garnett's brigades, which occurred before the latter received the order that brought its marchers off the oblique, presented a close-packed target the Union gunners did not neglect from point-blank range on the ridge ahead. "Don't crowd, boys!" a rebel captain shouted, his voice as lackadaisical amid the bursting shells as that of a dancing master. There was in fact a certain amount of formal politeness as the two brigades came together, Tennesseans on the one hand and Virginians on the other, under circumstances designed to favor havoc. Southern courtesy had never been more severely tried, yet such protest as was heard was mild in tone. It was here that the classic Confederate line was spoken: "Move on, cousins. You are drawing the fire our way."

Armistead was hard on Garnett's heels by now, and Kemper's men had drifted left, not only in an attempt to keep in touch with the latter's contracting line, but also in obedience to a natural inclination to flinch from the increasingly effective fire directed at their exposed flank from Little Round Top as well as from the south end of the Federal ridge, where McGilvery's seven batteries were massed. From close in rear of his advancing troops, Pickett saw his and Pettigrew's lead brigades, crowded into a blunted wedge perhaps five hundred yards in width, surge across the road and its two fences, taking severe losses from the opening blasts of canister loosed by guns that had been silent until now, and begin their climb up the slope toward the low stone wall behind which the blue infantry was crouched. He saw that his men were going to make it, a good part of them anyhow; but he saw, too—so heavy had their casualties been on the way across the valley, and so heavy were they going to be in storming the wall itself, which extended the length of the front and beyond—that unless the survivors were stoutly reinforced, and soon, they would not be able to hold what they were about to gain. Accordingly, he sent a courier to inform Longstreet of this close-up estimate of the situation.

The courier, a staff captain, galloped fast to find Old Peter, but even so he took time to draw rein in an attempt to rally some stragglers he found trotting toward the rear. "What are you running for?" he demanded, glaring down at them. One of the men looked up at him as if to say the question was a foolish waste of breath, though what he actually said was: "Why, good gracious, Captain, ain't you running yourself?" Too flustered to attempt an answer, the courier gave his horse the spur and continued on his mission, feeling rather baffled by the encounter.

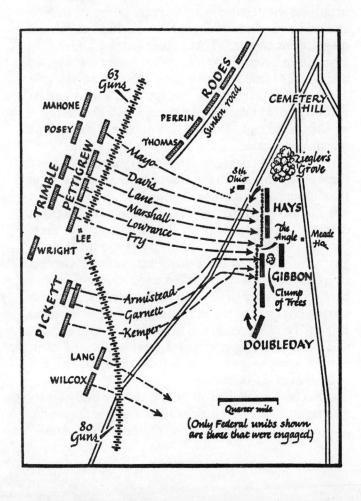

He found Old Peter still perched atop the snake rail fence, observing through his binoculars the action on the ridge. The general listened attentively to Pickett's message, but before he could reply a distinguished British visitor rode up: Lieutenant Colonel Arthur Fremantle, of Her Majesty's Coldstream Guards. Despite his high rank in a famous regiment, this was his first experience of battle. "General Longstreet," he said, breathless with excitement, "General Lee sent me here, and said you would place me in a position to see this magnificent charge." Then, observing for himself the struggle in progress on the ridge across the way, he exclaimed: "I wouldn't have missed this for anything!"

Old Peter laughed, an incongruous sound against that backdrop of death and destruction. "The devil you wouldn't!" he said; "I would like to have missed it very much. We've attacked and been repulsed. Look there." All the colonel could see, amid swirls of smoke on the slope at which the general was pointing, half a mile in the distance, was that men were fighting desperately; but Longstreet spoke as if the issue was no longer in doubt. "The charge is over," he said flatly. And then, having attended in his fashion to the amenities due a guest, he turned to the courier and added: "Captain Bright, ride to General Pickett and tell him what you have heard me say to Colonel Fremantle." The courier started off, but the general called after him: "Captain Bright!" Drawing rein, John Bright looked back and saw Old Peter pointing northward. "Tell General Pickett that Wilcox's brigade is in that orchard, and he can order him to his assistance."

The courier galloped off at last, and the burly Georgian returned to watching the final stages of the action, pausing only to countermand his recent order for Anderson's three reserve brigades to be committed. Wilcox and Lang could go forward, in accordance with Lee's original arrangements—Longstreet's final instructions, shouted after the courier when he first started back to Pickett, were more in the nature of a reminder than a command—but if what was happening on the ridge was only the prelude to a repulse, as he believed, then Anderson's three and Pender's two uncommitted brigades would be needed to meet the counterattack Meade would be likely to launch in the wake of the Confederates as they fell back down the slope and recrossed the valley. Fremantle marveled at his companion's self-possession under strain, remarking afterwards that "difficulties seem[ed] to make no other impression on him than to make him a little more savage." In point of fact, though Old Peter kept his binoculars trained on the flame-stabbed turmoil halfway up the enemy ridge, he watched the fighting not so much in suspense as to the outcome—for that had been settled already, at least to his own disgruntled satisfaction—as to study the manner in which it came about. Convinced that the attack had failed, even before the first signs of retreat were evident, he was mainly interested in seeing how many of his soldiers would survive it.

But they themselves had no such detached view of the holocaust in which they were involved. Massed as they were on a narrow front, flailed by canister from both flanks and dead ahead, the men of the five lead brigades were mingled inextricably; few of them had any knowledge of anything except in their immediate vicinity, and very little of that. "Everything was a wild kaleidoscopic whirl," a colonel would recall. Fry, for one, thought victory was certain. "Go on; it will not last five minutes longer!" he shouted as he fell, shot through the thigh while urging his brigade to hurry up the slope. Nearby a lieutenant waved his sword and exulted as if he saw the end of the war at hand. "Home, boys, home!" he cried. "Remember, home is over beyond those hills!"

Sheets of flame leaped out at the charging graybacks as the blue infantry opened fire along the wall, but they held their own fire until Garnett passed the word, which was taken up by officers all up and down the front: "Make ready. Take good aim. Fire low. *Fire!*" Uphill sheets of flame flashed in response and blue-capped heads dropped from sight beyond the wall. "Fire! Fire!" they could hear Federal officers shouting through the smoke and muzzle-flashes.

Still wrapped in his old army overcoat, Garnett rocked back in the saddle and fell heavily to the ground, dead, the Kernstown stain removed at last. Kemper meanwhile had turned and called to Armistead, who was close in his rear: "Armistead, hurry up! I am going to charge those heights and carry them, and I want you to support me!" His friend called back, "I'll do it!" and added proudly: "Look at my line. It never looked better on dress parade." But Kemper by then was in no condition to observe it; he had fallen, shot in the groin as he ordered the final assault.

Pickett thus was down to a single brigade commander, and Pettigrew was in the same condition on the left, where only Davis remained, Marshall having been killed at about the same time Fry went down. Unhorsed by a shell on his way across the valley, Pettigrew had crossed the Emmitsburg Road on foot and then had been wounded painfully in the hand as he began to climb the ridge. He remained in command, though his troops were mingled beyond the possibility of over-all control, even if he could have managed to make himself heard above the tremendous clatter of firing and the high screams of the wounded. Nevertheless, like Pickett's leaderless two on the right, his three brigades continued their uphill surge, eager to come to grips with their tormentors beyond the wall, and for the first time on this field today the rebel yell rang out.

On the Union right, near Ziegler's Grove, Hancock watched with admiration as Hays, whose northern flank considerably overlapped the enemy left, swung his end regiment forward, gatelike, to make contact with the Ohioans who had halted after routing Mayo and had taken up a position facing southwest with their left on the Emmitsburg Road. As a result of this pivoting maneuver, which was accompanied by two brass Napoleons firing double-shotted canister, some 450 men who otherwise would have had no share in the fighting after the rebels actually struck the blue defenses, well down the line and beyond their angle of sight, were placed where they could and did pump heavy volleys into the mangled flank of the attackers, adding greatly to the confusion and the carnage. Hancock shouted approval of this happy improvisation and took off southward at a gallop, intending to see whether the same could not be done at the opposite end of the position, which likewise extended well beyond the huddled mass of graybacks driving hard against his center.

He rode fast, but even so he had cause to fear he would be too late. The stone wall along which his five brigades were deployed ran due south for a couple of hundred yards from Ziegler's Grove, then turned sharply west for eighty yards, thus avoiding the clump of umbrella-shaped trees, before it made as sharp a turn again to resume its former direction. The jog in the wall—described thereafter as The Angle—had caused Gibbon's men to be posted eighty yards in advance of

Hays's, which meant that they would be struck first: as indeed they were. Galloping southward along the ridge, Hancock was hailed by Arthur Devereux, who commanded one of two regiments Gibbon had placed in reserve, well up the slope behind his center. "See, General!" Devereux cried, pointing. "They have broken through; the colors are coming over the stone wall. Let me go in there!"

Reining his horse in so abruptly that he brought the animal back on its haunches, Hancock looked and saw that the report was all too true. Less than two hundred yards away, due west and northwest of the clump of trees, which partly obscured his view, he saw a host of butternut soldiers, led by a gray-haired officer who brandished a sword with a black hat balanced on its point, boiling over the wall in hot pursuit of a blue regiment that had bolted. Some two hundred undefended feet of the south leg of the angle had been overrun. "Go in there pretty God-damned quick!" the general shouted, and spurred on southward to order Doubleday to repeat the flanking maneuver that was working so well at the far end of the line. That way, the breakthrough might at least be limited in width, and if Devereux got there in time it might even be contained.

Arriving, Hancock found that Doubleday, or anyhow the commander of the one I Corps brigade attached for defense of the Union center, had anticipated the order; G. J. Stannard, a former Vermont dry-goods merchant and militia officer, had already begun the pivot maneuver and was wheeling two of his three regiments into an advance position from which to tear the flank of the attackers pressing forward to exploit their narrow penetration of the south leg of the angle, directly in front of the clump of trees and less than two hundred yards north of the point where Stannard's gatelike swing was hinged. Vermonters all, the 900 men of these two out-sized regiments were nine-month volunteers; "nine monthlings hatched from $200 bounty eggs," scornful veterans had dubbed them on their recent arrival from the soft life of the Washington defenses. They had seen their first action yesterday and their army time was almost up, but they were determined to give a good account of themselves before returning home. Now the opportunity was at hand. Company by company, they opened fire as they wheeled into line, blasting the rebel flank, and as they delivered their murderous volleys they continued to move northward, closing the range until their officers were able to add the fire of their revolvers to the weight of metal thrown into the writhing mass of graybacks.

"Glory to God! Glory to God!" Doubleday shouted, swinging his hat in approval as he watched from up the slope. "See the Vermonters go it!"

Hancock too was delighted, but while he was con-gratulating Stannard on the success with which his green troops had executed the difficult maneuver, a bul-let passed through the pommel of his saddle and buried itself in the tender flesh of his inner thigh, along with several jagged bits of wood and a bent nail. Two officers caught him as he slumped, and when they had lowered him to the ground Stannard improvised a tourniquet—a knotted handkerchief wound tight with a pistol bar-rel—to stanch the flow of blood from the ugly wound. Hancock himself extracted the saddle nail unaided, though he mistook its source. "They must be hard up for ammunition when they throw such shot as that," he said wryly. Stretcher-bearers came on the run, but he refused to be carried off the field just yet. He insisted on staying to watch the action, which now was mounting swiftly toward a climax.

The gray-haired Confederate officer he had glimpsed through the screen of trees as he rode southward in rear of the center was his old friend Armistead, whom he had seen last in California and did not recognize now because of the distance and the smoke. Working his way forward to assume command of the frantic press of troops after Garnett and Kemper had fallen, Armistead found himself at the stone wall, midway of the 200-foot stretch from which a regiment of Pennsylvanians had bolted to avoid contact with the charging rebels. There the gray advance had stopped, or anyhow paused, while those in front knelt behind its welcome cover and poured a heavy fire into the secondary blue line up the slope. He saw, however, that it would not do to lose momentum or allow the Federals time to bring up reinforcements. "Come on, boys! Give them the cold steel!" he cried, and holding his saber high, still with the black hat balanced on its tip for a guidon, he stepped over the wall, yelling as he did so: "Follow me!"

Young Cushing's two guns were just ahead, unserved and silent because Cushing himself was dead by now, shot through the mouth as he called for a faster rate of fire, and Gibbon had been taken rearward, a bullet in his shoulder. Then Armistead fell too, killed as he reached with his free hand for the muzzle of one of the guns, and the clot of perhaps 300 men who had followed him over the wall was struck from the right front by the two regiments Devereux had brought down "pretty God-damned quick" from the uphill slope beyond the clump of trees. The fight was hand to hand along the fringes, while others among the defenders stood back, left and front and right, and fired into the close-packed, heav-

ing mass of rebel troops and colors. "Every man fought on his own hook," a bluecoat would recall, with little regard for rank or assignment, high or low. Even Hunt was there, on horseback, emptying his revolver into the crush. "See 'em! See 'em!" he cried as he pulled trigger. Then his horse went down, hoofs flailing, with the general underneath. Men on both sides were hollering as they milled about and fired, some cursing, others praying, and this, combined with the screams of the wounded and the moans of the dying, produced an effect which one who heard it called "strange and terrible, a sound that came from thousands of human throats, yet was not a commingling of shouts and yells but rather like a vast mournful roar."

Neither on the left nor on the right of the shallow penetration of the center, assailed as they were from north and south by the double envelopment Hays and Stannard had improvised, could the Confederates make real headway. Pettigrew's troops, advancing up their additional eighty yards of slope, which one of them noted incongruously was "covered with clover as soft as a Turkish carpet," were in fact outnumbered by the defenders of the two hundred yards of wall above the angle. Fry's brigade and part of Marshall's having gone in with the Virginians to the south, all that remained were Davis's brigade and Marshall's remnant, and though they kept coming on, torn by rifle fire and canister from the flank and dead ahead, they had not the slightest chance of scoring a breakthrough and they knew it. The most they could hope to accomplish was to keep the enemy units in their front from being shifted to meet the threat below the angle, and this they did, though at a cruel cost. A Mississippi regiment—including the University Greys, a company made up exclu-

sively of students from the state university, which suffered a precisely tabulated loss of 100% of its members
killed or wounded in the charge—managed to plant its
colors within arm's length of the Union line before it
was blasted out of existence, and a sergeant from a
North Carolina outfit, accompanied by one man bearing the regimental colors, got all the way up to the wall
itself, but only because the admiring defenders held
their fire as they drew near. "Come over to this side of
the Lord!" a bluecoat shouted: whereupon the two surrendered and crossed over with their flag. Some others
availed themselves of the same mercy at various points
along the line, but these were all. Except as captives, or
as corpses tumbling headlong under pressure from the
rear, not an attacker got over the wall north of the angle.

Blood dripping from his wounded hand, Pettigrew
sent word for Trimble to bring his two supporting
brigades forward and add their weight to the attack.
Trimble did so, ordering Lowrance to the right, against
the angle, and Lane to reinforce the battered left.
Mounted, he watched with pride as they swung past
him. "Charley, I believe those fine fellows are going into
the enemy's line," he told an aide. But he was wrong.
Moreover, as he watched them waver and recoil under
the impact of the heavy fire the Federals brought to
bear, he was hit a bone-splintering blow in the leg he
had nearly lost at Manassas, just over ten months back,
from a wound that had kept him all those fretful months
out of combat. He passed the command to Lane, whom
he had succeeded only four hours ago, but stayed to
watch the outcome of the action. Discouraged by what
he saw, the sixty-one-year-old Marylander, whose reputation for hard-handed aggressiveness was unsurpassed
by any man in either army, went rapidly into shock from

pain and loss of blood, and declined to permit his aide to attempt to rally the troops for a renewal of the assault, which he now perceived could not succeed.

"No," he said slowly, sadly, in response to the aide's request. "The best thing the men can do is get out of this. Let them go."

They did go, here and on the right and in the center—at any rate, those who had not surrendered and were still in any condition, either physical or mental, to undertake the long walk back across the shell-torn valley. This was harder for those within the angle, not only because they had to run the longest gauntlet between the two converging wings under Hays and Stannard, but also because they were the last to realize that the assault had failed. For them, the let-down was abrupt and sickening. "I looked to the right and left," a Virginia lieutenant would recall, "and felt we were disgraced. . . . We had, for the first time, failed to do our duty." It was only after he started back and saw for himself that the friends he missed were casualties, not skulkers, that he began to comprehend the nature of the failure, and "felt that after all we were not disgraced."

He made it back across, as did June Kimble, the Tennessee sergeant who had resolved to do his duty and had done it, but who now admitted frankly: "For about a hundred yards I broke the lightning speed record." Once more, however, his conscience intervened. With a horror of being shot in the back, he turned to face the bluecoats firing downhill at him and walked backwards until he was out of musket range, then turned again and plodded uphill amid shellbursts that plowed the farther reaches of what a Federal observer called "a square mile of Tophet."

Fortunately, the final stages of the withdrawal were favored somewhat by the advance of Wilcox and Lang, who came forward in response to calls from Pickett. Although Wilcox later reported that by the time he emerged from cover "not a man of the division that I was ordered to support could I see," his limited advance had at least the effect of causing Stannard, who was wounded too by now, to order his Vermonters back into line to meet this new menace to their flank, thus easing the pressure on those Confederates who were last to leave the angle and the more stubbornly defended portions of wall above and below it.

Even so, barely more than half of the 11,000 men in the nine-brigade assault force—including Mayo's defectors, whose losses had been comparatively light, and those disabled stalwarts who managed to hobble or crawl the westward distance across the valley—returned to the ridge they had left with such high hopes an hour ago. The rest, some 5000 in all, were either killed or captured. Further allowance for the wounded among the survivors, as well as for those who were killed or injured during the preliminary bombardment and in the belated advance of Lang and Wilcox, raised the total to about 7500 casualties, which amounted to sixty percent of the 12,500 Confederates engaged from first to last. In the five leading brigades under Pickett and Pettigrew the ratio of losses was considerably higher, no less indeed than seventy percent; so that it was no wonder that the former, writing five days later to his fiancée, spoke of "my spirit-crushed, wearied, cut-up people," especially if he had reference to his subordinate commanders. Not only had he lost all three of his brigadiers, but of his thirteen colonels eight were killed and all the rest were wounded. In fact, of his thirty-five officers above the rank of captain only one came back unhit, a one-armed major, and Pettigrew's losses were almost as grievous in that regard. In Fry's brigade two field officers escaped, in Marshall's only one, and in Davis's all were killed or wounded. Moreover, the Union infantry force, with half as many troops as came against them, suffered no more than 1500 casualties, barely one fifth of the number they inflicted while maintaining the integrity of their position. "We gained nothing but glory," a Virginia captain wrote home before the week was out; "and lost our bravest men."

The gloom that settled over the western ridge was more than matched, at least in intensity, by the elation of the victors on the one across the way. On Cemetery Hill, watching as the rebel lines began to come unhinged, a captain shouted: "By God, boys, we've got 'em now. They've broke all to hell!" And down on the blood-splotched ridge below, when it became apparent that such was indeed the case, a wild celebration got under way before the gunfire stopped. Hays, who had had two horses shot from under him and had lost all but six of his twenty orderlies, was so exuberant that he grabbed and kissed young David Shields, a lieutenant on his staff. "Boys, give me a flag!" he cried. "Get a flag, Corts, get a flag, Dave, and come on!" There was no shortage of such trophies; for of the 38 regimental flags that had been brought within musket range of the wall, here on the right and on the left, no less than 30 had been captured. Hays and the two staff officers he had invited to join him in a horseback victory dance rode up and down the division line, each trailing a stand of rebel colors in the dust behind his mount, cheered by those of their grinning soldiers who were not still busy taking pot shots at the butternut figures retreating in disorder

across the valley. Recalling his excitement, Shields wrote
later: "My horse seemed to be off the ground traveling
through the air." His impression was that if he could
survive what he had just been through, he could survive
almost anything, in or out of the catalogue of war. He
was going to live forever. "I felt though a shot as large
as a barrel should hit me in the back, it would be with no
more effect than shooting through a fog bank."

Meanwhile the nearly 4000 rebel prisoners, wounded
and unwounded, were being rounded up and sent to the
rear. "Smart, healthy-looking men," one Federal called
them, adding: "They move very quick, walk like horses."
It was strange to see them thus, close up and de-fanged,
without their guns and yells. They had a simple dignity
about them which their ragged clothes served more to
emphasize than lessen. Nor were all of them in rags.
"Many of their officers were well dressed, fine, proud
gentlemen," another observer wrote soon afterwards,
"such men as it would be a pleasure to meet, when the
war is over. I had no desire to exult over them, and pity
and sympathy were the general feelings of us all upon
the occasion."

This last was not entirely true. At least one Union
officer was alarmed by the thought that the prisoners—
who, after all, numbered only a few hundred less than
the surviving defenders of the ridge—might take it into
their heads to renew the fight with the discarded
weapons thickly strewn about the ground at their feet.
There was, as it turned out, no danger of this; but the
commander of a reserve battery, galloping forward in
response to belated orders to reinforce the badly
pounded guns along the center, received a different kind
of shock. As he came up the reverse slope of the ridge he
saw a mass of gray-clad men come over the crest ahead,

and his first thought was that the position had been overrun. He signaled a halt and was about to give the order to fall back, when he saw that the Confederates bore no arms and were under guard.

Meade had much the same original reaction. Arriving at last from Powers Hill, he too mistook the drove of prisoners for evidence of a breakthrough. Then, as he realized his mistake and rode on past them toward the crest, he encountered a lieutenant from Gibbon's staff. "How is it going here?" he asked eagerly, and received the reply: "I believe, General, the enemy's attack is repulsed." Meade could scarcely credit the information, welcome though it was. "What!" he exclaimed. "Is the assault already repulsed?" By that time he had reached the crest, however, and the lieutenant's assurance, "It is, sir," was confirmed by what he saw with his own eyes: more captives being herded into clusters along the left and right and center, his own troops cavorting with abandoned rebel flags, and the fugitives withdrawing amid shellbursts on the far side of the valley, all unmistakable evidence of a victory achieved. "Thank God," he said fervently. The lieutenant observed that Meade's right hand jerked involuntarily upward, as if to snatch off his slouch hat and wave it in exultation, but then his concern for dignity prevailed. Instead he merely waved his hand, albeit rather self-consciously, and cried, just once: "Hurrah!"

This done, he gave the staffer instructions for the posting of reinforcements expected shortly, "as the enemy might be mad enough to attack again." Adding: "If the enemy does attack, charge him in the flank and sweep him from the field," he rode on down the ridge, where he was greeted with cheers of recognition and tossed caps. A band had come up by now from somewhere, and when it broke into the strains of "Hail to the Chief" a correspondent remarked, not altogether jokingly: "Ah, General Meade, you're in very great danger of being President of the United States."

Despite the evidence spread before him that the Confederates were in a state of acute distress, and therefore probably vulnerable to attack, the northern commander's words had made it clear that he had no intention of going over to the offensive. No one on the other side of the valley had heard those words, however. If they had, their surprise and relief would have been at least as great as his had been on learning that their attempt to pierce his center had been foiled.

This was especially true of Longstreet. A counterpuncher himself, he expected Meade to attack without delay, and he moved at once to meet the threat as best he could, sending word for Wright, whom he had halted when he saw the charge must fail, to collect and rally the fugitives streaming back toward the center, while he himself attended to that same function on the right. Now that the painful thing he had opposed was over, he recovered his bluff and hearty manner. He rode among the returning troops and spoke reassuringly to them, meantime sending word for McLaws and Law to pull back to the line they had taken off from yesterday and thus place their divisions in position to assist in the defense of the weakened center. When one commander protested that his men could not be rallied, Old Peter mocked at his despair. "Very well; never mind then, General," he told him. "Just let them remain where they are. The enemy's going to advance, and will spare you the trouble."

Fremantle thought the Georgian's conduct "admirable," and when he paused at one point to ask if the colonel had anything to drink, the Britisher not only gave him a swig of rum from a silver flask but also insisted that he keep the rest, together with its container, as a token of his esteem. Longstreet thanked him, put the flask in his pocket for future reference, and continued to move among the fugitives with words of cheer and encouragement, preparing to meet the counterattack which he believed Meade would be delivering at any moment now.

But most of the survivors came streaming back the shortest way, straight across the valley toward the command post midway of its western rim, like hurt children in instinctive search of solace from a parent: meaning Lee. There the southern commander had remained throughout their advance and their brief, furious struggle on the distant ridge, until he saw them falter and begin their slow recoil; whereupon he rode forward to meet them coming back, to rally them with words of reassurance, and to share with them the ordeal of the counterattack he believed would soon be launched. Nor did he disappoint them in their expectations of solace and sustainment. "All this will come right in the end," he told them. "We'll talk it over afterwards. But in the meantime all good men must rally. We want all good and true men just now."

He made it clear to all he met that he considered the failure of the charge not their fault, but his, for having asked of them more than men could give. To Fremantle, who had ridden over from the right, he said: "This has been a sad day for us, Colonel. A sad day. But we can't always expect to win victories." After advising the visitor to find a safer point for observation, he continued to move among his soldiers in an attempt to brace them for the storm he thought was coming. "Very few failed to answer his appeal," Fremantle noted, "and I saw many badly wounded men take off their hats and cheer him."

One among the fugitives most in need of encouragement was Pickett, who came riding back with an expression of dejection and bewilderment on his face. Leading his division into battle for the first time he had seen two thirds of it destroyed. Not only had his great hour come to nothing; tactically speaking, it added up to considerably less than nothing. Lee met him with instructions designed to bring him back to the problem now at hand. "General Pickett, place your division in rear of this hill," he told him, "and be ready to repel the advance of the enemy should they follow up their advantage." At least one bystander observed that in his extremity Lee employed the words "the enemy" rather than his usual "those people." But Pickett was in no state to observe anything outside his personal loss and mortification.

"General Lee, I have no division now," he said tearfully; "Armistead is down, Garnett is down, and Kemper is mortally wounded—"

"Come, General Pickett," Lee broke in. "This has been my fight, and upon my shoulders rests the blame. The men and officers of your command have written the name of Virginia as high today as it has ever been written before. . . . Your men have done all that men can do," he added after a pause for emphasis. "The fault is entirely my own."

He repeated this as he rode from point to point about the field: "It's all my fault," "The blame is mine," and "You must help me." To Wilcox, who was about as unstrung as Pickett in reporting that he was not sure his troops would stand if the Federals attacked, Lee was particularly solicitous and tender. "Never mind, General," he told him, taking his hand as he spoke. "All this has been my fault. It is I who have lost this fight, and you must help me out of it the best way you can." Fremantle, who had not followed his advice to find a place of safety, thought it "impossible to look at him or listen to him without feeling the strongest admiration," and when he rode forward to the line of guns, the Britisher found the cannoneers ready to challenge any blue attack on the disrupted center. They had much the same reaction as his own to Lee's appeal. "We've not lost confidence in the old man," they assured him, speaking defiantly, almost angrily, as if someone had suggested otherwise. "This day's work will do him no harm. Uncle Robert will get us into Washington yet. You bet he will."

By no means all responded in that fashion, however— especially among the troops who had been all the way to the enemy ridge and back, as the artillerists had not— and even concerning those who did there was considerable doubt as to whether they would stand their ground, this soon after their delivery from chaos, if they were exposed to more than the possibility of further danger. In point of fact, there was strong evidence that they would not. When some officers managed to form a line along the forward slope of Seminary Ridge, still in plain view of the Union batteries, the rallied fugitives broke badly under the long-range fire their concentration drew. "Then commenced a rout, that increased to a stampede," an indignant witness later wrote. Fleeing rearward over the crest, the mass of several hundred fear-crazed men was funneled into a ravine along the western slope, and there, without regard for orders or appeals from their officers, who were swept along in the crush, they "pushed, poured, and rushed in a continuous stream, throwing away guns, blankets, and haversacks," until at last a straggler line, composed of the more stalwart few among them, was thrown across their path and "dammed [them] up."

Lee did not reproach them even then, knowing as he did that time alone could heal the wounds their morale had suffered in the hour just past. What was more, his ready acceptance of total blame for the failure of the assault was not merely a temporary burden he assumed for the sake of encouraging his troops to resist the counterattack he believed Meade was about to launch at them; he continued to say the same things in the future, after the immediate need for them was past and the quite different but altogether human need for self-justification might have been expected to set in. "It's all my fault. I thought my men were invincible," he told Longstreet the next day, perhaps by way of making specific admission that he had been wrong in overruling his chief lieutenant's objection that the charge was bound to fail. And in his official report to the President, forwarded on the last day of the month, he repeated for the record his assertion that such fault as might be found could not properly be applied to the men who had bled and died to sustain his pride in them. "The conduct of the troops was all that I could desire or expect," he wrote, "and they deserved success so far as it can be deserved by heroic valor and fortitude. More may have been required of them than they were able to perform, but my admiration of their noble qualities and confidence in their ability to cope successfully with the enemy has suffered no abatement from the issue of this protracted and sanguinary conflict."

★ 5 ★

Protracted the conflict had certainly been, and sanguinary too, three days of fighting having produced a combined total of about 50,000 casualties North and South. Nor was it quite over yet. Although Lee could not and Meade would not renew the infantry action, two indecisive and as it were extraneous cavalry engagements—one three miles east of Gettysburg, deep in the Federal right rear, and the other just west of Round Top, on the Confederate right flank—were, respectively, still to be ended and begun. The former, which reached a climax at about the time Pickett and Pettigrew surged up Cemetery Ridge, was the result of Jeb Stuart's attempt to carry out his instructions for placing his troopers in a position from which to harry the expected, or at any rate hoped-for, blue retreat; whereas the latter, fought about an hour after the gray attackers fell back across the valley, was the result of Judson Kilpatrick's attempt, in the absence of instructions, to strike while the tactical iron was hot and thus not only throw the rebels into retreat but also provoke a panic that would prevent them from achieving a getaway. Neither Stuart nor Kilpatrick, quite different in makeup and ability, but altogether similar in their thirst for action and applause, succeeded in accomplishing what he set out to do. In fact, as the two things turned out, both generals would have done better to remain within their respective lines, together with all their men: especially Kilpatrick.

At midday Stuart rode eastward out the York Pike with the brigades of Chambliss and Jenkins, the latter now under M. J. Ferguson since its regular commander had been wounded the day before; Hampton and Fitz Lee followed at a distance, bringing the total to just over 6000 sabers. One night's rest could scarcely have restored either the men or their mounts after a week on the go, but Jeb was eager for a fight. On Evelington Heights a year ago this morning, by way of providing the just-concluded drama of the Seven Days with an upbeat epilogue, he had opened fire with a single howitzer on McClellan's blue host encamped at Harrison's Landing, and though he had been criticized for flushing the game in this fashion, he would have liked nothing better today than another such opportunity, especially after the chilling reception his chief had given him yesterday when he rejoined the army that had been groping blindfold in his absence.

For more than two miles, however, he did not sight a single enemy soldier. The Pennsylvania countryside looked altogether peaceful, its rolling farmlands untouched by war, despite the thunder of the great cannonade behind him, south of Gettysburg, which began soon after 1 o'clock and continued to rumble without diminution as he turned south about 2.30 along Cress Ridge, which extended down to the Hanover Road and the Baltimore Pike beyond. Presently he spotted horsemen a mile to the east on the Low Dutch Road, a lane that paralleled the ridge, and promptly decided to defeat or drive them off, thus clearing his path to the Union rear. Accordingly, after posting Chambliss behind a screen of woods, he dismounted Ferguson's men and sent them forward to take position around a large barn on the farm of a family named Rummel. They would

serve as bait to draw the Federals, whose strength was so
far undisclosed, after which Stuart planned to attack
with Chambliss, then sweep the field with Hampton and
Lee, whom he warned by courier to remain under cover
of the ridge as they came up, thereby adding the shock
of surprise to the weight of their horseback assault on
the unsuspecting bluecoats whose attention would be
fixed on the dismounted and presumably vulnerable
band of graybacks in the Rummel barnyard.

It did not work out quite that way, for several reasons.
For one, the blue riders were in much greater numbers
than he knew. Two brigades of David Gregg's division,
reinforced by one brigade from Kilpatrick's, were at
hand, 5000 strong, armed with repeating carbines, and
apparently as eager for a clash as Stuart was. This by
itself would have been all right—the Confederates still
had the numerical advantage—but it presently developed that Ferguson's men, through a misinterpretation
of instructions, had drawn only ten rounds of ammunition each, with the result that they ran out of bullets
almost as soon as the fight got started. Stuart had to
send in Chambliss prematurely, in order to keep the bait
from being gobbled before he was set to spring the trap.
Even this was not too bad, or anyhow it need not have
been, if Hampton and Lee had come up as planned; but
they did not. Disclosing their presence while still too far
away to achieve surprise, they gave the Federals time to
fall back from the melee around the barn and form their
ranks to receive the charge. In fact, a good many of the
bluecoats did a great deal more than that. They moved
to meet it.

The brigade attached from Kilpatrick included four
Michigan regiments commanded by a recently promoted
brigadier named George A. Custer, bottom man in the

West Point class of '61, which had lost its top man yesterday on Little Round Top. Custer, whose love of combat was only exceeded by his ache for glory, saw the rebel
column approaching and moved fast. "Come on, you
Wolverines!" he shouted, four lengths in front of the lead
regiment, his long yellow ringlets streaming in the wind.
A Federal witness described what followed. "As the two
columns approached each other, the pace of each
increased, when suddenly a crash, like the falling of timber, betokened the crisis. So sudden and violent was the
collision that many of the horses were turned end over
end and crushed their riders beneath them. The clashing
of sabers, the firing of pistols, the demands for surrender and cries of the combatants now filled the air."

Gregg dealt ably with the situation that developed,
sending in other units to strike the flanks of the gray column which Custer had brought to a standstill by meet-
ing it head-on, and while the saber-to-saber conflict was
in progress, cannoneers on both sides threw in shell and
canister whenever they could do so without too great
risk of hitting their own men. Hampton went down with
a deep gash in his head, but was brought off the field in
time to prevent his capture. Stuart, perhaps reasoning
that it was not after all his mission to stage a cavalry
fight at this stage of the battle—which he had no way of
knowing was now at its climax, back on Cemetery
Ridge, with Armistead crying "Follow me!" as he
stepped over the low stone wall along Meade's center—
withdrew his troopers to the ridge from which they had
charged, and Gregg, who had cause to be well satisfied,
was content to let them go. The artillery exchange continued till past sundown, at which time the Confederates
retired northward and went unmolested into bivouac
alongside the York Pike, near the point where they had

left it six hours back. Gregg reported 254 casualties, most of them Custer's, whose Michiganders would suffer, before the war was over, a larger number of killed and wounded than any other cavalry brigade in the Union army. Stuart listed 181, but since this was exclusive of Ferguson's brigade and the artillery, the losses probably were about equal on both sides.

Jeb made the most of the affair in his report, praising the conduct of some of his regiments by saying that "the enemy's masses vanished before them like grain before the scythe." Yet the fact remained that, for once, he had failed to drive an outnumbered foe from a fair field of fight. "Defeated at every point, the enemy withdrew," Gregg declared, and while Stuart objected strenuously to the claim—he had withdrawn when he got good and ready, he maintained—there could be no denying that he had failed in his purpose of reaching the Union rear, even though it later developed that there was no retreat for him to harry and therefore no real work for him to do if he had been there.

Four miles southwest of the Rummel farm, the other cavalry action was over too by now. Beginning some two hours later, it ended some two hours earlier, and if, despite this brevity, its potential fruits were greater—the intention had been to throw Lee's right into confusion, hard on the heels of the Pickett-Pettigrew repulse, and thus set him up for a crumpling assault to be launched by the blue infantry from the western slopes of the Round Tops—so too was the failure, which amounted to nothing more or less than a fiasco.

Kilpatrick's remaining brigade, commanded by twenty-six-year-old Elon J. Farnsworth, was in position on the rebel flank, opposed by a skirmish line of Texans from Law's division, which extended from the base of

Round Top west to the Emmitsburg Road. A year older than Farnsworth, and four years older than Custer, who had been a West Point classmate, Kilpatrick rode back and forth among his troopers, expressing what one of them called "great impatience and eagerness for orders." There was nothing unusual in this, for that was his accustomed manner, all the way back to his boyhood in New Jersey. "A wiry, restless, undersized man with black eyes [and] a lantern jaw," as a fellow officer described him, he had stringy blond side whiskers, bandy legs that gave him a rolling gait, and a burning ambition which he attempted to assuage and advance with constant aggressiveness and bluster. The result was not uncomical, at least to some observers; Sherman, for one, was to call him "a hell of a damned fool," and a member of Meade's staff remarked that "it was hard to look at Kilpatrick without laughing." But this last was not always the case for those who served under him— "Kill Cavalry," they had dubbed him, somewhat rue-fully—and it was especially not the case today, so far as Farnsworth was concerned; for Kilpatrick kept insisting that he make horseback probes at the rebel skirmish line, despite the boulder-strewn terrain, which was highly unsuitable for cavalry operations, and the renowned marksmanship of the Texans, who had emptied a good many saddles by now and were backed up, moreover, by Law's old brigade of Alabamians, whose skill was scarcely less in that respect. However, the worst was still to come for Farnsworth and his men.

It came shortly before 5 o'clock, when an orderly arrived on a lathered horse from Cemetery Ridge, shout-ing as he drew near: "We turned the charge! Nine acres of prisoners!" That was enough for Kilpatrick. Though he had no instructions to go over to the offensive, he assumed that Meade was on the lookout for a chance to strike at the rebel line, especially if some part of it could be thrown into confusion beforehand, and he quickly determined to provide such an opportunity for the forces gazing down from the slopes of Round Top. Turning to Farnsworth, he told him to commit a West Virginia regiment at once, with orders to hack a gap in the butternut skirmish line, then go for the Confederate main body, deployed along the base of the height beyond Plum Run, opposing the blue infantry above. The West Virginians tried it and were repulsed, losing heavily when the Texans rose from behind a rail fence and slammed massed volleys at them. They tried it again— and again, by way of demonstration that the terrain was unsuited to horseback maneuver, were driven back.

Kilpatrick was not satisfied. Having often maintained that cavalry could "fight anywhere except at sea," he was out to prove it here today. He told Farnsworth to send in a second regiment, this time one of Vermonters who had suffered cruelly in the earlier skirmishing. Farnsworth had shown his mettle in some forty engagements since the first days of the war, and only four days ago he had been promoted from captain to brigadier in recognition of his bravery under fire. There could scarcely be any question of his courage, but after what they had both just seen he could not believe he had heard his chief aright.

"General, do you mean it?" he asked. "Shall I throw my handful of men over rough ground, through timber, against a brigade of infantry? The 1st Vermont has already been fought half to pieces. These are too good men to kill." But Kilpatrick not only meant it; he wanted it done without question or delay. "Do you refuse to obey my orders?" he snapped. "If you are afraid to lead this charge, I will lead it." Farnsworth rose in his stirrups, flushed with anger. "Take that back!" he cried, and an observer thought the tall young man "looked magnificent in his passion." Kilpatrick bristled back at him for a moment, but then repented and apologized. "I didn't mean it. Forget it," he said. Farnsworth's anger subsided as quickly as it had risen. "General, if you order the charge, I will lead it," he replied; "but you must take the responsibility." Kilpatrick nodded. "I take the responsibility," he said.

The Texans were even readier now than they had been before. Posted within earshot, they had overheard the hot exchange between the two young brigadiers: with the result that they not only had time to brace themselves for what was coming, but also time to pass the word along to Law that his rear would be threatened if the troopers managed to punch a hole in the widespread skirmish line. The Vermonters were prepared to do just that, though one of them later wrote: "Each man felt, as he tightened his saber belt, that he was summoned to a ride to death." Farnsworth having massed them in depth, they broke through on a narrow front about midway of the line, taking losses along both flanks as they made their penetration, then swung hard east to strike the rear of the rebel infantry on the far side of Plum Run, which was bone dry at this season. They crossed, still at a gallop, but it would have been far better for them if they had not. As they approached what they thought was the Confederate rear, their drawn sabers flashing sunlight, it was as if the head of the column struck a trip wire.

Oates, forewarned, had faced his Alabamians about, ignoring the enemy infantry uphill, and presented a solid front to the blue riders. The survivors turned

sharply north again, in an attempt to avoid a second volley; but that too was a mistake, since it carried them
directly along the line of marksmen who did not neglect
the rare opportunity for point-blank firing at cavalry in
profile. For some, indeed, it was like a return to happier
days. A company commander, seeing a horse collapse in
midstride with a bullet through the brain, heard a private alongside him shout: "Captain, I shot that black!"
Asked why he had not aimed for the rider instead of the
horse, the Alabamian grinned. "Oh, we'll get him anyhow," he said. "But I'm a hunter, and for two years I
haven't looked at a deer's eye. I couldn't stand it."

By that time Law had reinforced the skirmishers with
another regiment; so that when the blue survivors
turned back west and south, they found the entry gap
resealed. What had been intended as a havoc-spreading
charge now degenerated into a sort of circus, Roman
style, with the penned-in horsemen riding frantically in
large circles, ricocheting from cluster to cluster of
whooping rebels as they tried to find a way out of the
fire-laced coliseum. Farnsworth had his mount shot
from under him, took another from a trooper who was
glad to go afoot, and in final desperation—perhaps with
Kilpatrick's taunt still ringing in his ears—made a suicidal one-man charge, saber raised, against a solid mass
of Confederates who brought him down with five mortal wounds. Some 65 of his men had fallen with him by
the time the remnant found an exit and regained the
safety of the Union lines.

No earthly good had been accomplished, except by
way of providing a show for the spectators, blue and
gray, who had watched as in an amphitheater. Still, Kilpatrick did not regret having ordered the attempt; he
only regretted that the infantry onlookers, high on the

slopes of Round Top, had failed to seize the advantage offered them by the Vermonters on the plain below; in which case, he reported, "a total rout would have ensued." As for Farnsworth: "For the honor of his young brigade and the glory of his corps, he gave his life. . . . We can say of him, in the language of another, 'Good soldier, faithful friend, great heart, hail and farewell.' " Thus Kilpatrick, who had sent him to his death with words of doubt as to his courage.

The infantry had not come down to join the mix-up in the valley for the sufficient reason that it had received no instructions to do so, although there were those who urged this course on Meade in no uncertain terms. One such was Pleasonton, who was quite as cocky as his lieutenants. "I will give you half an hour to show yourself a great general," he told his chief, soon after the latter's arrival on Cemetery Ridge. "Order the army to advance, while I take the cavalry and get in Lee's rear, and we will finish the campaign in a week."

But Meade was having no part of such advice. Six days in command, he had spent the last three locked in mortal combat, all of it defensive on his side, and he had no intention of shifting to the offensive on short notice, even if that had been possible, simply because another in the sequence of all-out rebel assaults on his fishhook line had been repulsed. Besides, he was by no means convinced that this was the last of them. "How do you know Lee will not attack me again?" he replied. "We have done well enough." Pleasonton continued to press the point, maintaining that the Confederates, low on supplies by now and far from base, would be obliged to surrender if nailed down; to which Meade's only response was an invitation for the cavalryman to accompany him on the triumphal ride along the ridge to Little Round Top. It seemed to Pleasanton that the cheers of the troops "plainly showed they expected the advance," but the army commander did not swerve from the opinion he had just expressed: "We have done well enough."

Hancock made a similar appeal, with similar results. Lifted into an ambulance after the charge had been repulsed, he ordered the vehicle halted as soon as it reached the Taneytown Road, where shells from long-range Whitworths north of Gettysburg were still landing, and began to dictate a message to be delivered at once to Meade. After explaining that he had been "severely but I trust not seriously wounded," he made it clear that he had not left his troops "so long as a rebel was to be seen upright." Interrupted by the attending surgeon, who protested against the delay, especially under enfilading fire from the rebels, the wounded general replied testily: "We've enfiladed *them*, God damn 'em," and went on with his dictation. He urged his chief to hurl Sedgwick and Sykes at Seminary Ridge without delay—if, indeed, this had not been done already. "If the VI and V corps have pressed up, the enemy will be destroyed," he predicted, and he added, by way of reinforcing his claim that Lee was in no condition to withstand a determined attack: "The enemy must be short of ammunition, as I was shot with a tenpenny nail." However, all he heard from Meade was a verbal message that avoided the central issue altogether. "Say to General Hancock," his fellow Pennsylvanian replied, "that I regret exceedingly that he is wounded, and that I thank him for the country and for myself for the service he has rendered today."

By this time McLaws had begun the withdrawal

Longstreet ordered, and when the Federal skirmishers
followed the graybacks out to the Emmitsburg Road,
reclaiming the salient lost the day before, they were met
by heavy volleys from guns and rifles; which tended to
confirm the wisdom of Meade's decision, as he afterwards explained, not to advance on Seminary Ridge "in
consequence of the bad example [Lee] had set for me,
in ruining himself attacking a strong position."

Nor was the northern commander alone in this
belief. Henry Hunt, who had been pulled from under
his toppled horse at the climax of the rebel assault and
suffered only minor aches and pains from the injuries
received, sided absolutely with his chief. "A prompt
counter-charge after combat between two small bodies
of men is one thing," the artillerist later wrote; "the
change from the defensive to the offensive of an army,
after an engagement at a single point, is quite another.
To have made such a change to the offensive, on the
assumption that Lee had made no provision against a
reverse, would have been rash in the extreme." Warren
thought so, too. It was generally felt, he subsequently
declared, "that we had saved the country for the time
and that we had done enough; that we might jeopardize
all that we had done by trying to do too much." Such
were the opinions of the two surviving members of the
quartet of generals—the dead Reynolds and the
wounded Hancock were the other pair—who were
commonly given credit, then and later, for having done
most to prevent another defeat from being added to the
Union record: a defeat, moreover, which, given the time
and place, some would maintain the Union could not
have survived.

In point of fact, the greatest deterrent was the mute
but staggering testimony of the casualty lists. Including

Reynolds, Sickles, and Hancock, the three most aggressive of its corps commanders, a solid fourth of the Federal army had been killed or wounded or captured, and
well over half again as many skulkers and stragglers had
simply wandered off or been knocked loose from their
units. A head count next morning would show 51,414
present of all ranks. Of the more than 38,000 men who
thus were absent, the actual casualties numbered
23,049—precisely tabulated a few days later at 3155
killed, 14,529 wounded, 5365 captured—which left
some 15,000 not accounted for, just now at least, and
encouraged the belief that the losses had been even
greater than they were in fact. Moreover, they were
quite unevenly distributed. Of Meade's seven infantry
corps, the four led into action by Reynolds, Hancock,
Sickles, and Howard had suffered almost ninety percent
of the casualties, and if this had its brighter aspect—
Sedgwick's corps, the largest in the army, had scarcely
been engaged at all, and might therefore be considered
available for delivery of the counterstroke urged by
Pleasonton and Hancock—it also cast a corresponding
gloom over those who had done the bleeding. All in all,
when they became available, these figures did much to
support the judgment of the responsible commander
that, notwithstanding the tactical desirability of launching an immediate mass assault, which was as clear to him
as it was to any man on the field, the troops were in no
condition to sustain it.

On the other hand there was testimony from Lee's
own ranks that the Confederates were in no condition to
resist an assault if one had been made against them.
"Our ammunition was so low," Alexander confessed,
"and our diminished forces at the moment so widely dispersed along the unwisely extended line, that an advance

by a single fresh corps, [Sedgwick's] for instance, could
have cut us in two."

Few on that same side of the line agreed with this,
however. After all, it was not Lee's army that had been
shattered in the desperate charge that afternoon, but
only eight of his thirty-seven brigades, five of which—
Anderson's other three and Pender's two: the same number that had stood fast for Meade across the way—were
on hand to defend his center. Moreover, all his cavalry
was up by now, including Imboden's 2000 troopers who
had arrived at midday, and not one piece of artillery had
been lost. Far from being depressed by the repulse,
many along the rebel line had been angered by what
they had seen and were eager for revenge; they asked for
nothing better than a chance to serve the bluecoats in
the same manner, if they could be persuaded to attack.
"We'll fight them, sir, till hell freezes over," one grayback told an observer, "and then, sir, we will fight them
on the ice."

Indeed, adversity seemed to knit them closer together
as a family, which was what they had become in the past
year under Lee, and brought out the high qualities that
would stand them in good stead during the downhill
months ahead. Longstreet, for example, riding out after
dark to inspect his skirmish line, found a battery still in
position near the Peach Orchard, though he had
ordered all his artillery withdrawn to the cover of the
western ridge some time before. "Whose are these
guns?" he demanded; whereupon a tall man with a pipe
in his mouth stepped out of the shadows. "I am the captain," he said quietly, and when the general asked why
he had stayed out there in front of the infantry, the
artilleryman replied: "I am out here to have a little skirmishing on my own account, if the Yanks come out of

their holes." Amused by the prospect of a skirmish with 12-pounder howitzers, and heartened by such evidence of staunchness in a time of strain, Old Peter threw back his head and let his laugh ring out once more across that somber field.

Incongruous as his laughter had seemed that afternoon, just before the 11,000-man assault wave broke and began to ebb, it sounded even stranger now in the darkness, under cover of which the extent of the army's losses could begin to be assessed. From the top down, they were unremittingly grievous. Of the 52 Confederate generals who had crossed the Potomac in the past three weeks, no less than 17—barely under one third—had become casualties in the past three days. Five were killed outright or mortally wounded: Semmes and Barksdale, Pender, Armistead and Garnett. Two were captured: Archer, who had been taken on the first day, and Trimble, who had not been able to make it back across the valley today with a shattered leg: and this figure would be increased to three when the army began its withdrawal, since Kemper was too badly injured to be moved. Nine more were wounded: some lightly, such as Heth and Pettigrew, others gravely, such as Hood, whose arm might have to be taken off, and Hampton, who had received not one but two head cuts and also had some shrapnel in his body. When the list was lengthened by 18 colonels killed or captured, many of them officers of high promise, slated for early promotion, it was obvious that the Army of Northern Virginia had suffered a loss in leadership from which it might never recover.

A British observer was of this opinion. He lauded the offensive prowess of Lee's soldiers, who had marched out as proudly as if on parade in their eagerness to come to grips with their opponents on the ridge across the way; "But they will never do it again," he predicted. And he told why. He had been with the army since Fredericksburg, ticking off the illustrious dead from Stonewall Jackson down, and now on the heels of Gettysburg he asked a rhetorical question of his Confederate friends: "Don't you see your system feeds upon itself? You cannot fill the places of these men. Your troops do wonders, but every time at a cost you cannot afford."

That might well be. Certainly there was no comfort in a comparison of the representation on the list of those of less exalted rank. Here, too, no less than a third had fallen—and possibly more, for the count was incomplete. Lee recorded his losses as 2592 killed, 12,709 wounded, and 5150 captured or missing, a total of 20,451: which was surely low, for a variety of reasons. For one, a few units that had fought made no report, and for another he had directed in mid-May that troops so lightly wounded that they could remain with their regiments were not to be listed as casualties, although such men were included in the Federal tabulations. Moreover, his figure for the number captured or missing could not be reconciled with the prisoner-of-war records in the Adjutant General's office at Washington, which bore the names of 12,227 Confederates captured July 1–5. The true total of Lee's losses in Pennsylvania could hardly have been less than 25,000 and quite possibly was far heavier; 28,063 was the figure computed by one meticulous student of such grisly matters, in which case the butcher's bill for Gettysburg, blue and gray together, exceeded 50,000 men. This was more than Shiloh and Sharpsburg combined, with Ball's Bluff and Belmont thrown in for good measure. And while there was considerably less disparity of bloodshed among the several corps of the attackers—Hill had suffered most and Ewell least, but both were within a thousand of Longstreet, who had lost perhaps 8500—this was by no means true of smaller units within the corps. Gordon's exultation, "The Almighty has covered my men with his shield and buckler," could scarcely have been echoed by any commander of the eight brigades that went up Cemetery Ridge and even within these there was a diversity of misfortune.

Most regiments came back across the valley with at least a skeleton cadre to which future recruits or conscripts could be attached; but not all. The 14th Tennessee, for example, had left Clarksville in 1861 with 960 men on its muster roll, and in the past two years, most of which time their homeland had been under Union occupation, they had fought on all the major battlefields of Virginia. When Archer took them across Willoughby Run on the opening day of Gettysburg they counted 365 bayonets; by sunset they were down to barely 60. These five dozen survivors, led by a captain on the third day, went forward with Fry against Cemetery Ridge, and there—where the low stone wall jogged west, then south, to form what was known thereafter as The Angle—all but three of the remaining 60 fell. This was only one among the forty-odd regiments in the charge; there were others that suffered about as cruelly; but to those wives and sweethearts, parents and sisters and younger brothers who had remained at its point of origin, fifty miles down the Cumberland from Nashville, the news came hard. "Thus the band that once was the pride of Clarksville has fallen," a citizen lamented, and he went on to explain something of what he and those around him felt. "A gloom rests over the city; the hopes and affections of the people were wrapped in the regi-

ment. . . . Ah! what a terrible responsibility rests upon
those who inaugurated this unholy war."

No one felt the responsibility harder than Lee,
though, far from inaugurating, he had opposed the war
at the outset, when some who now were loudest in their
lamentations had called for secession or coercion, whatever the consequences, and had allowed themselves to
be persuaded that all the blood that would be shed
could be mopped up with a congressman's pocket handkerchief; whereas it now turned out that, at the modest
rate of a quart for every dead man and a pint for each
of the wounded, perhaps not all the handkerchiefs in
the nation, or both nations, would suffice to soak up the
blood that had been spilled at Gettysburg alone. Such
macabre calculations might be of particular interest
down the years—a fit subject, perhaps, for a master's
thesis when centennial time came round—but Lee's
tonight were of a different nature. From the moment
he saw the shattered brigades of Pickett and Pettigrew
begin their stumble back across the valley, it was obvious that what was left of his army, low on food and with
only enough ammunition on hand for one more day of
large-scale action, would have to retreat.

After riding forward to help rally the fugitives and
thus present as bold a front as possible to discourage a
counterattack, he went to his tent and there, by candle-
light, resumed his study of the maps over which he had
pored throughout the hectic week preceding the blindfold commitment to battle. If his problems now were no
less difficult, they were at least much simpler, having
been reduced to the logistics of withdrawing his survivors, together with his wounded, his supply train, and
his prisoners, from the immediate front of a victorious
opponent deep in hostile territory. He chose his routes,

decided on the order of march, and then, despite the lateness of the hour and his bone-deep weariness after three days of frustration, went in person to make certain that his plans were understood by the responsible commanders.

By dawn, Ewell and Longstreet were to have their troops disposed along Seminary Ridge, north and south of Hill's present position in the center. All day tomorrow, whether Meade attacked or not, they were to hold their ground and thus afford a head start for the wounded, as well as for the supply train and the captives; after which they were to take up the march themselves, under cover of darkness, with Hill in the lead, followed by Longstreet, and Ewell bringing up the rear. Pickett's remnant—a scant 800 of his badly shaken men would be on hand at daylight—was assigned to guard the 5000-odd Federal prisoners on the return, and Imboden's troopers would escort the miles-long column of ambulances and forage wagons loaded with such of the wounded as the surgeons judged could survive the long ride home. By this arrangement, the last infantry division to reach the field, as well as the last cavalry brigade, would be the first to depart. Before leaving his tent, Lee sent word for Imboden to report to headquarters and wait for his return, intending to give him detailed instructions for the conduct of the march. Then he went out into the night.

Unlike the vague and discretionary orders he had issued throughout the week leading up to battle and even during the past three days of fighting, in the course of which his messages had been verbal and for the most part tentative, his instructions now were written and precise, allowing no discretion whatsoever to anyone at all. In Hill's case, moreover, since his was the corps that would mark the route and set the pace, Lee took the added precaution of conferring with him in person, tracing for him the line of march on the map and making certain there was no possibility of a misunderstanding. This might have waited for morning; the infantry movement would not begin until the following evening at the earliest; but evidently Lee felt that he should not, or could not, sleep until the matter had been disposed of to his satisfaction. Delegation of authority, under orders that not only permitted but encouraged a wide degree of latitude in their execution by subordinates, had been the basis for his greatest triumphs, particularly during the ten months he had had Jackson to rely on; Second Manassas and Chancellorsville were instances in point. But at Gettysburg, with Stonewall just seven weeks in his grave, the system had failed him, and his actions tonight were an acknowledgment of the fact. Though he would return to the system in time, out of necessity as well as from choice, on this last night of his greatest and worst-fought battle he abandoned it entirely. He relied on no one but himself.

It was late, well after midnight, by the time he left Hill and rode back through the quiet moonlit camps along Seminary Ridge to his headquarters beside the Chambersburg Pike. Imboden was waiting for him there, as instructed, though no one else was stirring; his staff had gone to sleep so tired that not even a sentry had been posted. Lee drew rein and sat motionless for a time, apparently too weary to dismount, but as the cavalryman stepped forward, intending to assist him, he swung down and leaned for another long moment against Traveller, head bowed and one arm thrown across the saddle for more rest.

Imboden watched him, awed by the tableau—"The

moon shone full upon his massive features and revealed an expression of sadness that I had never before seen upon his face"—then, hoping, as he said later, "to change the silent current of his thoughts," ventured to speak of his obvious fatigue: "General, this has been a hard day on you." Lee raised his head, and his fellow Virginian saw grief as well as weariness in his eyes. "Yes, this has been a sad, sad day to us," he replied, emphasizing the word he had used that afternoon in speaking to Fremantle. Again he fell silent, but presently he "straightened up to his full height" and spoke "with more animation and excitement" than Imboden had ever seen him display: "I never saw troops behave more magnificently than Pickett's division of Virginians did today in that grand charge upon the enemy. And if they had been supported as they were to have been—but, for some reason not yet fully explained to me, were not— we would have held the position and the day would have been ours." This last was a strange thing for him to say, for he himself had denied Hill permission to throw his whole corps into the assault. However, there was no mistaking the extent of his regret. "Too bad; too bad," he groaned; "Oh, too bad!"

Suppressing his emotion, he invited Imboden into his tent for a study of the map and the long road home, which he was about to take. "We must now return to Virginia," he said.

★ 6 ★

All next morning, having completed the perilous nighttime disengagement of both wings in order to form a continuous line of defense along Seminary Ridge, from Oak Hill on the north to the confronting loom of Round Top on the south, the Confederates awaited the answer to the question that was uppermost in their minds: Would the Federals attack? Apparently they would not. "What o'clock is it?" Longstreet finally asked an artillerist standing beside him. "11.55," the officer replied, and ventured a prediction: "General, this is the 'Glorious Fourth.' We should have a salute from the other side at noon." Noon came and went but not a gun was fired. Old Peter believed he knew why. "Their artillery was too much crippled yesterday to think of salutes," he said with satisfaction. "Meade is not in good spirits this morning."

Presently there was evidence that he was wrong. Across the way, in the vicinity of the Peach Orchard, a Union brigade was seen deploying for battle. Nothing came of this, however; for just at that time—about 1 o'clock—rain began to fall, first a drizzle, then a steady downpour; the bluecoats jammed their fixed bayonets into the ground to keep the water from running down their rifle barrels, then squatted uncomfortably beside them, shoulders hunched against the rain. Obviously they had abandoned all notion of attack, if indeed they had had any such real intention in the first place. On their separate ridges, an average mile apart, the men of both armies peered at one another through the transparent curtain of rain as it sluiced the bloodstains from the grass and rocks where they had fought so savagely the past three days, but would not fight today.

Lee appeared calm and confident as he watched the departure of the long column of wounded at the height of the afternoon rainstorm and continued his preparations for the withdrawal of the infantry and artillery that night. Beneath the surface, however, he was testy: as was shown by his response to a well-meant pleasantry from one of Ewell's young staff officers who came to headquarters with a report from his chief. "General," he said encouragingly, "I hope the other two corps are in as good condition for work as ours is this morning." Lee looked at him hard and said coldly, "What reason have you, young man, to suppose they are not?"

Even before it became evident that the Federals were not going to attack he proposed, by means of a flag of truce, a man-for-man exchange of prisoners, thus risking a disclosure of his intentions in hope of lightening his burden on the march. Nothing came of this; Meade prudently declined, on grounds that he had no authority in such matters, and Lee continued his preparations for the withdrawal, prisoners and all. Imboden and the wounded were to return by way of Cashtown and Chambersburg, Greencastle and Hagerstown, for a Potomac crossing near Williamsport, a distance of forty-odd miles, while the infantry would follow a route some dozen miles shorter, southwest through Fairfield to Hagerstown for a crossing at the same point, its left flank protected by units of Stuart's cavalry on the road to Emmitsburg.

Though he felt confident that his opponent would be

restricted in maneuver by the continuing obligation to cover Baltimore and Washington, Lee recognized the impending retrograde movement as probably the most hazardous of his career. His troops did not seem greatly dispirited by the failure of the campaign, but their weariness was apparent to even a casual eye and a good third of those who had headed north with such high hopes a month ago would not be returning. Including the walking wounded who remained with their commands, he had fewer than 50,000 effectives of all arms. Moreover, Meade by now must have received heavy reinforcements from the surrounding northern states, as well as from his nearby capital: whereas Lee could expect no such transfusions of strength until he crossed the Potomac, if at all.

Leaving his campfires burning on the ridge, Hill began the withdrawal soon after nightfall. Longstreet followed, still in a driving rain that served to muffle the sound of the army's departure from its opponent across the valley. There were delays, however, and it was 2 o'clock in the morning before Ewell began his march. By now the roads were troughs of mud, which made for heavy going: so heavy, indeed, that it was 4 o'clock in the afternoon by the time the lead elements of the Second Corps plodded into Fairfield, only nine miles from the now deserted ridge just west of Gettysburg. Part of the delay was caused by free-swinging Union troopers, who got among the trains and captured a number of wagons, together with their guards and drivers. Old Bald Head was so outraged by this development that he was for facing about and fighting, then and there. But Lee would not agree. "No, no, General Ewell," he said; "we must let those people alone for the present. We will try them again some other time."

Hill and Longstreet, well beyond Fairfield before sundown, had no such difficulties. The latter, in fact, was in high good spirits when he called a halt that evening, conveniently near a roadside tavern where his staff had arranged for dinner to be served. Apparently the troops outside were getting theirs, too, for in the course of the meal there was a sound of scuffling in the adjoining chamber, followed by the appearance of a hard-faced farmwife who pushed her way into the dining room, exclaiming as she advanced: "Which is the General? Where is the great officer? Good heavens, they are killing our fat hogs! Our milk cows now are going!" On the march northward, such a complaint would have brought sudden and heavy reprisal on the offenders, but not now. "Yes, Madam," Old Peter told her, shaking his head in disapproval, "it's very sad; very sad. And this sort of thing has been going on in Virginia for more than two years. Very sad."

He took over the lead from Hill next day, July 6, and though the rain continued to fall and the mud to deepen, the men stepped out smartly once they were clear of Monterey Pass and beyond South Mountain. "Let him who will say it to the contrary," a Texan wrote home, "we made Manassas time from Pennsylvania." At 5 p.m. Longstreet entered Hagerstown, and Lee, who rode with him as usual, was relieved to learn that the train of wounded had passed through earlier that day and should have reached the Potomac by now, half a dozen miles away.

Imboden had made good speed with his 17-mile-long column, though at the cost of much suffering by the wounded, whose piteous cries to be left by the road to die were ignored by the drivers in obedience to orders that there were to be no halts for any reason

whatever, by day or night. Many of the injured men had
been without food for thirty-six hours, he later wrote,
and "their torn and bloody clothing, matted and hard-
ened, was rasping the tender, inflamed, and still oozing
wounds. Very few of the wagons had even a layer of
straw in them, and all were without springs. . . . From
nearly every wagon as the teams trotted on, urged by
whip and shout, came such cries and shrieks as these:
'Oh, God! Why can't I die?' 'My God, will no one have
mercy and kill me?' 'Stop! Oh, for God's sake, stop just
for one minute; take me out and let me die on the roadside!' 'I am dying, I am dying!' . . . During this one
night," the cavalryman added, "I realized more of the
horrors of war than I had in all the two preceding
years."

Bypassing Chambersburg in the darkness, the lead
escort regiment rode through Greencastle at dawn, and
when the troopers were a mile beyond the town, which
had offered no resistance at all in the course of the
march north the week before, some thirty or forty citizens rushed out of their houses and "attacked the train
with axes, cutting the spokes out of ten or a dozen
wheels and dropping the wagons in the streets." Imboden sent a detachment of troopers back, and this put an
end to the trouble there. Beyond Hagerstown, however,
the Union cavalry appeared in strength from Frederick
and began to harass the column. At Williamsport, finding the pontoon bridge destroyed by raiders from
downstream on the opposite bank, Imboden called a
halt and deployed his men and vehicles in the style
employed by wagon trains when attacked by Indians on
the plains. Arming his drivers with spare rifles and placing his 23 guns at regular intervals along the half-circle
of wagons, he faced northeast, the river at his back, and

managed to hold off the attackers until Fitz Lee arrived and drove them away.

The army commander got there the following morning, still riding with Longstreet at the head of the infantry column, and though he was pleased to learn that Imboden and his nephew Fitz had staved off the immediate threat by the blue horsemen, who had greatly outnumbered the defenders until now, he could see for himself that his predicament, here on the north bank of the river he had marched so hard to reach, was worse by far than the one in which he had found himself three days ago at Gettysburg, after the failure of his final attempt to break the Union fishhook. Not only was the pontoon bridge destroyed, but the recent torrential rains had swollen the Potomac well past fording. Low on food, as well as ammunition for its guns, the army was cut off from Virginia, together with its prisoners and its wounded. Lee's first thought was for these last; he directed that all the ferryboats in the region were to be collected and used in transporting the injured men to the south bank; the wagons, like the infantry and the artillery, would have to wait until the river subsided or the bridge could be rebuilt. Meanwhile, if Meade attacked, the Confederates, with small chance to maneuver and none at all to retreat, would have to give him battle under conditions whereby victory would yield but little profit and defeat would mean annihilation.

Accordingly, the engineers began their task of laying out a system of defense that extended some three miles in each direction, upstream and down from Williamsport, where in normal times a man could wade across. Both of its extremities well covered, the six-mile curve of line was anchored north on Conococheague Creek and south on the Potomac below Falling Waters, the site of the

wrecked bridge. As at Gettysburg, Hill took the center
and Ewell and Longstreet the left and right—they had by
now about 35,000 effectives between them, including the
cannoneers whose limber chests were nearly empty—
while Stuart's troopers reinforced the flanks and
patrolled the front. By next day, July 8, the dispositions
were complete, though the men continued to improve
them with their shovels, and Lee received the welcome
news that ammunition for his guns was on the way from
Winchester; it would arrive tomorrow and could be
brought across by the ferries already hard at work transporting the wounded to the Virginia bank. Foam-flecked
and swollen, the river was still on the boom, however,
farther than ever past fording and with no decrease predicted.

So far, Meade's infantry had not appeared, but Lee
did not believe it would be long in coming—and in
strength much greater than his own. He kept up a show
of calmness, despite a precarious shortage of food and
the personal strain of having been informed that his son
Rooney, taken to Hanover County to recover from his
Brandy Station wound, had been captured by raiders
and hauled off to Fort Monroe, where he was being held
as a hostage to insure the safety of some Federal prisoners charged with various crimes against the people of
the Old Dominion. Despite the fret of such distractions,
Lee wrote that night to the President, proposing once
more that Beauregard's "army in effigy" march at once
for the Rappahannock and thus create a diversion in his
favor through this anxious time of waiting for the
Potomac to subside.

"I hope Your Excellency will understand that I am not
in the least discouraged," he added, somewhat apolo-
getic over this second appeal for help from outside his

department, "or that my faith in the protection of an all-merciful Providence, or in the fortitude of this army, is at all shaken. But, though conscious that the enemy has been much shattered in the recent battle, I am aware that he can be easily reinforced, while no addition can be made to our numbers. The measure, therefore, that I have recommended is altogether one of a prudential nature."

Learning from scouts the following evening that the Federal main body was on the march from Frederick, he was convinced that his army would soon have to fight for its survival, which in turn meant the survival of the Confederacy itself. In this extremity he occupied himself with the inspection and improvement of his defenses, the distribution of the newly arrived ammunition for his batteries, and the nerving of his troops for the shock he believed was coming. Though the river continued to rise in his rear and food and forage were getting scarcer by the hour—the men were now on half rations and the horses were getting nothing to eat but grass and standing grain—he kept up a show of confidence and good cheer.

Only those who knew him best detected his extreme concern: Alexander, for example, who later testified that he had never seen his chief so deeply anxious as he appeared on July 10, one week after the guns of Gettysburg stopped roaring. This did not show, however, in a dispatch the general sent Davis that night from his still bridgeless six-mile bridgehead on the north bank of the still-unfordable Potomac. "With the blessing of Heaven," he told the President, "I trust that the courage and fortitude of the army will be found sufficient to relieve us from the embarrassment caused by the unlooked-for natural difficulties of our situation, if not to secure more valuable and substantial results. Very respectfully, your obedient servant, R. E. Lee."

In all this time, Sunday through Saturday, no two opposing infantrymen had looked at one another along the barrels of their rifles, and the source of this week-long lethargy on the part of those who should have been pursuers lay in the make-up of the man who led them. His caution, which had given the blue army its first undeniable large-scale victory to balance against the five major defeats it had suffered under as many different leaders in the past two years, was more enlarged than reduced by the discovery, on the morning of July 5, that the Confederates were no longer in position on the ridge across the way; so that while the first half of Lee's prediction—"General Meade will commit no blunder on my front"—had been fulfilled, the second half—"If I make one, he will make haste to take advantage of it"—had not. Not that there was no occasion for this increase of caution. The defenders had suffered heavily in the three-day conflict, particularly in the loss of men of rank. Schimmelfennig, who emerged from his wood-shed hiding place when Gettysburg was reoccupied on the 4th, was meager compensation for the sixteen brigade and division commanders killed or wounded in the battle, let alone for the three corps commanders who had fallen. Besides, avoidance of risk having gained him so much so far, Meade had no intention of abandoning that policy simply because the winds of chance appeared to have shifted in his favor for the moment.

Whether they had in fact shifted, or had merely been made to seem to, was by no means certain. Lee was foxy, as Meade well knew from old acquaintance. He was known to be most dangerous when he appeared least so:

particularly in retreat, as McClellan had discovered while pursuing him under similar circumstances, back in September, after presuming to have taken his measure at South Mountain. Moreover, he was not above tampering with the weather vane, and there was evidence that such was the case at present. Francis Barlow, who had been wounded and captured on the opening day of battle while commanding one of Howard's overrun divisions north of town, was left behind in Gettysburg when the rebels withdrew to their ridge on the night of July 3. He got word to headquarters next morning that Lee's plan, as he had overheard it from his sick-bed, was to feign retreat, then waylay his pursuers.

Meade took the warning much to heart and contented himself that afternoon, at the height of the sudden rainstorm, with issuing a congratulatory order to the troops "for the glorious result of the recent operations." That those operations had not ended was evident to all, for the graybacks were still on Seminary Ridge, less than a mile across the rain-swept valley. "Our task is not yet accomplished," the order acknowledged, "and the commanding general looks to the army for greater efforts to drive from our soil every vestige of the presence of the invader."

It was read to all regiments that evening. In one, when the reading was over, the colonel waved his hat and called for three cheers for Meade. But the men were strangely silent. This was not because they had no use for their new chief, one of them afterwards observed; it was simply because they did not feel like cheering, either for him or for anyone else, rain or no rain. Many of them had been engaged all day in burying the dead and bringing in the wounded of both armies, and this was scarcely the kind of work that put them in the frame of mind for tossing caps and shouting hurrahs. Mostly though, as the man explained, the veterans, "with their lights and experiences, could not see the wisdom or the occasion for any such manifestation of enthusiasm." They had done a great deal of cheering over the past two years, for Hooker and Burnside and Pope and McDowell, as well as for Little Mac, and in the course of time they had matured; or as this witness put it, their "business sense increased with age." Someday, perhaps, there would be a reason for tossing their caps completely away and cheering themselves hoarse, but this did not seem to them to be quite it. So they remained silent, watching the colonel swing his hat for a while, then glumly put it back on his head and dismiss them.

That evening the corps commanders voted five to two to hold their present ground until it was certain that Lee was retreating. Next morning—Sunday: Meade had been just one week in command—they found that he was indeed gone, but there was doubt as to whether he was retreating or maneuvering for a better position from which to renew the contest. Sedgwick moved out in the afternoon, only to bog down in the mud, and fog was so heavy the following morning that he could determine nothing except that the Confederates had reached Monterey Pass, southwest of Fairfield. "As soon as possible," Meade wired Halleck, "I will cross South Mountain and proceed in search of the enemy." On second thought, however, and always bearing in mind his instructions to "maneuver and fight in such a manner as to cover the capital and Baltimore," he decided that his best course would be to avoid a direct pursuit, which might necessitate a costly storming of the pass, and instead march south into Maryland, then westward in an attempt to come up with Lee before he effected a crossing near

Williamsport, where blue raiders from Harpers Ferry had wrecked the pontoon bridge the day before.

In Frederick by noon of July 7, fifty-odd hours after finding that his opponent had stolen away from his front under cover of darkness, the northern commander indulged himself in the luxury of a hot bath in a hotel and put on fresh clothes for the first time in ten days. This afforded him considerable relief, but it also provided a chance for him to discover how profoundly tired he was. "From the time I took command till today," he wrote his wife, "I. . . have not had a regular night's rest, and many nights not a wink of sleep, and for several days did not even wash my face and hands, no regular food, and all the time in a state of mental anxiety. Indeed, I think I have lived as much in this time as in the last thirty years."

The men, of course, were in far worse shape from their exertions. Four of the seven corps had been shot almost to pieces, and some of the survivors had trouble recognizing their outfits, so unequal had been the losses in the various commands, including more than 300 field and company grade officers lost by the quick subtractive action of shells and bullets and clubbed muskets. III Corps veterans, who were among the hardest hit in this respect, sardonically referred to themselves as "the III Corps as we understand it." Their uniforms were in tatters and their long marches through dust and mud, to and from the three-day uproar, had quite literally worn the shoes off their feet. Meade's regular army soul was pained to see them, though the pain was salved considerably by a wire received that afternoon from Halleck: "It gives me pleasure to inform you that you have been appointed a brigadier general in the Regular Army, to rank from July 3, the date of your brilliant victory."

This welcome message was followed however by two
more from Old Brains that were not so welcome, suggesting as they did a lack of confidence in his aggressive
qualities. "Push forward and fight Lee before he can
cross the Potomac," one directed, while the other was
more specific: "You have given the enemy a stunning
blow at Gettysburg. Follow it up, and give him another
before he can reach the Potomac. . . . There is strong
evidence that he is short of artillery ammunition, and if
vigorously pressed he must suffer."

Meade wanted it understood that the suffering was
unlikely to be as one-sided as his superior implied. He
too was having his troubles and he wanted them known
to those above him, who presumed to hand down judg-
ments from a distance. "My army is assembling slowly,"
he replied, still in Frederick on July 8. "The rains of yesterday and last night have made all roads but pikes
almost impassable. Artillery and wagons are stalled; it
will take time to collect them together. A large portion of
the men are barefooted. . . . I expect to find the enemy
in a strong position, well covered with artillery, and I do
not desire to imitate his example at Gettysburg and
assault a position where the chances were so greatly
against success. I wish in advance to moderate the expectations of those who, in ignorance of the difficulties to be
encountered, may expect too much. All that I can do
under the circumstances I pledge this army to do."

Apparently Halleck did not like the sound of this, for
he replied within the hour: "There is reliable information that the enemy is crossing at Williamsport. The
opportunity to attack his divided forces should not be
lost. The President is urgent and anxious that your army
should move against him by forced marches." Meade
had not heard a word from Lincoln, either of thanks for

his recent victory or of encouragement in his present exertions, and now there was this indirect expression of a lack of confidence. Forced marches! The Pennsylvanian bristled. "My army is and has been making forced marches, short of rations and barefooted," he wired back, pointing out in passing that the information as to a rebel crossing differed from his own, and added: "I take occasion to repeat that I will use my utmost efforts to push forward this army."

Old Brains protested that he had been misconceived. "Do not understand me as expressing any dissatisfaction," he replied; "on the contrary, your army has done most nobly. I only wish to give you opinions formed from information received here." But having entered this disclaimer he returned to his former tone, ignoring Meade's denial that any appreciable part of the rebel force had crossed the Potomac, either at Williamsport or elsewhere. "If Lee's army is so divided by the river," he persisted, "the importance of attacking the part on this side is incalculable. Such an opportunity may never occur again. . . . You will have forces sufficient to render your victory certain. My only fear now is that the enemy may escape."

At Middletown on July 9, having replaced Butterfield with Humphreys as chief of staff and thus got rid of the last reminder of Hooker's luckless tenure, Meade was pleased that no rain had fallen since early the day before. Though the Potomac remained some five feet above its normal level and therefore well past fording, the roads were drying fast and permitted better marching. Moreover, Halleck was keeping his word as to reinforcements. The army had 85,000 men present for duty and 10,000 more on the way, which meant that its Gettysburg losses had been made good, although a number of short-term militia and grass-green conscripts were included. "This army is moving in three columns," Meade informed Halleck before midday, "the right column having in it three corps. . . . I think the decisive battle of the war will be fought in a few days. In view of the momentous consequences, I desire to adopt such measures as in my judgment will tend to insure success, even though these may be deemed tardy."

Delighted to hear that Meade was in motion again, however tardy, the general-in-chief was careful to say nothing that might cause him to stop and resume the telegraphic argument. "Do not be influenced by any dispatch from here against your own judgment," he told him. "Regard them as suggestions only. Our information here is not always correct." In point of fact, now that contact seemed imminent, it was Old Brains who was urging caution. More troops were on the way, he wired next day, and he advised waiting for them. "I think it will be best for you to postpone a general battle till you can concentrate all your forces and get up your reserves and reinforcements. . . . Beware of partial combats. Bring up and hurl upon the enemy all your forces, good and bad."

Meade agreed. He spent the next two days, which continued fair, examining the curved shield of Lee's defenses and jockeying for a position from which to "hurl" his army upon them. By early afternoon of July 12—Sunday again: he now had been two full weeks in command—he was ready, though the skies again were threatening rain.

Selected divisions from the II, V, and VI Corps confronted a rebel-held wheat field, pickets out, awaiting the signal to go forward, when a Pennsylvania chaplain rode up to the command post and protested the violation of the Sabbath. Couldn't the battle be fought as well tomorrow? he demanded. For once Meade kept his temper, challenged thus by a home-state man of the cloth, and explained somewhat elaborately that he was like a carpenter with a contract to construct a box, four sides and the bottom of which had been completed; now the lid was ready to be put on. The chaplain was unimpressed. "As God's agent and disciple I solemnly protest," he declared fervently. "I will show you that the Almighty will not permit you to desecrate His sacred day. . . . Look at the heavens; see the threatening storm approaching!" Whereupon there were sudden peals of thunder and zigzags of lightning, as in a passage from the Old Testament, and rain began to pour down on the wheat field and the troops who were about to move against it. Meade canceled the probing action, returned to his quarters, and got off a wire to Halleck. "It is my intention to attack them tomorrow," he wrote; but then—perhaps with the chaplain's demonstration in mind—he added, "unless something intervenes to prevent it."

So he said. But a council of war he called that evening showed that his chief subordinates were opposed to launching any attack without a further examination of Lee's position. Only Wadsworth, commanding the I Corps in the absence of Newton, who was sick, agreed with Meade wholeheartedly in favoring an assault, although Howard, anxious as always to retrieve a damaged reputation, expressed a willingness to go along with the plan. Despite reports that the Potomac was falling rapidly after four days of fair weather, Meade deferred to the judgment of five of his seven corps commanders, postponed the scheduled advance, and spent the next day conducting a further study of the rebel dispositions. Informing Halleck of the outcome of the council of war, he told him: "I shall continue these reconnaissances with the expectation of finding some weak point upon which, if I succeed, I shall hazard an attack."

Old Brains was prompt to reply that he disapproved of such flinching now that the two armies were once more face to face. "You are strong enough to attack and defeat the enemy before he can effect a crossing," he wired. "Act upon your own judgment and make your generals execute your orders. Call no council of war. It is proverbial that councils of war never fight. Reinforcements are pushed on as rapidly as possible. Do not let the enemy escape."

It was plain that the advice as to councils of war amounted to an attempt to lock the stable after the pony had been stolen. And so too did the rest of it, as the thing turned out. When Meade at last went forward next morning, July 14, he found the rebel trenches empty and all but a rear-guard handful of graybacks already on the far bank of the Potomac. Aside from a number of stragglers picked up in the rush, together with two mud-stalled guns—the only ones Lee lost in the whole campaign—attacks on the remnant merely served to hasten the final stages of the crossing, after which the delivered Confederates cut their rebuilt pontoon bridge loose from the Maryland shore and looked mockingly back across the swirling waters, which were once more on the rise as a result of the two-day rainstorm the chaplain had invoked.

Meade was not greatly disappointed, or at any rate he did not seem so in a dispatch informing Halleck of Lee's escape before it had even been completed. The closing sentence was downright bland: "Your instructions as to further movements, in case the enemy are entirely across the river, are desired."

For Lee, threatened in front by twice his number and menaced within the perimeter by starvation, the past three days had been touch and go, all the time with the receding but still swollen Potomac mocking his efforts to escape. In the end it was Jackson's old quartermaster, John Harman, who managed the army's extraction and landed it safe on the soil of Virginia, having improvised pontoons by tearing down abandoned houses for their timbers and floating the finished products down to Falling Waters, where they were linked and floored; "a good bridge," Lee called the result, and though a more

critical staff officer termed it a "crazy affair," it served its
purpose. Its planks overlaid with lopped branches to
deaden the sound of wheels and boots, it not only permitted the secret withdrawal of the guns and wagons in
the darkness; it also made possible the dry-shod crossing
of the two corps under Longstreet and Hill, while Ewell
managed to use the ford at Williamsport, his tallest men
standing in midstream, armpit deep, to pass the shorter
waders along. By dawn the Second Corps was over, but
the First and Third were still waiting for the trains to
clear the bridge. At last they did, and Longstreet crossed
without interference, followed by Hill's lead division: at
which point guns began to roar.

"There!" Lee exclaimed, turning his head sharply in
the direction of the sound. "I was expecting it—the
beginning of the attack."

He soon learned, however, that Heth, who had recovered from his head injury and returned to the command
of his division, had faced his men about and was holding off the attackers while Hill's center division completed the crossing; whereupon Heth turned and
followed, fighting as he went. It was smartly done.
Despite an official boast by Kilpatrick that he captured a
1500-man Confederate brigade, only about 300 stragglers failed to make it over the river before the bridge
was cut loose from the northern bank, and the loss of
the two stalled guns, while regrettable, was more than
made up for by the seven that had been taken in Pennsylvania and brought back.

Another loss was more grievous. On Heth's return to
duty, Johnston Pettigrew had resumed command of
what was left of his brigade, which served this morning
as rear guard. He had his men in line, awaiting his turn
at the bridge, when suddenly they were charged by a

group of about forty Union cavalrymen who were thought at first to be Confederates brandishing a captured flag, so foolhardy was their attack. Pettigrew, one of whose arms was still weak from his Seven Pines wound, while the other was in a sling because of the hand that had been hit at Gettysburg, was tossed from his startled horse. He picked himself up and calmly directed the firing at the blue troopers, who were dashing about and banging away with their carbines. Eventually all of them were killed—which made it difficult to substantiate or disprove the claim that they were drunk—but meantime one took a position on the flank and fired so effectively that the general himself drew his revolver and went after him in person. Determined to get so close he could not miss, Pettigrew was shot in the stomach before he came within easy pistol range. He made it over the bridge, refusing to be left behind as a prisoner, and lived for three days of intense suffering before he died at Bunker Hill, Virginia, the tenth general permanently lost to the army in the course of the invasion. The whole South mourned him, especially his native North Carolina, and Lee referred to him in his report as "an officer of great merit and promise."

Saddened by this last-minute sacrifice of a gallant fighter, but grateful for its delivery from immediate peril, the army continued its march that day and the next to Bunker Hill, twenty miles from the Potomac, and there it went into camp, as Lee reported, for rest and recruitment. "The men are in good health and spirits," he informed Richmond, "but want shoes and clothing badly. . . . As soon as these necessary articles are obtained we shall be prepared to resume operations." That he was still feeling aggressive, despite the setback he had suffered, was shown by his reaction on July 16 to information that the enemy was preparing to cross the river at Harpers Ferry. "Should he follow us in this direction," Lee wrote Davis, "I shall lead him up the Valley and endeavor to attack him as far from his base as possible."

Meade's exchanges with his government, following his laconic report of a rebel getaway, were of a different nature. Halleck was plainly miffed. "I need hardly say to you," he wired, "that the escape of Lee's army without another battle has created great dissatisfaction in the mind of the President, and it will require an active and energetic pursuit on your part to remove the impression that it has not been sufficiently active before." This was altogether more than Meade could take, particularly from Lincoln, who still had sent him no word of appreciation or encouragement, by way of reward for the first great victory in the East, but only second-hand expressions of doubt and disappointment. The Pennsylvanian stood on his dignity and made the strongest protest within his means. "Having performed my duty conscientiously and to the best of my ability," he declared, "the censure of the President conveyed in your dispatch . . . is, in my judgment, so undeserved that I feel compelled most respectfully to ask to be immediately relieved from the command of this army."

There Halleck had it, and Lincoln too. They could either refrain from such goadings or let the victorious general depart. Moreover, Meade strengthened his case with a follow-up wire, sent half an hour later, in which he passed along Kilpatrick's exuberant if erroneous report of capturing a whole rebel brigade on the near bank of the Potomac. Old Brains promptly backtracked, as he always seemed to do when confronted with vigorous opposition from anyone, blue or gray, except Joe

Hooker. "My telegram, stating the disappointment of the President at the escape of Lee's army, was not intended as a censure," he replied, "but as a stimulus to an active pursuit. It is not deemed a sufficient cause for your application to be relieved."

In the end Meade withdrew his resignation, or at any rate did not insist that it be accepted, and on July 17, 18, and 19—the last date was a Sunday: he now had been three weeks in command—he crossed the Potomac at Harpers Ferry and Berlin, half a dozen miles downstream, complying with his instructions to conduct "an active and energetic pursuit," although he was convinced that such a course was over-risky. "The proper policy for the government would have been to be contented with driving Lee out of Maryland," he wrote his wife, "and not to have advanced till this army was largely reinforced and reorganized and put on such a footing that its advance was sure to be successful."

In point of fact, however, he had already been "largely reinforced." His aggregate present on July 20 was 105,623 men, including some 13,500 troopers, while Lee on that same date, exclusive of about 9000 cavalry, had a total of 50,178, or barely more than half as many infantry and cannoneers as were moving against him. Confronted with the danger of being cut off from Richmond, he abandoned his plan for drawing the enemy up the valley and instead moved eastward through Chester Gap. On July 21—the second anniversary of First Manassas, whose twice-fought-over field lay only some thirty miles beyond the crest of the Blue Ridge—Federal lookouts reported dust clouds rising; the rebels were on the march. Lee reached Culpeper two days later, and Meade, conforming, shifted to Warrenton, from which point he sent a cavalry and infantry column across the Rappahannock on the last night of the month. Gray horsemen opposed the advance, but Lee, aware of the odds against him and unwilling to take the further risk of remaining within the V of the two rivers, decided to fall back beyond the Rapidan. This was accomplished by August 4, ending the sixty days of marching and fighting which comprised the Gettysburg campaign. Both armies were back at their approximate starting points, and Meade did not pursue.

He had at last received from Washington the accolade that had been withheld so long, though the gesture still was not from Lincoln. "Take it altogether," Halleck wrote, "your short campaign has proved your superior generalship, and you merit, as you will receive, the confidence of the government and the gratitude of your country." But Meade had already disclaimed such praise from other sources. "The papers are making a great deal too much fuss about me," he wrote home. "I claim no extraordinary merit for this last battle, and would prefer waiting a little while to see what my career is to be before making any pretensions. . . . I never claimed a victory," he explained, "though I stated that Lee was defeated in his efforts to destroy my army." Thin-skinned and testy as he was, he found it hard to abide the pricks he received from his superiors. He doubted, indeed, whether he was "sufficiently phlegmatic" for the leadership of an army which he now perceived was commanded from Washington, and he confided to his wife that he would esteem it the best of favors if Lincoln would replace him with someone else. Who that someone might be he did not say, but he could scarcely have recommended any of his present subordinates, whose lack of energy he deplored. Most of all, he missed his fellow Pennsylvanians, the dead Reynolds and the con-

valescing Hancock. "Their places are not to be supplied," he said.

With ten of his best generals gone for good, and
eight more out with wounds of various depth and grav-
ity, Lee had even greater cause for sadness. Just now,
though, his energies were mainly confined to refitting
his army, preparing it for a continuation of the struggle he had sought to end with one hard blow, and incidentally in putting down a spirit of contention among
his hot-tempered subordinates as to where the blame
for the recent defeat should go. Few were as frank as
Ewell, who presently told a friend that "it took a dozen
blunders to lose Gettysburg and [I] committed a good
many of them," or as selfless as Longstreet, who wrote
to a kinsman shortly after the battle: "As General Lee is
our commander, he should have the support and influence we can give him. If the blame, if there is any, can
be shifted from him to me, I shall help him and our
cause by taking it. I desire, therefore, that all the
responsibility that can be put upon me shall go there,
and shall remain there." Later he would vigorously
decline the very chance he said he hoped for, but that
was in the after years, where there was no longer any
question of sustaining either the army commander or
the cause.

Others not only declined it now but were quick to
point out just where they thought the blame should rest:
Pickett, for instance, whose report was highly critical of
the other units involved in the charge tradition would
give his name to. Lee returned the document to him
with the suggestion that it be destroyed, together with
all copies. "You and your men have covered yourselves
with glory," he told him, "but we have the enemy to
fight and must carefully, at this critical moment, guard

against dissensions which the reflections in your report would create. . . . I hope all will yet be well."

His own critique of the battle, from the Confederate point of view, was given five years later to a man who was contemplating a school history. Referring the writer to the official accounts, Lee avoided personalities entirely. "Its loss was occasioned by a combination of circumstances," he declared. "It was commenced in the absence of correct intelligence. It was continued in the effort to overcome the difficulties by which we were surrounded, and [a success] would have been gained could one determined and united blow have been delivered by our whole line. As it was, victory trembled in the balance for three days, and the battle resulted in the infliction of as great an amount of injury as was received and in frustrating the Federal campaign for the season." Reticent by nature in such matters, he was content to let it go at that, except for once when he was out riding with a friend. Then he did speak of personalities, or anyhow one personality. "If I had had Stonewall Jackson with me," he said, looking out over the peaceful fields, "so far as man can see, I should have won the battle of Gettysburg."

That was still in the future, however. For the present he reserved his praise for the men who had been there. "The army did all it could," he told one of his numerous cousins in late July. "I fear I required of it impossibilities. But it responded to the call nobly and cheerfully, and though it did not win a victory it conquered a success. We must now prepare for harder blows and harder work."

List of Maps

(Maps drawn by George Annand, from originals by the author. All are oriented north.)

A Note on the Type

The principal text of this Modern Library edition
was set in a digitized version of Janson, a typeface that dates
from about 1690 and was cut by Nicholas Kis,
a Hungarian working in Amsterdam. The original matrices have
survived and are held by the Stempel foundry in Germany.
Hermann Zapf redesigned some of the weights and sizes for
Stempel, basing his revisions on the original design.